The Tragedy of
HAMLET

with Related Readings

SERIES EDITORS

Dom Saliani   Chris Ferguson   Dr. Tim Scott

NELSON

NELSON

ISBN-13: 978-0-17-604813-6
ISBN-10: 0-17-604813-8

Cataloguing in Publication Data

Shakespeare, William, 1564-1616
    Hamlet with related readings

(The global Shakespeare series)
ISBN 0-17-604813-8

1. Shakespeare, William, 1564-1616. Hamlet.
I. Saliani, Dom.   II. Title. III. Series.

PR2823.A2S24   1996   822.3'3   C96-990041-1

Project Managers:	TARA STEELE (CANADA)
	JACKIE TIDEY (AUSTRALIA)
	LAURIE WENDELL (U.S.A.)
Series Designer:	LIZ HARASYMCZUK
Cover Illustrator:	WAYNE MONDOK
Production Editors:	JULIA KEELER, KATHLEEN FFOLLIOTT,
	MARCIA MIRON, KAREN ALLISTON
Composition Analyst:	ZENAIDA DIORES
Production Coordinator:	DONNA BROWN
Permissions:	VICKI GOULD
Research:	LISA BRANT

Printed and bound in Canada

17 18 19 20   21 20 19 18

Contents

Features of the *Global Shakespeare Series*

Introduction to the Play: Information on the date, sources, themes, and appeal of the play, notes on Shakespeare's use of verse and prose, and common stage directions all help to set a context for the play.

The Text: The *Global Shakespeare Series* is faithful to Shakespeare's full original texts. Spelling and punctuation have been modernized to make the plays accessible to today's readers. For the last 200 years, many editors have chosen to arrange and rearrange Shakespeare's words to create a consistent iambic pentameter in the text. For example, a dialogue involving short speeches would look like this:

GHOST: Mark me.
HAMLET: I will.
GHOST: My hour is almost come.

The three lines make up 10 syllables. In some cases, editors have even taken words from one line and combined them with words from another line to create the iambic pentameter pattern. Shakespeare did not do this in his original text. The *Global Shakespeare Series* has not adopted this convention. What you see is what Shakespeare wrote.

Dramatis Personae: The list of characters is organized by families or by loyalty affiliations.

Scene Summaries: Brief synopses help you to follow and anticipate developments in the plot.

Artwork and Graphics: Original artwork has been created and designed for this series by internationally acclaimed artists.

Marginal Notes: Generous notes define difficult or archaic vocabulary. In some cases, entire sentences of Shakespeare are paraphrased into modern idiom — these are identified with quotation marks.

Notes of Interest: Longer notes provide background information on Shakespeare's times or interesting interpretations of various speeches or characters.

Quotable Notables: Brief comments on various aspects of the play by authors, celebrities, and highly regarded literary critics and professors are included. The views do not necessarily reflect the views of the editors; they are merely springboards for discussion, debate, and reflection.

Related Reading References: These references indicate that there is a piece of literature in the latter part of the book that relates well to a specific scene or speech.

Considerations: Each Act is followed by a series of scene-specific "considerations." Some involve analysis and interpretation; others will offer opportunities to be creative and imaginative.

Related Readings: The second half of the text contains poems, short stories, short drama, and non-fiction pieces that are directly related to the play. These can be read for enjoyment or for enrichment. They emphasize the continuing relevance of Shakespeare in today's society.

The 10 Most Difficult Questions One Can Ask: These challenging questions are ideal for developing into research or independent study projects.

Introduction to *Hamlet*

The Appeal of *Hamlet*

If Shakespeare is indeed the world's greatest playwright, then *Hamlet* may be the greatest play ever written.

Hamlet, however, is much more than an enduring cultural monument – it is a living and popular work of drama. For 400 years, it has dominated stages all over the world and feature film versions of this masterpiece continue to be produced.

Why do people never tire of *Hamlet*? Perhaps its appeal can be attributed to the story itself. The plotline seems to have all the elements necessary for an engaging story. Horatio seems to be speaking for the author when he promises late in the play, to tell

Of carnal, bloody, and unnatural acts,
Of accidental judgments, casual slaughters,
Of deaths put on by cunning and forced
*   cause,*
And, in this upshot, purposes mistook
Fallen on the inventors' heads.(Act 5, sc. 2)

However, more exciting plots have been devised and forgotten. We must look elsewhere to explain the appeal of the play. Perhaps what continues to draw people to the play is the character of Hamlet himself. In 1817, William Hazlitt recognized Hamlet's timeless and universal appeal when he declared that "It is we who are Hamlet."

Hamlet as a Revenge Play

By genre, *Hamlet* is as much a revenge play as it is a tragedy. A typical revenge plot would involve:

a. a hero, usually informed by a ghost of an injury or crime that needs to be revenged
b. the hero accepting the challenge to revenge and beginning to plot it
c. the hero confronting the villain and overcoming obstacles standing in the way of revenge
d. the revenge finally being achieved in a bloody and horrifying manner

Frequently, revenge plays would also include a play within a play and a protagonist who pretends to be insane in order to enact his revenge.

Date and Sources of the Play

Shakespeare wrote at least 37 plays. Of these, 18 appeared in *quarto* form. A quarto is a book that is produced by folding a large sheet into four and then binding the sheets. The result would be a book about the size of today's paperbacks.

In 1603, *Hamlet* appeared in print in quarto form. However it was a "bad" quarto. Scholars believe that the actor who played Marcellus recreated what he could remember of the play and sold it to an unscrupulous printer. This "bad" First Quarto was about half the length of the more authoritative Second Quarto which appeared in print the following year.

In 1623, the complete works of Shakespeare appeared in a single volume we now refer to as the First Folio. A *folio* is a book produced by folding large printed sheets in half and then binding the sheets.

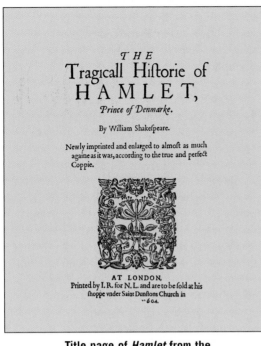

Title page of *Hamlet* from the

Second Quarto, 1604

The First Folio version of the play differed significantly from that printed in the Second Quarto. Editors usually base their texts on a combination of the Second Quarto and the First Folio versions.

Scholars are divided as to when the play was actually written. Some place it as early as 1589 and others as late as 1601.

Saxo Grammaticus, a 12th century Danish monk wrote the first history of Amleth. In this version, the hero, Amleth, succeeds in revenging the murder of his father, claims the throne and in effect "lives happily ever after" with his English princess. See page 152 in the Related Readings sections of this text for the complete story.

In 1570, Belleforest translated Saxo Grammaticus into French. This work, entitled *Histoires Tragiques,* became very popular in England. Shakespeare may have read this French version, because an English translation of Belleforest did not become available until 1608.

Shakespeare's Verse and Prose

Many students find Shakespeare difficult to read and understand. They often ask whether or not the Elizabethans really spoke the way Shakespeare's characters do. The answer is, of course, no. Shakespeare wrote using a poetic form known as *blank verse*. This produces an elevated style which would have been very different from everyday speech during the Elizabethan period.

Furthermore, the blank verse contains a rhythmic pattern known as *iambic pentameter*. What this means is that most lines contain five feet (pentameter) and each foot contains an unstressed and a stressed syllable (an iamb). In other words, as Shakespeare wrote, playing in the back of his mind would be a rhythm pattern that would sound like:

da DA da DA da DA da DA da DA

Hamlet's first line in the play would look like this in terms of stressed and unstressed syllables:

~ / ~ / ~ / ~ / ~ /
A little more than kin, and less than kind

The play *Hamlet* is approximately 4000 lines long and of these, a full quarter are written in prose. Prose contrasts strongly with the elevated style of blank verse. Persons of noble birth speak in verse and servants and members of the lower classes usually speak in prose. However, Hamlet speaks in prose when he addresses commoners. Letters and documents, scenes of comic relief, and scenes involving madness are also usually written in prose.

The Text and Stage Directions

The edition for this text is based on the 1604 Second Quarto and the 1623 First Folio. In some cases, however, the First Quarto is relied upon to clarify ambiguity and for expanded stage directions. Spelling and punctuation have been modernized to make the reading more accessible to today's readers.

Shakespeare used stage directions very sparingly in his plays. Because he was directly involved in the production of the plays, there was little need to record the stage directions. However, the First Quarto of *Hamlet* includes many stage directions that do not appear in the more authoritative version. Several of these directions are included in this edition as they provide some insight on how the play was first performed.

In this edition, the stage directions that appear in italics are Shakespeare's. Directions that are included in square brackets [ ] have been added by the editor.

The following stage directions appear frequently in Shakespeare's plays:

Above, aloft – scene played in the balcony above the stage level or from up in the loft

Alarum – a loud shout, a signal call to arms

Aside – spoken directly to the audience and not heard by the others on the stage

Below, beneath – speech or scene played from below the surface of the stage. The actor stands inside an open trap-door

Exit – he/she leaves the stage

Exeunt – they leave the stage

Flourish – fanfare of trumpets; usually announces the entrance of royalty

Hautboys – musicians enter, playing wind instruments

Omnes – all; everyone

Within – words spoken off-stage in what the audience would assume is an unseen room, a corridor, or the outdoors

NORTHERN EUROPE

NORWAY

SWEDEN

SCOTLAND

North
Sea

IRELAND

DENMARK

• Elsinore

Baltic
Sea

• Copenhagen

WALES

POLAND

ENGLAND

• Wittenberg

NORMANDY

• Paris

The setting for *HAMLET*

Dramatis Personae

Royal House of Denmark:

CLAUDIUS   King of Denmark
GERTRUDE   Queen of Denmark
HAMLET   Prince of Denmark

GHOST   of Hamlet's father

House of the Lord Chamberlain:

POLONIUS   Lord Chamberlain
LAERTES   Son to Polonius
OPHELIA   Daughter to Polonius

REYNALDO   Servant to Polonius

University Friends of Hamlet:

HORATIO   A scholar

ROSENCRANTZ   Student and courtier
GUILDENSTERN   Student and courtier

Danish Courtiers and Soldiers:

CORNELIUS   Danish courtier and
   Ambassador

VOLTEMAND   Danish courtier and
   Ambassador
OSRIC   Danish courtier
GENTLEMAN   Danish courtier

BARNARDO   Officer in the Danish army
MARCELLUS   Officer in the Danish
   army
FRANCISCO   A soldier in the Danish army

Others of Denmark:

GRAVE-DIGGER: Played by the Clown
OTHER   Grave-digger's companion
PLAYERS   Actors
A PRIEST
SAILORS
MESSENGERS AND OTHER
   ATTENDANTS

Others of Norway and England:

FORTINBRAS   Prince of Norway
CAPTAIN   In the Norwegian army

ENGLISH AMBASSADORS

Act One
Scene 1

Denmark.
Castle at Elsinore, upon the battlements.

Enter Barnardo and Francisco, two sentinels.
[Francisco is at his post. Barnardo enters to him.]

BARNARDO: Who's there?
FRANCISCO: Nay, answer me. Stand and unfold yourself.
BARNARDO: Long live the King!
FRANCISCO: Barnardo?
BARNARDO: He.
FRANCISCO: You come most carefully upon your hour.
BARNARDO: 'Tis now struck twelve. Get thee to bed, Francisco.
FRANCISCO: For this relief much thanks. 'Tis bitter cold,
    And I am sick at heart.
BARNARDO: Have you had quiet guard?   10
FRANCISCO: Not a mouse stirring.
BARNARDO: Well, good night.
    If you do meet Horatio and Marcellus,
    The rivals of my watch, bid them make haste.

Enter Horatio and Marcellus.

FRANCISCO: I think I hear them. Stand ho! Who is there?
HORATIO: Friends to this ground.
MARCELLUS: And liegemen to the Dane.
FRANCISCO: Give you good night.
MARCELLUS: O, farewell, honest soldier.
    Who hath relieved you?   20
FRANCISCO: Barnardo hath my place.
    Give you good night.

Exit Francisco.

MARCELLUS: Holla, Barnardo!

2. "Stop and identify yourself."

6. *carefully* – precisely on time

RELATED READING

8 – 9. *The Night Watch* – poem by James McLean (page 158)

14. *rivals* – partners, relief

17. *liegemen* – soldiers, loyal subjects

"Now I shall relish Hamlet more than I ever have done."
– John Keats (1795 – 1821), British Romantic poet

25. *A piece of him* – Horatio's attempt at levity, which may suggest his reluctance to be there, or his skepticism about ghosts.

31. *touching* – concerning

35. *approve our eyes* – confirm what we have seen

38. *assail your ears* – force you to listen

39. *fortified* – set, resistant

44. *pole* – North Star

50. *Thou art a scholar* – This may explain why they have asked Horatio, a scholar and not a military man, to join them. If the ghost were a demon, Horatio would be able to speak in Latin and say the right things to deal with the evil spirit.

52. *harrows* – distresses; lacerates, as a plough does the earth

harrow

53. *It would be spoke to* – According to popular belief, "A ghost has not the power to speak till it has been spoken to" (Brand, *Popular Antiquities*).

BARNARDO: Say, what is Horatio there?

HORATIO: A piece of him.

BARNARDO: Welcome, Horatio. Welcome, good Marcellus.

HORATIO: What, has this thing appeared again to-night?

BARNARDO: I have seen nothing.

MARCELLUS: Horatio says 'tis but our fantasy,
    And will not let belief take hold of him,   30
    Touching this dreaded sight twice seen of us.
    Therefore I have entreated him along
    With us to watch the minutes of this night,
    That if again this apparition come,
    He may approve our eyes and speak to it.

HORATIO: Tush, tush, 'twill not appear.

BARNARDO: Sit down a while,
    And let us once again assail your ears
    That are so fortified against our story,
    What we have two nights seen.   40

HORATIO: Well, sit we down,
    And let us hear Barnardo speak of this.

BARNARDO: Last night of all,
    When yond same star that's westward from the pole
    Had made his course to illume that part of heaven
    Where now it burns, Marcellus and myself,
    The bell then beating one —

Enter Ghost.

MARCELLUS: Peace, break thee off. Look where it comes again!

BARNARDO: In the same figure like the King that's dead.

MARCELLUS: Thou art a scholar, speak to it, Horatio.   50

BARNARDO: Looks it not like the King? Mark it, Horatio.

HORATIO: Most like. It harrows me with fear and wonder.

BARNARDO: It would be spoke to.

MARCELLUS: Speak to it, Horatio.

HORATIO: What art thou that usurp'st this time of night,
    Together with that fair and warlike form
    In which the majesty of buried Denmark
    Did sometimes march? By heaven I charge thee speak.

MARCELLUS: It is offended.

BARNARDO: See, it stalks away.   60

HORATIO: Stay, speak, speak, I charge thee speak!

Exit Ghost.

MARCELLUS: 'Tis gone, and will not answer.

BARNARDO: How now, Horatio? You tremble and look pale.

Is not this something more than fantasy?
What think you on it?

HORATIO: Before my God, I might not this believe
Without the sensible and true avouch
Of mine own eyes.

MARCELLUS: Is it not like the King?

HORATIO: As thou art to thyself.   70
Such was the very armour he had on
When he the ambitious Norway combated.
So frowned he once when in an angry parle
He smote the sledded Polacks on the ice.
'Tis strange.

MARCELLUS: Thus twice before, and jump at this dead hour,
With martial stalk hath he gone by our watch.

HORATIO: In what particular thought to work I know not,
But in the gross and scope of mine opinion,
This bodes some strange eruption to our state.   80

MARCELLUS: Good now, sit down and tell me, he that knows,
Why this same strict and most observant watch
So nightly toils the subject of the land,
And why such daily cast of brazen cannon,
And foreign mart for implements of war,
Why such impress of shipwrights, whose sore task
Does not divide the Sunday from the week,
What might be toward, that this sweaty haste
Doth make the night joint-labourer with the day,
Who is it that can inform me?   90

HORATIO: That can I,
At least the whisper goes so. Our last King,
Whose image even but now appeared to us,
Was, as you know, by Fortinbras of Norway,
Thereto pricked on by a most emulate pride,
Dared to the combat; in which our valiant Hamlet
(For so this side of our known world esteemed him)
Did slay this Fortinbras, who, by a sealed compact
Well ratified by law and heraldy,
Did forfeit with his life, all those his lands   100
Which he stood seized of, to the conqueror.
Against the which a moiety competent
Was gaged by our king, which had returned
To the inheritance of Fortinbras,
Had he been vanquisher; as by the same covenant
And carriage of the article designed,
His fell to Hamlet. Now, sir, young Fortinbras,
Of unimproved mettle hot and full,

67. *avouch* – testimony
73. *parle* – argument
74. *sledded* – travelled on sleds

"sledded Polacks"

76. "In this manner, twice before and precisely at this late hour of night"
77. *martial stalk* – warlike march
79. "It is my opinion"

85. *mart* – trading
86. *impress* – forced service
87. *divide* – distinguish
88. *toward* – in preparation

95. *emulate* – envious; eager to outdo
98. *sealed compact* – signed contract
101. *seized of* – in possession of
102. *moiety competent* – sufficient or equal portion
103. *gaged* – pledged
105 – 106. *covenant/And carriage* – agreement and conveyance of the details
108. *unimproved mettle* – courage not tempered by experience

109. *skirts* – outlying areas; outskirts

110. "Assembled indiscriminately a band of outlaws"

118. *head* – reason, source

119. *post-haste and rummage* – activity

121. *portentous* – foreboding

124. *mote* – speck of dust

125. *palmy* – glorious. The palm symbolizes victory.

126. *ere* – before

129. *stars with trains of fire* – comets

comet

130. *moist star* – moon

131. *Neptune's empire stands* – the seas depend. Neptune was the Roman god of the oceans.

133. *precurse* – forerunners

134. *harbingers* – messengers

137. *climatures* – regions

140–151. Horatio applies his scholarly knowledge of why ghosts appear. Notice that all three reasons imply that the ghost is not an evil spirit.

148. *uphoarded* – hoarded

Hath in the skirts of Norway here and there
Sharked up a list of lawless resolutes,   110
For food and diet, to some enterprise
That hath a stomach in it, which is no other,
As it doth well appear unto our state,
But to recover of us, by strong hand
And terms compulsatory, those foresaid lands
So by his father lost. And this, I take it,
Is the main motive of our preparations,
The source of this our watch, and the chief head
Of this post-haste and rummage in the land.

BARNARDO: I think it be no other but even so.   120
Well may it sort that this portentous figure
Comes armed through our watch so like the King
That was and is the question of these wars.

HORATIO: A mote it is to trouble the mind's eye.
In the most high and palmy state of Rome,
A little ere the mightiest Julius fell,
The graves stood tenantless and the sheeted dead
Did squeak and gibber in the Roman streets.
As stars with trains of fire, and dews of blood,
Disasters in the sun; and the moist star   130
Upon whose influence Neptune's empire stands
Was sick almost to doomsday with eclipse.
And even the like precurse of feared events,
As harbingers preceding still the fates
And prologue to the omen coming on,
Have heaven and earth together demonstrated
Unto our climatures and countrymen.

Enter Ghost.

But soft, behold! Lo where it comes again!

Ghost spreads his arms.

I'll cross it though it blast me. Stay, illusion!
If thou hast any sound or use of voice,   140
Speak to me.
If there be any good thing to be done
That may to thee do ease, and grace to me,
Speak to me.
If thou art privy to thy country's fate,
Which happily foreknowing may avoid,
O speak!
Or if thou hast uphoarded in thy life

Extorted treasure in the womb of earth,
For which, they say, your spirits oft walk in death,　150
Speak of it, stay and speak! Stop it, Marcellus.

The cock crows.

MARCELLUS: Shall I strike it with my partisan?
HORATIO: Do, if it will not stand.
BARNARDO: 'Tis here!
HORATIO: 'Tis here!
MARCELLUS: 'Tis gone!

Exit Ghost.

We do it wrong, being so majestical,
To offer it the show of violence,
For it is as the air, invulnerable,
And our vain blows malicious mockery.　160
BARNARDO: It was about to speak when the cock crew.
HORATIO: And then it started like a guilty thing
Upon a fearful summons. I have heard
The cock, that is the trumpet to the morn,
Doth with his lofty and shrill-sounding throat
Awake the god of day, and at his warning,
Whether in sea or fire, in earth or air,
The extravagant and erring spirit hies
To his confine; and of the truth herein
This present object made probation.　170
MARCELLUS: It faded on the crowing of the cock.
Some say that ever 'gainst that season comes
Wherein our Saviour's birth is celebrated,
This bird of dawning singeth all night long,
And then they say no spirit dare stir abroad,
The nights are wholesome, then no planets strike,
No fairy takes, nor witch hath power to charm,
So hallowed, and so gracious, is that time.
HORATIO: So have I heard and do in part believe it.
But look, the morn in russet mantle clad　180
Walks over the dew of yon high eastward hill.
Break we our watch up, and by my advice
Let us impart what we have seen to-night
Unto young Hamlet, for, upon my life,
This spirit, dumb to us, will speak to him.
Do you consent we shall acquaint him with it,
As needful in our loves, fitting our duty?
MARCELLUS: Let's do it, I pray, and I this morning know
Where we shall find him most convenient.

Exeunt.

15

Act One • Scene 1

149. *extorted* – wrongfully obtained
152. *partisan* – pike or long-handled weapon

partisan

160. *malicious mockery* – feeble imitation of one who intends to cause harm
167. *sea ... air* – the four elements of which all matter is composed
168. *extravagant and erring* – wandering and lost
169. *confine* – place of confinement
170. *object made probation* – ghost made proof

174. *This bird of dawning* – rooster

177. *takes* – uses its magical powers

180. *russet mantle clad* – cloaked in reddish brown

Act One
Scene 2

A room of state in the castle.

Claudius, the newly crowned King of Denmark, holds court. He talks about his recent marriage to the wife of his brother, the previous King, and then about the activities of young Fortinbras. He grants Laertes, the son of his chief adviser, permission to return to his studies in Paris but denies a similar request from his nephew Hamlet. Later in the scene, Horatio and the two sentinels tell Hamlet what they have seen upon the battlements.

Enter Claudius King of Denmark, Gertrude the Queen, Hamlet, Polonius, Laertes, Voltemand, Cornelius, Lords, and Attendants.

KING: Though yet of Hamlet our dear brother's death
    The memory be green, and that it us befitted
    To bear our hearts in grief and our whole kingdom
    To be contracted in one brow of woe,
    Yet so far hath discretion fought with nature
    That we with wisest sorrow think on him,
    Together with remembrance of ourselves.
    Therefore our sometime sister, now our queen,
    The imperial jointress to this warlike state,
    Have we, as 'twere with a defeated joy,   10
    With an auspicious and a dropping eye,
    With mirth in funeral and with dirge in marriage,
    In equal scale weighing delight and dole,
    Taken to wife. Nor have we herein barred
    Your better wisdoms, which have freely gone
    With this affair along. For all, our thanks.
    Now follows, that you know, young Fortinbras,
    Holding a weak supposal of our worth,
    Or thinking by our late dear brother's death
    Our state to be disjoint and out of frame,   20
    Colleagued with the dream of his advantage,
    He hath not failed to pester us with message,
    Importing the surrender of those lands
    Lost by his father, with all bonds of law,
    To our most valiant brother. So much for him.
    Now for ourself and for this time of meeting,
    Thus much the business is. We have here writ
    To Norway, uncle of young Fortinbras, —

9. *jointress* – partner

12 – 13. *With mirth ... dole* – Claudius is able to rejoice and mourn at the same time. The two phrases contain oxymorons. An oxymoron is a phrase which contains at least two words that express contradictory meanings, e.g., Led Zeppelin, eloquent silence.

18. *weak supposal* – low opinion
20. *disjoint ... frame* – disordered, chaotic
21. *Colleagued* – together
23. *Importing* – dealing with
26. *ourself* – As befits a monarch, Claudius uses the royal plural throughout.

Who, impotent and bedrid, scarcely hears
Of this his nephew's purpose, — to suppress   30
His further gait herein, in that the levies,
The lists and full proportions, are all made
Out of his subject. And we here dispatch
You, good Cornelius, and you, Voltemand,
For bearers of this greeting to old Norway,
Giving to you no further personal power
To business with the king more than the scope
Of these delated articles allow.
Farewell, and let your haste commend your duty.

CORNELIUS:
VOLTEMAND: } In that and all things will we show our duty.   40

KING: We doubt it nothing. Heartily farewell.

Exeunt Voltemand and Cornelius.

And now, Laertes, what's the news with you?
You told us of some suit. What is it, Laertes?
You cannot speak of reason to the Dane,
And lose your voice. What wouldst thou beg, Laertes,
That shall not be my offer, not thy asking?
The head is not more native to the heart,
The hand more instrumental to the mouth,
Than is the throne of Denmark to thy father.
What wouldst thou have, Laertes?   50

LAERTES: My dread lord,
    Your leave and favour to return to France.
    From whence though willingly I came to Denmark,
    To show my duty in your coronation,
    Yet now, I must confess, that duty done,
    My thoughts and wishes bend again toward France
    And bow them to your gracious leave and pardon.

KING: Have you your father's leave? What says Polonius?

POLONIUS: He hath, my lord, wrung from me my slow leave
    By laboursome petition, and at last   60
    Upon his will I sealed my hard consent.
    I do beseech you, give him leave to go.

KING: Take thy fair hour, Laertes. Time be thine,
    And thy best graces spend it at thy will.
    But now, my cousin Hamlet, and my son —

HAMLET: A little more than kin, and less than kind.

KING: How is it that the clouds still hang on you?

HAMLET: Not so, my lord. I am too much in the sun.

QUEEN: Good Hamlet, cast thy nighted colour off,

---

29. *impotent and bedrid* – weak and confined to bed

30 – 31. *to ... herein* – to halt his going further with these kinds of action

31. *in that* – on the basis of the fact that

32 – 33. *all ... subject* – The army that young Fortinbras has raised is made up of old King Norway's subjects.

38. *delated* – set forth in full

39. *commend* – be evidence of

44. *Dane* – King of the Danes

45. *lose your voice* – waste your words

47. *native* – closely connected

51. *dread* – dreaded, esteemed

61. *sealed my hard consent* – agreed reluctantly to give consent

66. With Hamlet's first speech, we notice his tendency to play with words. Here, he not only puns on the two meanings of "kind" but also offers his version of the old proverb "The nearer in kin, the less in kindness."

68. *in the sun* – Hamlet once again puns. Does he mean sun or son?

Act One • Scene 2

78. *Seems, ... seems* –
This speech introduces one
of Shakespeare's most
prevalent themes – the
discrepancy between
appearance and reality.
Hamlet has no patience, it
seems, with mere appear-
ances.

83. *haviour* – expression

87. *passes show* –
surpasses appearance
88. *trappings* – clothing,
adornments

94. *obsequious sorrow* –
appropriate mourning

101. *most ... sense* – most
ordinary thing knowable to
our common sense

111. *most ... throne* –
Hamlet is hereby declared
Claudius' heir and next in
line for the throne.

And let thine eye look like a friend on Denmark.   70
Do not for ever with thy vailed lids
Seek for thy noble father in the dust.
Thou knowest 'tis common. All that lives must die,
Passing through nature to eternity.
HAMLET: Ay, madam, it is common.
QUEEN: If it be,
Why seems it so particular with thee?
HAMLET: Seems, madam? Nay it is. I know not 'seems.'
'Tis not alone my inky cloak, good mother,
Nor customary suits of solemn black,   80
Nor windy suspiration of forced breath,
No, nor the fruitful river in the eye,
Nor the dejected haviour of the visage,
Together with all forms, moods, shapes of grief,
That can denote me truly. These indeed seem,
For they are actions that a man might play.
But I have that within which passes show
These but the trappings and the suits of woe.
KING: 'Tis sweet and commendable in your nature, Hamlet,
To give these mourning duties to your father.   90
But, you must know, your father lost a father.
That father lost, lost his, and the survivor bound
In filial obligation for some term
To do obsequious sorrow. But to persever
In obstinate condolement is a course
Of impious stubbornness. 'Tis unmanly grief.
It shows a will most incorrect to heaven,
A heart unfortified, a mind impatient,
An understanding simple and unschooled.
For what we know must be and is as common   100
As any the most vulgar thing to sense,
Why should we in our peevish opposition
Take it to heart? Fie! 'Tis a fault to heaven,
A fault against the dead, a fault to nature,
To reason most absurd, whose common theme
Is death of fathers, and who still hath cried,
From the first corpse till he that died to-day,
'This must be so.' We pray you, throw to earth
This unprevailing woe, and think of us
As of a father. For let the world take note,   110
You are the most immediate to our throne,
And with no less nobility of love
Than that which dearest father bears his son,
Do I impart toward you. For your intent

In going back to school in Wittenberg,
It is most retrograde to our desire,
And we beseech you bend you to remain
Here in the cheer and comfort of our eye,
Our chiefest courtier, cousin, and our son.

QUEEN: Let not thy mother lose her prayers, Hamlet. 120
I pray thee, stay with us. Go not to Wittenberg.

HAMLET: I shall in all my best obey you, madam.

KING: Why, 'tis a loving and a fair reply.
Be as ourself in Denmark. Madam, come.
This gentle and unforced accord of Hamlet
Sits smiling to my heart. In grace whereof
No jocund health that Denmark drinks to-day,
But the great cannon to the clouds shall tell,
And the King's rouse the heavens all bruit again,
Re-speaking earthly thunder. Come away. 130

Exeunt all but Hamlet.

HAMLET: O, that this too too sullied flesh would melt
Thaw and resolve itself into a dew,
Or that the Everlasting had not fixed
His canon 'gainst self-slaughter! O God! God!
How weary, stale, flat and unprofitable,
Seem to me all the uses of this world!
Fie on it, ah fie. 'Tis an unweeded garden,
That grows to seed. Things rank and gross in nature
Possess it merely. That it should come to this!
But two months dead — nay, not so much, not two — 140
So excellent a king, that was, to this
Hyperion to a satyr, so loving to my mother
That he might not beteem the winds of heaven
Visit her face too roughly. Heaven and earth,
Must I remember? Why, she would hang on him,
As if increase of appetite had grown
By what it fed on. And yet, within a month —
Let me not think on it — Frailty, thy name is woman —
A little month, or ere those shoes were old
With which she followed my poor father's body, 150
Like Niobe, all tears — why she, even she —
O, God, a beast, that wants discourse of reason
Would have mourned longer — married with my uncle,
My father's brother, but no more like my father
Than I to Hercules. Within a month,
Ere yet the salt of most unrighteous tears

115. *Wittenberg* — anachronism. This university was not built until almost 500 years after the events of the original Hamlet story. Wittenberg was known as the birthplace of Protestantism.

126. *grace* — thanksgiving
127. *jocund health* — joyful toast
128. "The cannons will be fired" (every time Claudius drinks)
129. *bruit* — echo
131. *sullied* — defiled
136. *uses* — customs
142. *Hyperion … satyr* — Hamlet compares his father to a sun god (Hyperion) and his uncle to a beast — half man, half goat (satyr).

satyr

143. *beteem* — allow

151. *Niobe* — In Greek mythology, Niobe wept so inconsolably over the death of her children that she was turned to stone.
155. *Hercules* — in Greek mythology, a hero of great strength

157. *galled* – sore

Had left the flushing in her galled eyes,
She married. O, most wicked speed, to post
With such dexterity to incestuous sheets!
It is not nor it cannot come to good.   160
But break, my heart, for I must hold my tongue.

Enter Horatio, Marcellus, and Barnardo.

HORATIO: Hail to your lordship.
HAMLET: I am glad to see you well.
    Horatio, — or I do forget myself.
HORATIO: The same, my lord, and your poor servant ever.
HAMLET: Sir, my good friend. I'll change that name with you.
    And what make you from Wittenberg, Horatio?—
    Marcellus.
MARCELLUS: My good lord.
HAMLET: I am very glad to see you.—Good even, sir.—   170
    But what, in faith, make you from Wittenberg?
HORATIO: A truant disposition, good my lord.
HAMLET: I would not hear your enemy say so,
    Nor shall you do mine ear that violence,

175. *truster* – a believer

    To make it truster of your own report
    Against yourself. I know you are no truant.
    But what is your affair in Elsinore?
    We'll teach you to drink deep ere you depart.
HORATIO: My lord, I came to see your father's funeral.
HAMLET: I pray thee, do not mock me, fellow-student.   180
    I think it was to see my mother's wedding.
HORATIO: Indeed, my lord, it followed hard upon.
HAMLET: Thrift, thrift, Horatio. The funeral baked meats
    Did coldly furnish forth the marriage tables.
    Would I had met my dearest foe in heaven
    Or ever I had seen that day, Horatio.
    My father — methinks I see my father —
HORATIO: Where, my lord?
HAMLET: In my mind's eye, Horatio.
HORATIO: I saw him once; he was a goodly king.   190
HAMLET: He was a man, take him for all in all.
    I shall not look upon his like again.
HORATIO: My lord, I think I saw him yesternight.
HAMLET: Saw? Who?
HORATIO: My lord, the king your father.
HAMLET: The king my father!

197. "Control your aston-
ishment for a while"
198. *attent* – attentive

HORATIO: Season your admiration for awhile
    With an attent ear, till I may deliver,

Upon the witness of these gentlemen,
This marvel to you.   200

HAMLET: For God's love, let me hear!

HORATIO: Two nights together had these gentlemen,
Marcellus and Barnardo, on their watch,
In the dead waste and middle of the night,
Been thus encountered. A figure like your father,
Armed at point exactly, cap-à-pe,
Appears before them, and with solemn march
Goes slow and stately by them. Thrice he walked
By their oppressed and fear-surprised eyes,
Within his truncheon's length, whilst they, distilled   210
Almost to jelly with the act of fear,
Stand dumb and speak not to him. This to me
In dreadful secrecy impart they did,
And I with them the third night kept the watch,
Where, as they had delivered, both in time,
Form of the thing, each word made true and good,
The apparition comes. I knew your father;
These hands are not more like.

HAMLET: But where was this?

MARCELLUS: My lord, upon the platform where we watch.   220

HAMLET: Did you not speak to it?

HORATIO: My lord, I did,
But answer made it none. Yet once methought
It lifted up its head and did address
Itself to motion, like as it would speak.
But even then the morning cock crew loud,
And at the sound it shrunk in haste away
And vanished from our sight.

HAMLET: 'Tis very strange.

HORATIO: As I do live, my honoured lord, 'tis true,   230
And we did think it writ down in our duty
To let you know of it.

HAMLET: Indeed, indeed, sirs, but this troubles me.
Hold you the watch to-night?

MARCELLUS: }
BARNARDO: } We do, my lord.

HAMLET: Armed, say you?

MARCELLUS: }
BARNARDO: } Armed, my lord.

HAMLET: From top to toe?

MARCELLUS: }
BARNARDO: } My lord, from head to foot.

HAMLET: Then saw you not his face?   240

206. "Fully armed from head to toe"

209. *oppressed* – overwhelmed

210. *truncheon* – staff of office

210. *distilled* – dissolved

215. "Where, as they had reported, both in time of appearance"

"We all sympathize with Hamlet, and that is understandable, because almost every one of us recognizes in the prince, our own characteristics."
– Ivan Turgenev (1818 – 1883) Russian novelist and playwright

241. *beaver* – visor

helmet, beaver down

243. *countenance* – facial expression

251. *tell* – count to

259. *warrant* – guarantee

260. Note that Hamlet admits the possibility that the apparition may be a devil and not his father's ghost.

264. *tenable* – kept secret

267. *requite* – reward

273. *doubt* – suspect
274. *rise* – rise to the surface
275. *overwhelm them* – attempt to cover them up

HORATIO: O, yes, my lord, he wore his beaver up.
HAMLET: What, looked he frowningly?
HORATIO: A countenance more in sorrow than in anger.
HAMLET: Pale or red?
HORATIO: Nay, very pale.
HAMLET: And fixed his eyes upon you?
HORATIO: Most constantly.
HAMLET: I would I had been there.
HORATIO: It would have much amazed you.
HAMLET: Very like, very like. Stayed it long?   250
HORATIO: While one with moderate haste might tell a
    hundred.
MARCELLUS: } Longer, longer.
BARNARDO:
HORATIO: Not when I saw it.
HAMLET: His beard was grizzled, no?
HORATIO: It was, as I have seen it in his life,
    A sable silvered.
HAMLET: I will watch to-night.
    Perchance 'twill walk again.
HORATIO: I warrant it will.
HAMLET: If it assume my noble father's person,   260
    I'll speak to it, though hell itself should gape
    And bid me hold my peace. I pray you all,
    If you have hitherto concealed this sight,
    Let it be tenable in your silence still.
    And whatsoever else shall hap to-night,
    Give it an understanding, but no tongue.
    I will requite your loves. So, fare you well.
    Upon the platform, 'twixt eleven and twelve,
    I'll visit you.
ALL: Our duty to your honour.   270
HAMLET: Your loves, as mine to you. Farewell.

Exeunt all but Hamlet.

My father's spirit in arms! All is not well.
I doubt some foul play. Would the night were come.
Till then sit still, my soul. Foul deeds will rise,
Though all the earth overwhelm them, to men's eyes.

Exit.

Act One
Scene 3

A room in Polonius' house.

Enter Laertes and Ophelia his sister.

LAERTES: My necessaries are embarked. Farewell,
And, sister, as the winds give benefit
And convoy is assistant, do not sleep,
But let me hear from you.
OPHELIA: Do you doubt that?
LAERTES: For Hamlet and the trifling of his favour,
Hold it a fashion and a toy in blood,
A violet in the youth of primy nature,
Forward, not permanent, sweet, not lasting,
The perfume and suppliance of a minute,   10
No more.
OPHELIA: No more but so?
LAERTES: Think it no more.
For nature, crescent, does not grow alone
In thews and bulk, but, as this temple waxes,
The inward service of the mind and soul
Grows wide withal. Perhaps he loves you now,
And now no soil nor cautel doth besmirch
The virtue of his will. But you must fear,
His greatness weighed, his will is not his own.   20
For he himself is subject to his birth:
He may not, as unvalued persons do,
Carve for himself, for on his choice depends
The safety and health of this whole state.
And therefore must his choice be circumscribed
Unto the voice and yielding of that body
Whereof he is the head. Then if he says he loves you,
It fits your wisdom so far to believe it
As he in his particular act and place

Before departing for Paris, Laertes bids farewell to his sister Ophelia. He suggests to her that she keep her distance from Hamlet. Polonius offers his son some parting words of wisdom and then he turns his attention to Ophelia. Upon hearing that Hamlet has expressed his love for her, Polonius admonishes Ophelia and commands her to avoid Hamlet in the future.

1. *necessaries* – baggage
2 – 3. *as ... assistant* – whenever the winds and ships are available
7. "Consider it a passing fancy and a trick of youth"
9. *forward* – premature flowering
10. *suppliance* – pastime

14. *crescent* – as it grows
15 – 17. "In physical strength, but as this body grows, the power of the mind and soul increases also."
18. *cautel* – deceit
20. *greatness weighed* – social rank considered
22. *unvalued* – common
23. *carve* – choose
25. *circumscribed* – determined
26. *voice and yielding* – opinion and consent

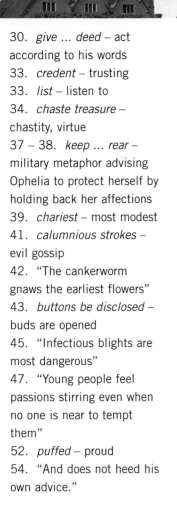

30. *give ... deed* – act according to his words

33. *credent* – trusting

33. *list* – listen to

34. *chaste treasure* – chastity, virtue

37 – 38. *keep ... rear* – military metaphor advising Ophelia to protect herself by holding back her affections

39. *chariest* – most modest

41. *calumnious strokes* – evil gossip

42. "The cankerworm gnaws the earliest flowers"

43. *buttons be disclosed* – buds are opened

45. "Infectious blights are most dangerous"

47. "Young people feel passions stirring even when no one is near to tempt them"

52. *puffed* – proud

54. "And does not heed his own advice."

61. *stayed for* – waited for

62. *precepts* – rules of conduct

63. *character* – inscribe

64. *unproportioned* – unruly

65. "Be sociable but don't lower yourself by being too friendly with anyone."

66. *adoption tried* – friendship tested

68. *dull thy palm* – shake hands with; make friends

May give his saying deed; which is no further   30
Than the main voice of Denmark goes withal.
Then weigh what loss your honour may sustain,
If with too credent ear you list his songs,
Or lose your heart, or your chaste treasure open
To his unmastered importunity.
Fear it, Ophelia, fear it, my dear sister,
And keep you in the rear of your affection
Out of the shot and danger of desire.
The chariest maid is prodigal enough
If she unmask her beauty to the moon.   40
Virtue itself escapes not calumnious strokes.
The canker galls the infants of the spring
Too oft before their buttons be disclosed,
And in the morn and liquid dew of youth
Contagious blastments are most imminent.
Be wary then. Best safety lies in fear.
Youth to itself rebels, though none else near.

OPHELIA: I shall the effect of this good lesson keep
As watchman to my heart. But, good my brother,
Do not, as some ungracious pastors do,   50
Show me the steep and thorny way to heaven,
Whiles like a puffed and reckless libertine
Himself the primrose path of dalliance treads,
And recks not his own rede.

LAERTES: O, fear me not.
I stay too long.

Enter Polonius.

But here my father comes.
A double blessing is a double grace.
Occasion smiles upon a second leave.

POLONIUS: Yet here, Laertes? Aboard, aboard, for shame.
The wind sits in the shoulder of your sail,   60
And you are stayed for. There; my blessing with thee.
And these few precepts in thy memory
See thou character. Give thy thoughts no tongue,
Nor any unproportioned thought his act.
Be thou familiar, but by no means vulgar.
Those friends thou hast, and their adoption tried,
Grapple them to thy soul with hoops of steel,
But do not dull thy palm with entertainment
Of each new-hatched, unfledged comrade. Beware
Of entrance to a quarrel, but being in,   70

Bear it that the opposed may beware of thee.
Give every man thy ear, but few thy voice.
Take each man's censure, but reserve thy judgment.
Costly thy habit as thy purse can buy,
But not expressed in fancy; rich, not gaudy,
For the apparel oft proclaims the man,
And they in France of the best rank and station
Are of a most select and generous chief in that.
Neither a borrower nor a lender be,
For loan oft loses both itself and friend,   80
And borrowing dulls the edge of husbandry.
This above all: to thine own self be true,
And it must follow, as the night the day
Thou canst not then be false to any man.
Farewell. My blessing season this in thee.

LAERTES: Most humbly do I take my leave, my lord.

POLONIUS: The time invites you. Go. Your servants tend.

LAERTES: Farewell, Ophelia; and remember well
    What I have said to you.

OPHELIA: 'Tis in my memory locked,   90
    And you yourself shall keep the key of it.

LAERTES: Farewell.

Exit.

POLONIUS: What is it, Ophelia, be hath said to you?

OPHELIA: So please you, something touching the Lord Hamlet.

POLONIUS: Marry, well bethought.
    'Tis told me, he hath very oft of late
    Given private time to you, and you yourself
    Have of your audience been most free and bounteous.
    If it be so, as so 'tis put on me,
    And that in way of caution, I must tell you,   100
    You do not understand yourself so clearly
    As it behoves my daughter and your honour.
    What is between you? Give me up the truth.

OPHELIA: He hath, my lord, of late made many tenders
    Of his affection to me.

POLONIUS: Affection! Pooh! You speak like a green girl,
    Unsifted in such perilous circumstance.
    Do you believe his tenders, as you call them?

OPHELIA: I do not know, my lord, what I should think.

POLONIUS: Marry, I'll teach you. Think yourself a baby,   110
    That you have taken these tenders for true pay,
    Which are not sterling. Tender yourself more dearly

---

71. *Bear it* – conduct yourself in such a way
73. *censure* – opinion
74. *habit* – clothing
81. *husbandry* – skill in money management
85. *season* – ripen

"The best part in the whole picture was when old Ophelia's brother – the one that gets in the duel with Hamlet at the very end – was going away and his father was giving him a lot of advice. While the father kept giving him a lot of advice, old Ophelia was sort of horsing around with her brother, taking his dagger out of the holster, and teasing him and all while he was trying to look interested in the bull his father was shooting. That was nice. I got a big bang out of that."
– J.D. Salinger (b. 1919), American novelist, author of *The Catcher in the Rye*

95. *bethought* – remembered

104. *tenders* – offers
106. *green* – naive
107. *unsifted* – untried, inexperienced

111. *tenders* – Polonius puns on the other meanings of tender: money or legal tender, and to render.

Act One • Scene 3

113. *crack the wind* – run it out of breath, overwork (as a horse)
115. *importuned* – urged

118. *countenance* – evidence, confirmation
120. *springes ... woodcocks* – traps to capture foolish birds
122. *blazes* – passions

127 – 128. "Do not agree to see Hamlet just because he asks to talk to you."
130. *tether* – freedom
131. *In few* – In short
132. *brokers* – agents
133. *dye* – nature, quality
133. *investments* – clothing, vestments
134. *implorators* – urgers
135. *bawds* – prostitutes. Notice the oxymoron in "pious bawds."
136. *beguile* – deceive

Or — not to crack the wind of the poor phrase,
Running it thus — you'll tender me a fool.

OPHELIA: My lord, he hath importuned me with love
In honourable fashion.

POLONIUS: Ay, fashion you may call it. Go to, go to.

OPHELIA: And hath given countenance to his speech, my lord,
With almost all the holy vows of heaven.

POLONIUS: Ay, springes to catch woodcocks. I do know,   120
When the blood burns, how prodigal the soul
Lends the tongue vows. These blazes, daughter,
Giving more light than heat, extinct in both
Even in their promise as it is a-making,
You must not take for fire. From this time
Be somewhat scanter of your maiden presence,
Set your entreatments at a higher rate
Than a command to parley. For Lord Hamlet,
Believe so much in him, that he is young
And with a larger tether may he walk   130
Than may be given you. In few, Ophelia,
Do not believe his vows, for they are brokers,
Not of that dye which their investments show,
But mere implorators of unholy suits,
Breathing like sanctified and pious bawds,
The better to beguile. This is for all.
I would not, in plain terms, from this time forth,
Have you so slander any moment leisure,
As to give words or talk with the Lord Hamlet.
Look to it, I charge you. Come your ways.   140

OPHELIA: I shall obey, my lord.

Exeunt.

Act One
Scene 4

The platform.

Enter Hamlet, Horatio, and Marcellus.

HAMLET: The air bites shrewdly; it is very cold.
HORATIO: It is a nipping and an eager air.
HAMLET: What hour now?
HORATIO: I think it lacks of twelve.
HAMLET: No, it is struck.
HORATIO: Indeed? I heard it not. It then draws near the season
    Wherein the spirit held his wont to walk.

A flourish of trumpets,
and two pieces of ordnance go off.

    What does this mean, my lord?
HAMLET: The king doth wake to-night and takes his rouse,
    Keeps wassail, and the swaggering upspring reels;   10
    And, as he drains his draughts of Rhenish down,
    The kettle-drum and trumpet thus bray out
    The triumph of his pledge.
HORATIO: Is it a custom?
HAMLET: Ay, marry, is it,
    But to my mind, though I am native here
    And to the manner born, it is a custom
    More honoured in the breach than the observance.
    This heavy-headed revel east and west
    Makes us traduced and taxed of other nations —   20
    They clepe us drunkards, and with swinish phrase
    Soil our addition; and indeed it takes
    From our achievements, though performed at height,
    The pith and marrow of our attribute.
    So, oft it chances in particular men,

It is almost midnight and Hamlet is upon the battlement with Horatio and Marcellus. The ghost appears and beckons Hamlet to go with him. The others try to prevent Hamlet from following the apparition, fearing that it is malevolent and may lead Hamlet to his destruction.

1. *shrewdly* – sharply

6. *season* – time of night

9 – 10. "The King is up late tonight, partying and drinking; he drinks toasts and dances wildly."
13. Claudius is triumphant in his ability to drain dry long drafts as he offers various toasts (pledge).
19 – 20. "This overindulgence in drink enables people, east and west, to malign and criticize us."
21. *clepe* – name, call
22. *addition* – reputation
23. *at height* – the highest level
24. "The heart or core of our reputation."

26. *mole of nature –* natural blemish

29. *overgrowth –* overdevelopment

29. *complexion –* temperament, trait

30. *pales and forts –* barriers and defences

31 – 32. *over-leavens ... manners –* corrupts the form of pleasing actions

34. *nature's ... livery –* something they are born with

36. *undergo –* possess

37. *censure –* opinion

38 – 40. "One's noble nature is put into disrepute because of a small fault."

46. During the Elizabethan period, it was believed that devils assumed pleasing shapes to tempt people. In 1594, Thomas Nashe speculated why the devil often appeared in the likeliness of a parent or relative: "No other reason can be given of it but this, that in those shapes which he supposeth most familiar unto us, and that we are inclined to with a natural kind of love, we will sooner harken to him than otherwise."

That for some vicious mole of nature in them,
As, in their birth wherein they are not guilty,
(Since nature cannot choose his origin),
By their overgrowth of some complexion,
Oft breaking down the pales and forts of reason,   30
Or by some habit that too much over-leavens
The form of plausive manners, that these men,
Carrying, I say, the stamp of one defect,
Being nature's livery, or fortune's star,
His virtues else, be they as pure as grace,
As infinite as man may undergo
Shall in the general censure take corruption
From that particular fault. The dram of evil
Doth all the noble substance of a doubt
To his own scandal.   40

Enter Ghost.

HORATIO: Look, my lord, it comes!
HAMLET: Angels and ministers of grace defend us!
  Be thou a spirit of health or goblin damned,
  Bring with thee airs from heaven or blasts from hell,
  Be thy intents wicked or charitable,
  Thou com'st in such a questionable shape
  That I will speak to thee. I'll call thee Hamlet,
  King, father, royal Dane. O, answer me.

Let me not burst in ignorance, but tell
Why thy canonized bones, hearsed in death,   50
Have burst their cerements, why the sepulchre,
Wherein we saw thee quietly interred,
Hath oped his ponderous and marble jaws,
To cast thee up again. What may this mean,
That thou, dead corpse, again in complete steel
Revisits thus the glimpses of the moon,
Making night hideous, and we fools of nature
So horridly to shake our disposition
With thoughts beyond the reaches of our souls?
Say, why is this? Wherefore? What should we do?   60

Ghost beckons Hamlet.

HORATIO: It beckons you to go away with it,
    As if it some impartment did desire
    To you alone.
MARCELLUS: Look, with what courteous action
    It waves you to a more removed ground,
    But do not go with it.
HORATIO: No, by no means.
HAMLET: It will not speak. Then I will follow it.
HORATIO: Do not, my lord.
HAMLET: Why, what should be the fear?   70
    I do not set my life in a pin's fee;
    And for my soul, what can it do to that,

50. *hearsed* – buried
51. *cerements* – funeral clothing, sheets

57. *fools of nature* – playthings, puppets of nature

62. *impartment* – communication

71. *pin's fee* – price of a pin

Act One • Scene 4

75. *flood* – sea

77. *beetles* – overhangs

81. *toys of desperation* –
foolish thoughts of suicide

92. *Nemean lion* – a
reference to Hercules' killing
of the Nemean Lion
94. *lets* – hinders

96. *waxes* – grows

101. Marcellus is not
content, as is Horatio
momentarily, to leave heaven
to sort out the issue. He
believes they should follow
Hamlet.

Being a thing immortal as itself?
It waves me forth again. I'll follow it.

HORATIO: What if it tempt you toward the flood, my lord,
Or to the dreadful summit of the cliff
That beetles over his base into the sea,
And there assume some other horrible form,
Which might deprive your sovereignty of reason
And draw you into madness? Think of it.   80
The very place puts toys of desperation,
Without more motive, into every brain
That looks so many fathoms to the sea
And hears it roar beneath.

HAMLET: It waves me still.
Go on, I'll follow thee.

MARCELLUS: You shall not go, my lord.

HAMLET: Hold off your hands.

HORATIO: Be ruled. You shall not go.

HAMLET: My fate cries out   90
And makes each petty artery in this body
As hardy as the Nemean lion's nerve.
Still am I called. Unhand me, gentlemen.
By heaven, I'll make a ghost of him that lets me!
I say, away. — Go on. I'll follow thee.

Exeunt Ghost and Hamlet.

HORATIO: He waxes desperate with imagination.

MARCELLUS: Let's follow. 'Tis not fit thus to obey him.

HORATIO: Have after. To what issue will this come?

MARCELLUS: Something is rotten in the state of Denmark.

HORATIO: Heaven will direct it.   100

MARCELLUS: Nay, let's follow him.

Exeunt.

Act One
Scene 5

Another part of the platform.

Enter Ghost and Hamlet.

HAMLET: Where wilt thou lead me? Speak! I'll go no further.
GHOST: Mark me.
HAMLET: I will.
GHOST: My hour is almost come
When I to sulphurous and tormenting flames
Must render up myself.
HAMLET: Alas, poor ghost.
GHOST: Pity me not, but lend thy serious hearing
To what I shall unfold.
HAMLET: Speak, I am bound to hear.   10
GHOST: So art thou to revenge, when thou shalt hear.
HAMLET: What?
GHOST: I am thy father's spirit,
Doomed for a certain term to walk the night,
And for the day confined to fast in fires,
Till the foul crimes done in my days of nature
Are burnt and purged away. But that I am forbid
To tell the secrets of my prison-house,
I could a tale unfold whose lightest word
Would harrow up thy soul, freeze thy young blood,   20
Make thy two eyes, like stars, start from their spheres,
Thy knotted and combined locks to part
And each particular hair to stand on end,
Like quills upon the fretful porpentine.
But this eternal blazon must not be
To ears of flesh and blood. List, list, O, list!
If thou didst ever thy dear father love —
HAMLET: O God!
GHOST: Revenge his foul and most unnatural murder.

Hamlet learns from the ghost of his dead father that Claudius murdered him as he slept in the orchard. The ghost commands Hamlet to revenge this wicked deed and Hamlet seems prepared to do so immediately. When joined by his friends, Hamlet swears them to secrecy, especially in regard to the false show of madness that he will be exhibiting.

14. The ghost is in purgatory, the middle ground between heaven and hell. Souls go there to purge away their sins before being admitted to heaven.
16. *days of nature* – natural life
20. *harrow up* – rip up
21. *spheres* – sockets
24. *porpentine* – porcupine
25. *eternal blazon* – divulging of the mysteries of the eternal

"We feel not only the virtues, but the weaknesses of Hamlet as our own."
– Henry MacKenzie (1745 – 1831), Scottish author

36. *I find thee apt* – The ghost is content with Hamlet's apparent readiness to execute swift revenge.

38. *Lethe* – river in Hades that causes forgetfulness

42. *forged process* – false account

46. *O my prophetic soul* – In Act 1, Scene 2, l.273 Hamlet suspected "some foul play." Here he discovers that his intuition was right.

47. *adulterate* – Some scholars, J. Dover Wilson in particular, suggest that the use of "adulterate" in this speech implies that Claudius and Gertrude had an affair before the death of King Hamlet.

55. *decline* – sink down to

58. "Just as virtue will never be moved or shaken"

59. *shape of heaven* – an angelic form assumed by the devil to tempt humans

61. *sate* – satisfy itself completely

62. *prey* – feed

66. *secure hour* – time free from care or worry

67. *hebenon* – poison

68. *porches* – openings

73. *posset* – thicken (A posset was a hot milk drink thickened and curdled with ale or wine.)

HAMLET: Murder! 30

GHOST: Murder most foul, as in the best it is,
But this most foul, strange and unnatural.

HAMLET: Haste me to know it, that I, with wings as swift
As meditation or the thoughts of love
May sweep to my revenge.

GHOST: I find thee apt,
And duller shouldst thou be than the fat weed
That roots itself in ease on Lethe wharf,
Wouldst thou not stir in this. Now, Hamlet, hear.
'Tis given out that, sleeping in my orchard, 40
A serpent stung me. So the whole ear of Denmark
Is by a forged process of my death
Rankly abused. But know, thou noble youth,
The serpent that did sting thy father's life
Now wears his crown.

HAMLET: O my prophetic soul! My uncle!

GHOST: Ay, that incestuous, that adulterate beast,
With witchcraft of his wit, with traitorous gifts —
O wicked wit and gifts, that have the power
So to seduce! — won to his shameful lust 50
The will of my most seeming-virtuous queen.
O Hamlet, what a falling-off was there,
From me, whose love was of that dignity
That it went hand in hand even with the vow
I made to her in marriage, and to decline
Upon a wretch whose natural gifts were poor
To those of mine.
But virtue, as it never will be moved,
Though lewdness court it in a shape of heaven,
So lust, though to a radiant angel linked, 60
Will sate itself in a celestial bed,
And prey on garbage.
But, soft! Methinks I scent the morning air.
Brief let me be. Sleeping within my orchard,
My custom always of the afternoon,
Upon my secure hour thy uncle stole
With juice of cursed hebenon in a vial,
And in the porches of my ears did pour
The leperous distilment, whose effect
Holds such an enmity with blood of man 70
That swift as quicksilver it courses through
The natural gates and alleys of the body,
And with a sudden vigour doth posset
And curd, like eager droppings into milk,

The thin and wholesome blood. So did it mine,
And a most instant tetter barked about,
Most lazar-like, with vile and loathsome crust
All my smooth body.
Thus was I, sleeping, by a brother's hand
Of life, of crown, of queen, at once dispatched.   80
Cut off even in the blossoms of my sin,
Unhouseled, disappointed, unaneled,
No reckoning made, but sent to my account
With all my imperfections on my head.
O, horrible! O, horrible! Most horrible!
If thou hast nature in thee, bear it not.
Let not the royal bed of Denmark be
A couch for luxury and damned incest.
But, howsoever thou pursuest this act,
Taint not thy mind, nor let thy soul contrive   90
Against thy mother aught. Leave her to heaven
And to those thorns that in her bosom lodge,
To prick and sting her. Fare thee well at once!
The glow-worm shows the matin to be near
And gins to pale his uneffectual fire.
Adieu, adieu, adieu. Remember me.

Exit.

HAMLET: O all you host of heaven! O earth! What else?
And shall I couple hell? O, fie! Hold, hold, my heart;
And you, my sinews, grow not instant old,
But bear me stiffly up. Remember thee!   100
Ay, thou poor ghost, while memory holds a seat
In this distracted globe. Remember thee?
Yea, from the table of my memory
I'll wipe away all trivial fond records,
All saws of books, all forms, all pressures past,
That youth and observation copied there.
And thy commandment all alone shall live
Within the book and volume of my brain,
Unmixed with baser matter. Yes, by heaven!
O most pernicious woman!   110
O villain, villain, smiling, damned villain!
My tables, meet it is I set it down
That one may smile, and smile, and be a villain —
At least I'm sure it may be so in Denmark.

Writing.

Margin notes:

76 – 78. "And almost instantly, a leprous vile rash, like the bark of a tree, crusted over all my smooth body."

81. "Murdered with all my sins still with me"

82. "Not having received benefit of holy communion, confession, and extreme unction." Extreme unction, the last rites, involves being anointed with holy oil.

90. *contrive* – plot

91. *aught* – in any respect

94. *matin* – morning

95. *uneffectual* – The glowworm's light becomes ineffectual because of the brightness of the day.

98. *couple* – add

102. *distracted globe* – confused head

105. "All wisdom to be gained by books, all forms or shapes, all impressions of the past"

112. "My notebook – it is fitting that I write it down"

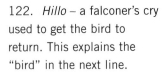

So, uncle, there you are. Now to my word.
It is 'Adieu, adieu! remember me.'
I have sworn it.
HORATIO: *[Within]* My lord, my lord,
MARCELLUS: *[Within]* Lord Hamlet,
HORATIO: *[Within]* Heaven secure him!   120
HAMLET: So be it!
HORATIO: *[Within]* Hillo, ho, ho, my lord!
HAMLET: Hillo, ho, ho, boy! Come, bird, come.

Enter Horatio and Marcellus.

MARCELLUS: How is it, my noble lord?
HORATIO: What news, my lord?
HAMLET: O, wonderful!
HORATIO: Good my lord, tell it.
HAMLET: No, you'll reveal it.
HORATIO: Not I, my lord, by heaven.
MARCELLUS: Nor I, my lord.   130
HAMLET: How say you, then. Would heart of man once
   think it — But you'll be secret?
HORATIO:
MARCELLUS: } Ay, by heaven.
HAMLET: There's never a villain dwelling in all Denmark
   But he's an arrant knave.
HORATIO: There needs no ghost, my lord, come from the grave
   To tell us this.
HAMLET: Why, right, you are in the right,
   And so, without more circumstance at all,
   I hold it fit that we shake hands and part.   140
   You, as your business and desire shall point you —
   For every man has business and desire,
   Such as it is — and for mine own poor part,
   Look you, I'll go pray.
HORATIO: These are but wild and whirling words, my lord.
HAMLET: I'm sorry they offend you, heartily —
   Yes, faith heartily.
HORATIO: There's no offence, my lord.
HAMLET: Yes, by Saint Patrick, but there is, Horatio,
   And much offence too. Touching this vision here,   150
   It is an honest ghost, that let me tell you.
   For your desire to know what is between us,
   Overmaster it as you may. And now, good friends,
   As you are friends, scholars and soldiers,
   Give me one poor request.

122. *Hillo* – a falconer's cry used to get the bird to return. This explains the "bird" in the next line.

131. *once* – ever

135. *arrant knave* – complete and utter rascal

149. *Saint Patrick* – patron saint of Ireland; often associated with visions of purgatory
153. "Overcome the urge (to know) as best you can"

HORATIO: What is it, my lord? We will.

HAMLET: Never make known what you have seen to-night.

HORATIO:
MARCELLUS: } My lord, we will not.

HAMLET: Nay, but swear it.

HORATIO: In faith, my lord, not I.   160

MARCELLUS: Nor I, my lord, in faith.

HAMLET: Upon my sword.

MARCELLUS: We have sworn, my lord, already.

HAMLET: Indeed, upon my sword, indeed.

GHOST: *[From beneath the stage]* Swear.

HAMLET: Ah ha, boy! Say'st thou so? Art thou there, truepenny?
    Come on, you hear this fellow in the cellarage.
    Consent to swear.

HORATIO: Propose the oath, my lord.

HAMLET: Never to speak of this that you have seen,   170
    Swear by my sword.

GHOST: *[Beneath]* Swear.

HAMLET: *Hic et ubique?* Then we'll shift our ground.
    Come hither, gentlemen,
    And lay your hands again upon my sword.
    Never to speak of this that you have heard,
    Swear by my sword.

GHOST: *[Beneath]* Swear.

HAMLET: Well said, old mole! Canst work in the earth
    so fast?   180
    A worthy pioner! Once more remove, good friends.

HORATIO: O day and night, but this is wondrous strange!

HAMLET: And therefore as a stranger give it welcome.
    There are more things in heaven and earth, Horatio,
    Than are dreamt of in your philosophy.
    But come,
    Here, as before, never, so help you mercy,
    How strange or odd so ever I bear myself,
    As I perchance hereafter shall think meet
    To put an antic disposition on —   190
    That you, at such times seeing me, never shall,
    With arms encumbered thus, or this headshake,
    Or by pronouncing of some doubtful phrase,
    As 'Well, well, we know,' or 'We could, and if we would,'
    Or 'If we list to speak,' or 'There be, and if they might,'
    Or such ambiguous giving out, to note
    That you know aught of me. This do swear,
    So grace and mercy at your most need help you.

GHOST: *[Beneath]* Swear.

---

166. *truepenny* – trusty or good fellow

173. *Hic et ubique?* – Here and everywhere?

181. *pioner* – foot soldier whose task it often is to dig trenches

183. "And therefore, welcome it as (the Bible says) we should welcome a stranger."

190. "To put on a show of madness"

194. *and if* – if only
195. *list* – choose
196. *giving out* – hint

They swear.

HAMLET: Rest, rest, perturbed spirit! So, gentlemen,   200
With all my love I do commend me to you,
And what so poor a man as Hamlet is
May do, to express his love and friending to you,
God willing, shall not lack. Let us go in together.
And still your fingers on your lips, I pray.
The time is out of joint. O cursed spite,
That ever I was born to set it right.
Nay, come, let's go together.

Exeunt.

৯৯ ৯৯ ৯৯

206. *out of joint* – in total disorder; out of its natural order

"Hamlet is the most baffling of the great plays. It is the tragedy of a man and an action continually baffled by wisdom. The man is too wise ... The task set by the dead is a simple one. All tasks are simple to the simple-minded. To the delicate and complex mind so much of life is bound up with every act that any violent act involves not only a large personal sacrifice of ideal, but a tearing up of the roots of half the order of the world."
– John Masefield (1878 – 1967), British poet laureate

Act One Considerations

ACT ONE Scene 1

▶ Why did Marcellus and Barnardo ask Horatio to join them during their watch? What character traits does Horatio possess that would suggest they were right in asking him to join them?

▶ To what extent is Shakespeare successful in attracting the audience's or reader's attention in this first scene? How does he accomplish this?

ACT ONE Scene 2

▶ Imagine you are a talk show host, interviewing the newly crowned Claudius, King of Denmark. In a series of questions and answers, review the information provided in the first 65 lines of this scene.

▶ What different aspects of Hamlet's character are revealed in this scene? In pairs or groups of four, discuss the evidence which would suggest that Hamlet is either in his teens or his late twenties.

ACT ONE Scene 3

▶ Imagine you are an advice columnist and you have received a question that deals with either Ophelia's or Laertes' situation. Write the question and the response using the points made in this scene. You may use some of the original phrases from the play.

▶ Write a diary entry in which Ophelia or Laertes recounts some of the advice she or he has received and how she or he feels about the advice.

ACT ONE Scene 4

▶ In the notes on page 28, Thomas Nashe offers reasons why Hamlet should not trust the apparition. Hamlet's friends do likewise. Summarize these reasons. How does Hamlet respond and what does this show about his character?

ACT ONE Scene 5

▶ Knowing what he now knows, could Hamlet march into the castle and accuse Claudius of murder? What would happen if Hamlet attempted to kill Claudius immediately? Write a short account of a scene following this one in which Hamlet either accuses Claudius or attempts to kill him.

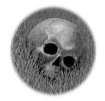

Act Two
Scene 1

A room in Polonius' house.

Enter Polonius and Reynaldo.

POLONIUS: Give him this money and these notes, Reynaldo.

REYNALDO: I will, my lord.

POLONIUS: You shall do marvellous wisely, good Reynaldo,
Before you visit him, to make inquire
Of his behaviour.

REYNALDO: My lord, I did intend it.

POLONIUS: Marry, well said, very well said. Look you, sir,
Inquire me first what Danskers are in Paris,
And how, and who, what means, and where they keep,
What company, at what expense. And finding   10
By this encompassment and drift of question
That they do know my son, come you more nearer
Than your particular demands will touch it.
Take you, as it were, some distant knowledge of him,
As thus, 'I know his father and his friends,
And in part him.' Do you mark this, Reynaldo?

REYNALDO: Ay, very well, my lord.

POLONIUS: 'And in part him.' But, you may say, 'not well.
But, if it be he I mean, he's very wild,
Addicted so and so' — and there put on him   20
What forgeries you please — marry, none so rank
As may dishonour him — take heed of that —
But, sir, such wanton, wild and usual slips
As are companions noted and most known
To youth and liberty.

REYNALDO: As gaming, my lord?

POLONIUS: Ay, or drinking, fencing, swearing,
Quarrelling, drabbing — you may go so far.

REYNALDO: My lord, that would dishonour him.

POLONIUS: Faith, no, as you may season it in the charge.   30

8. "First, find out for me what Danes are in Paris."

11. "And by this roundabout course of questioning"

14. *Take you* – assume, pretend you have

28. *drabbing* – visiting prostitutes
30. *Season* – moderate; tone down

You must not put another scandal on him,
That he is open to incontinency —
That's not my meaning. But breathe his faults so quaintly
That they may seem the taints of liberty,
The flash and outbreak of a fiery mind,
A savageness in unreclaimed blood,
Of general assault.

36 – 37. "A wildness
common in all youth."

REYNALDO: But, my good lord —
POLONIUS: Wherefore should you do this?
REYNALDO: Ay, my lord, I would know that.   40
POLONIUS: Marry, sir, here's my drift,
And I believe, it is a fetch of warrant.

42. "And I believe, it is a
clever device"

You laying these slight sullies on my son,

43. *sullies* – stains,
blemishes

As it were a thing a little soiled in the working,

44. *working* – handling

Mark you,

46 – 47. "You should
question the person with
whom you are conversing,
and if he has ever seen
Laertes involved in such low
activities as previously
mentioned"
49. "He will agree with you
using words such as:"
51. *addition* – title or form
of address

Your party in converse, him you would sound,
Having ever seen in the prenominate crimes
The youth you breathe of guilty, be assured
He closes with you in this consequence:
'Good sir,' or so, or 'friend,' or 'gentleman,'   50
According to the phrase or the addition
Of man and country.
REYNALDO: Very good, my lord.
POLONIUS: And then, sir, does he this — he does —
what was I about to say? By the mass, I was about to
say something. Where did I leave?
REYNALDO: At 'closes in the consequence,'
At 'friend or so,' and 'gentleman.'
POLONIUS: At 'closes in the consequence,' ay, marry.
He closes thus: 'I know the gentleman,   60
I saw him yesterday,' or 'the other day,'
Or then, or then, with such, or such, 'and as you say,
There was he gaming', 'there overtook in his rouse'
'There falling out at tennis' or perchance,
'I saw him enter such a house of sale,' —

66. *Videlicet* – namely
69. "And thus do we who
are wise and able"
70. *windlasses* – roundabout
means
70. *assays of bias* – a lawn
bowling term. In lawn
bowling, one does not aim
directly at the target (jack).
One must use the bias to get
the bowl to curve toward the
jack.

Videlicet, a brothel, or so forth.
See you now,
Your bait of falsehood takes this carp of truth,
And thus do we of wisdom and of reach,
With windlasses and with assays of bias,   70
By indirections find directions out.
So by my former lecture and advice,
Shall you my son. You have me, have you not?
REYNALDO: My lord, I have.
POLONIUS: God be with you. Fare you well.

REYNALDO: Good my lord!
POLONIUS: Observe his inclination in yourself.
REYNALDO: I shall, my lord.
POLONIUS: And let him ply his music.
REYNALDO: Well, my lord.   80
POLONIUS: Farewell!

Exit Reynaldo. Enter Ophelia.

How now, Ophelia, what's the matter?
OPHELIA: O, my lord, my lord, I have been so affrighted.
POLONIUS: With what, in the name of God?
OPHELIA: My lord, as I was sewing in my closet,
        Lord Hamlet, with his doublet all unbraced,
        No hat upon his head, his stockings fouled,
        Ungartered, and down-gyved to his ankle,
        Pale as his shirt, his knees knocking each other,
        And with a look so piteous in purport   90
        As if he had been loosed out of hell
        To speak of horrors, he comes before me.
POLONIUS: Mad for thy love?
OPHELIA: My lord, I do not know,
        But truly, I do fear it.
POLONIUS: What said he?
OPHELIA: He took me by the wrist and held me hard.
        Then goes he to the length of all his arm,
        And, with his other hand thus over his brow,
        He falls to such perusal of my face   100
        As he would draw it. Long stayed he so.
        At last, a little shaking of mine arm
        And thrice his head thus waving up and down,
        He raised a sigh so piteous and profound
        As it did seem to shatter all his bulk
        And end his being. That done, he lets me go,
        And, with his head over his shoulder turned,
        He seemed to find his way without his eyes,
        For out of doors he went without their helps,
        And to the last bended their light on me.   110
POLONIUS: Come, go with me. I will go seek the king.
        This is the very ecstasy of love,
        Whose violent property fordoes itself
        And leads the will to desperate undertakings
        As oft as any passion under heaven
        That does afflict our natures. I am sorry —
        What, have you given him any hard words of late?

85. closet – small private room

88. down-gyved – fallen down

90. purport – expression

105. bulk – trunk of the body

110. bended their light – directed his gaze

113. property fordoes – characteristic destroys

123. *quoted* – observed
124. *beshrew my jealousy!* – a curse on my suspicions!
125 – 126. "By heaven, it is as normal for old persons to suspect more than they actually have evidence for"
129 – 130. "This news of Hamlet's madness caused by love, if concealed, might cause more grief than it would offence if it is revealed."

"Polonius is a man bred in courts, exercised in business, stored with observations, confident in his knowledge, proud of his eloquence, and declining into dotage."
– Samuel Johnson (1709 – 1784), British essayist, biographer, and developer of the first English dictionary

OPHELIA: No, my good lord, but, as you did command,
    I did repel his letters and denied
    His access to me.   120
POLONIUS: That hath made him mad.
    I am sorry that with better heed and judgment
    I had not quoted him. I feared he did but trifle,
    And meant to wreck thee. But, beshrew my jealousy!
    By heaven, it is as proper to our age
    To cast beyond ourselves in our opinions
    As it is common for the younger sort
    To lack discretion. Come, go we to the King.
    This must be known, which, being kept close, might move
    More grief to hide than hate to utter love.   130

Exeunt.

Act Two
Scene 2

A room in the castle

Enter King and Queen, Rosencrantz, Guildenstern, and Attendants.

KING: Welcome, dear Rosencrantz and Guildenstern!
    Moreover that we much did long to see you,
    The need we have to use you did provoke
    Our hasty sending. Something have you heard
    Of Hamlet's transformation — so I call it,
    Since not the exterior nor the inward man
    Resembles that it was. What it should be,
    More than his father's death, that thus hath put him
    So much from the understanding of himself,
    I cannot dream of. I entreat you both,   10
    That, being of so young days brought up with him,
    And since so neighboured to his youth and haviour,
    That you vouchsafe your rest here in our court
    Some little time. So by your companies
    To draw him on to pleasures and to gather,
    So much as from occasion you may glean,
    Whether aught to us unknown afflicts him thus
    That, opened, lies within our remedy.

QUEEN: Good gentlemen, he hath much talked of you,
    And sure I am, two men there are not living   20
    To whom he more adheres. If it will please you
    To show us so much gentry and good will
    As to expend your time with us awhile,
    For the supply and profit of our hope,
    Your visitation shall receive such thanks
    As fits a king's remembrance.

ROSENCRANTZ: Both your Majesties
    Might, by the sovereign power you have of us,

Hamlet's university friends arrive at court and are commissioned by the King to spy on Hamlet. Polonius reports that the cause of Hamlet's madness is unrequited love for Ophelia. The King is skeptical, but agrees to test the theory. Hamlet appears and engages in seemingly nonsensical banter with Polonius. Hamlet's friends are warmly welcomed, and he quickly determines that they are in the employ of Claudius. A company of actors arrive, and Hamlet is elated when they agree to put on a play. In private conference, he bids one of the actors to insert several lines into the play.

13. *vouchsafe your rest* – consent to remain

15 – 18. The King enlists the aid of Rosencrantz and Guildenstern to spy on Hamlet to determine the cause of his madness. The King tells them that once the cause is discovered, he will try to find a remedy for the illness.

Put your dread pleasures more into command
Than to entreaty.   30
GUILDENSTERN: But we both obey,
    And here give up ourselves in the full bent
    To lay our service freely at your feet
    To be commanded.
KING: Thanks, Rosencrantz and gentle Guildenstern.
QUEEN: Thanks, Guildenstern and gentle Rosencrantz
    And I beseech you instantly to visit
    My too much changed son. Go, some of you,
    And bring these gentlemen where Hamlet is.

40. *practices* – doings

GUILDENSTERN: Heavens make our presence and our practices 40
    Pleasant and helpful to him!
QUEEN: Ay, amen.

Exeunt Rosencrantz, Guildenstern [and an Attendant.]
Enter Polonius.

POLONIUS: The ambassadors from Norway, my good lord,
    Are joyfully returned.
KING: Thou still hast been the father of good news.
POLONIUS: Have I, my lord? I assure my good liege
    I hold my duty as I hold my soul,
    Both to my God and to my gracious King,
    And I do think, or else this brain of mine

50. "Pursues not the art of statecraft as well"

    Hunts not the trail of policy so sure   50
    As it hath used to do, that I have found
    The very cause of Hamlet's lunacy.
KING: O, speak of that! That do I long to hear.
POLONIUS: Give first admittance to the ambassadors.
    My news shall be the fruit to that great feast.
KING: Thyself do grace to them, and bring them in.

56. *grace* – The King continues the food metaphor begun by Polonius and puns on the double meaning of the word "grace."

Exit Polonius.

He tells me, my dear Gertrude, he hath found
The head and source of all your son's distemper.

59. *doubt* – suspect

QUEEN: I doubt it is no other but the main,
    His father's death, and our overhasty marriage.   60
KING: Well, we shall sift him.

61. *sift him* – question Polonius closely

Enter Polonius, with Voltemand and Cornelius.

Welcome, my good friends.
Say, Voltemand, what from our brother Norway?

VOLTEMAND: Most fair return of greetings and desires.
    Upon our first, he sent out to suppress
    His nephew's levies, which to him appeared
    To be a preparation against the Polack.
    But, better looked into, he truly found
    It was against your highness, whereat grieved,
    That so his sickness, age and impotence   70
    Was falsely borne in hand, sends out arrests
    On Fortinbras, which he, in brief, obeys,
    Receives rebuke from Norway, and in fine
    Makes vow before his uncle never more
    To give the assay of arms against your Majesty.
    Whereon old Norway, overcome with joy,
    Gives him three thousand crowns in annual fee
    And his commission to employ those soldiers
    So levied as before, against the Polack,
    With an entreaty, herein further shown,   80

[Gives him a paper.]

    That it might please you to give quiet pass
    Through your dominions for this enterprise
    On such regards of safety and allowance
    As therein are set down.
KING: It likes us well,
    And at our more considered time we'll read,
    Answer, and think upon this business.
    Meantime we thank you for your well-took labour.
    Go to your rest. At night we'll feast together.
    Most welcome home!   90

Exeunt Voltemand and Cornelius.

POLONIUS: This business is well ended.
    My liege, and madam, to expostulate
    What majesty should be, what duty is,
    Why day is day, night night, and time is time,
    Were nothing but to waste night, day and time.
    Therefore, since brevity is the soul of wit,
    And tediousness the limbs and outward flourishes,
    I will be brief. Your noble son is mad.
    Mad call I it, for, to define true madness,
    What is it but to be nothing else but mad?   100
    But let that go.
QUEEN: More matter, with less art.

65. *Upon our first* – upon first raising the issue

69. *grieved* – offended
71. *borne in hand* – deceived
71. *arrests* – orders for Fortinbras to stop his activities
75. *assay* – challenge, threat

81. *quiet pass* – safe passage

POLONIUS: Madam, I swear I use no art at all.
    That he is mad, 'tis true; 'tis true 'tis pity;
    And pity 'tis 'tis true. A foolish figure —
    But farewell it, for I will use no art.
    Mad let us grant him, then. And now remains
    That we find out the cause of this effect,
    Or rather say the cause of this defect,
    For this effect defective comes by cause.   110
    Thus it remains, and the remainder thus.
    Perpend.
    I have a daughter — have while she is mine —
    Who in her duty and obedience, mark,
    Hath given me this. Now gather, and surmise.

[Reads:]

    'To the celestial and my soul's idol, the most
    beautified Ophelia,'— That's an ill phrase,
    a vile phrase, 'beautified' is a vile phrase.
    But you shall hear. Thus: *[Reads:]*
    'In her excellent white bosom, these, &c.'   120
QUEEN: Came this from Hamlet to her?
POLONIUS: Good madam, stay awhile, I will be faithful.
[Reads:]   *'Doubt thou the stars are fire;*
      Doubt that the sun doth move;
      Doubt truth to be a liar;
      But never doubt I love.

110. *comes by cause* – must have a cause

112. *Perpend* – Take careful note

"Polonius's mishandling of language parallels his mismanagement of human affairs."
– Gladys Veidemanis

123. *doubt* – means either to call into question or to suspect. Perhaps Shakespeare was ahead of his time in questioning the orthodox belief that the sun moved round the earth.

O dear Ophelia, I am ill at these numbers.
I have not art to reckon my groans. But that
I love thee best, O most best, believe it. Adieu.
    'Thine evermore, most dear lady, whilst   130
    this machine is to him,   *Hamlet.'*

This in obedience hath my daughter shown me,
And, more above, hath his solicitings,
As they fell out by time, by means, and place,
All given to mine ear.
KING: But how hath she received his love?
POLONIUS: What do you think of me?
KING: As of a man faithful and honourable.
POLONIUS: I would fain prove so. But what might you think,
    When I had seen this hot love on the wing —   140
    As I perceived it, I must tell you that,
    Before my daughter told me — what might you
    Or my dear majesty your queen here think,
    If I had played the desk or table-book,
    Or given my heart a winking mute and dumb,
    Or looked upon this love with idle sight —
    What might you think? No, I went round to work,
    And my young mistress thus I did bespeak:
    'Lord Hamlet is a prince, out of thy star.
    This must not be.' And then I prescripts gave her,   150
    That she should lock herself from his resort,
    Admit no messengers, receive no tokens.

127. *numbers* – verse making

131. *machine* – body

144. "If I had remained silent"
145. *winking* – closed one's eyes to the matter

149. *out of thy star* – far above you in rank
151. *resort* – access

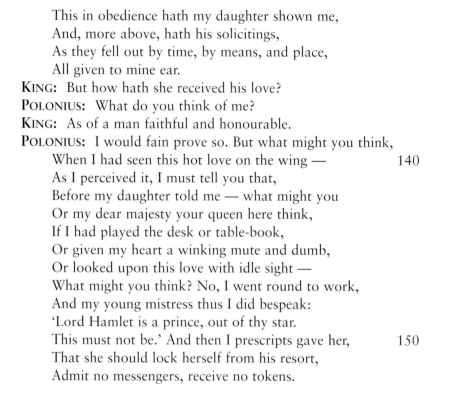

47

154 – 158. Polonius lists the classic symptoms of madness: depression, poor appetite, insomnia, fatigue, and disorientation.

169. *Within the centre* – the centre of the earth
170. *try* – test (the theory)
175. *loose* – to release animals into the same enclosure to mate

180. This imagery is consistent with the farming connotations of the word "loose" in line 175.

arras

176. *arras* – a large wall-sized tapestry

188. *fishmonger* – Hamlet is a punster. A fishmonger to the Elizabethans meant a seller of fish; a pimp; or it may even be a reference to Lord Burleigh, Queen Elizabeth's chief adviser, who benefited financially by having Wednesdays declared "fishdays" by Parliament.

Which done, she took the fruits of my advice,
And he, repelled — a short tale to make —
Fell into a sadness, then into a fast,
Thence to a watch, thence into a weakness,
Thence to a lightness, and, by this declension,
Into the madness wherein now he raves,
And all we mourn for.
KING: Do you think 'tis this?   160
QUEEN: It may be, very likely.
POLONIUS: Hath there been such a time, I would fain know that,
That I have positively said "'Tis so,'
When it proved otherwise?
KING: Not that I know.
POLONIUS: *[Pointing to his head and shoulder.]*
Take this from this, if this be otherwise.
If circumstances lead me, I will find
Where truth is hid, though it were hid indeed
Within the centre.
KING: How may we try it further?   170
POLONIUS: You know, sometimes
He walks four hours together, here
In the lobby.
QUEEN: So he does indeed.
POLONIUS: At such a time I'll loose my daughter to him.
Be you and I behind an arras then,
Mark the encounter. If he love her not
And be not from his reason fallen thereon,
Let me be no assistant for a state,
But keep a farm and carters.   180
KING: We will try it.
QUEEN: But, look, where sadly the poor wretch comes reading.
POLONIUS: Away, I do beseech you, both away.
I'll board him presently. O, give me leave.

[Exeunt King, Queen and Attendants.]
Enter Hamlet, reading.

How does my good Lord Hamlet?
HAMLET: Well, God-a-mercy.
POLONIUS: Do you know me, my lord?
HAMLET: Excellent well. You are a fishmonger.
POLONIUS: Not I, my lord.
HAMLET: Then I would you were so honest a man.   190
POLONIUS: Honest, my lord.

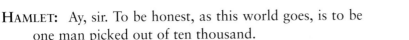

HAMLET: Ay, sir. To be honest, as this world goes, is to be one man picked out of ten thousand.

POLONIUS: That's very true, my lord.

HAMLET: For if the sun breed maggots in a dead dog, being a good kissing carrion — Have you a daughter?

POLONIUS: I have, my lord.

HAMLET: Let her not walk in the sun. Conception is a blessing, but not as your daughter may conceive. Friend, look to it.   200

POLONIUS: *[Aside]* How say you by that? Still harping on my daughter. Yet he knew me not at first. He said I was a fishmonger. He is far gone, far gone, and truly in my youth I suffered much extremity for love, very near this. I'll speak to him again. What do you read, my lord?

HAMLET: Words, words, words.

POLONIUS: What is the matter, my lord?

HAMLET: Between who?

POLONIUS: I mean, the matter that you read, my lord.   210

HAMLET: Slanders, sir. For the satirical rogue says here that old men have grey beards, that their faces are wrinkled, their eyes purging thick amber and plum-tree gum and that they have a plentiful lack of wit, together with most weak hams. All which, sir, though I most powerfully and potently believe, yet I hold it not honesty to have it thus set down, for yourself, sir, shall grow old as I am, if like a crab you could go backward.

POLONIUS: *[Aside]* Though this be madness, yet there is method in it. — Will you walk out of the air, my lord?   220

HAMLET: Into my grave.

POLONIUS: Indeed, that is out of the air.

[Aside] How pregnant sometimes his replies are! A happiness that often madness hits on, which reason and sanity could not so prosperously be delivered of. I will leave him and suddenly contrive the means of meeting between him and my daughter. — My lord, I will most humbly take my leave of you.

HAMLET: You cannot, sir, take from me any thing that I will more willingly part withal — except my life, except my   230 life, except my life.

POLONIUS: Fare you well, my lord.

HAMLET: These tedious old fools!

Enter Rosencrantz and Guildenstern.

195 – 196. *For ... carrion* – Hamlet talks what appears to be nonsense to convince Polonius of his madness. The carrion (carcass), according to Hamlet, is good for kissing.

213. *purging* – discharging

223. *pregnant* – quick-witted, full of meaning

226. *suddenly* – immediately

Act Two • Scene 2

POLONIUS: You go to seek the Lord Hamlet. There he is.
ROSENCRANTZ: *[To Polonius]* God save you, sir!

Exit Polonius.

GUILDENSTERN: My honoured lord.
ROSENCRANTZ: My most dear lord.
HAMLET: My excellent good friends. How dost thou, Guildenstern? Ah, Rosencrantz! Good lads, how do ye both?   240
ROSENCRANTZ: As the indifferent children of the earth. Happy, in that we are not over-happy. On fortune's cap we are not the very button.
HAMLET: Nor the soles of her shoe?
ROSENCRANTZ: Neither, my lord.
HAMLET: Then you live about her waist, or in the middle of her favours?
GUILDENSTERN: Faith, her privates we.
HAMLET: In the secret parts of fortune? O, most true, she is a strumpet. What news?   250
ROSENCRANTZ: None, my lord, but that the world's grown honest.
HAMLET: Then is doomsday near. But your news is not true. Let me question more in particular. What have you, my good friends, deserved at the hands of fortune, that she sends you to prison hither?
GUILDENSTERN: Prison, my lord?
HAMLET: Denmark's a prison.
ROSENCRANTZ: Then is the world one.
HAMLET: A goodly one, in which there are many confines,   260
wards and dungeons, Denmark being one of the worst.
ROSENCRANTZ: We think not so, my lord.
HAMLET: Why, then, it is none to you, for there is nothing either good or bad but thinking makes it so. To me it is a prison.
ROSENCRANTZ: Why then, your ambition makes it one. 'Tis too narrow for your mind.
HAMLET: O God, I could be bounded in a nutshell and count myself a king of infinite space, were it not that I have bad dreams.   270
GUILDENSTERN: Which dreams indeed are ambition, for the very substance of the ambitious is merely the shadow of a dream.
HAMLET: A dream itself is but a shadow.
ROSENCRANTZ: Truly, and I hold ambition of so airy

242. *indifferent* – ordinary; in other words, fine
244. *very button* – highest point

and light a quality that it is but a shadow's shadow.

HAMLET: Then are our beggars bodies, and our monarchs and outstretched heroes the beggars' shadows. Shall we to the court? For, by my fay, I cannot reason.

ROSENCRANTZ:
GUILDENSTERN: } We'll wait upon you.   280

HAMLET: No such matter. I will not sort you with the rest of my servants, for, to speak to you like an honest man, I am most dreadfully attended. But, in the beaten way of friendship, what make you at Elsinore?

ROSENCRANTZ: To visit you, my lord, no other occasion.

HAMLET: Beggar that I am, I am even poor in thanks, but I thank you. And sure, dear friends, my thanks are too dear a halfpenny. Were you not sent for? Is it your own inclining? Is it a free visitation? Come, deal justly with me. Come, come. Nay, speak.   290

GUILDENSTERN: What should we say, my lord?

HAMLET: Why, any thing but to the purpose. You were sent for, and there is a kind of confession in your looks which your modesties have not craft enough to colour. I know the good King and Queen have sent for you.

ROSENCRANTZ: To what end, my lord?

HAMLET: That you must teach me. But let me conjure you, by the rights of our fellowship, by the consonancy of our youth, by the obligation of our ever-preserved love,   300
and by what more dear a better proposer could charge you withal, be even and direct with me, whether you were sent for, or no.

ROSENCRANTZ: *[Aside to Guildenstern]* What say you?

HAMLET: *[Aside]* Nay, then I have an eye of you. If you love me, hold not off.

GUILDENSTERN: My lord, we were sent for.

HAMLET: I will tell you why. So shall my anticipation prevent your discovery, and your secrecy to the King and Queen moult no feather. I have of late, but   310
wherefore I know not, lost all my mirth, forgone all custom of exercises; and indeed it goes so heavily with my disposition that this goodly frame, the earth, seems to me a sterile promontory, this most excellent canopy, the air, look you, this brave overhanging firmament, this majestical roof fretted with golden fire, why, it appeareth nothing to me but a foul and pestilent congregation of vapours. What a piece of work is a man, how noble in reason, how infinite in faculties,

---

277 – 278. Hamlet takes Rosencrantz's comments to their most absurd lengths. What he concludes in essence is that since ambition is as substantial as a shadow, then beggars who are without ambition are more real than kings and heroes, who have ambition, and who therefore are less real than beggars. They are beggars' shadows.

298. *conjure you* – ask
299 – 300. *consonancy … youth* – the closeness we shared as youths
305. "Nay, then, I'll keep my eyes on you." Hamlet knows that his friends have been enlisted by the King.
308 – 310. "So shall my accurate guess as to why you were sent for make unnecessary your betraying any of the King or Queen's secrets."
311. *forgone* – given up

314. *sterile promontory* – barren piece of land
314. *canopy* – covering

320. *express* – exact
321. *apprehension* – understanding
322. *paragon* – model of perfection
323. *quintessence* – finest or purest form of

331. The theatres in Shakespeare's day were closed during Lent.

332. *coted* – passed
336. *target* – small shield
337. *gratis* – for nothing
337. *humorous* – ruled by violent dispositions
339. *tickled ... sere* – easily provoked to laughter

340. *halt* – scan poorly
344. *residence* – permanent base

346 – 347. *inhibition ... innovation* – They have been prevented from acting because of the latest trend.

352 – 353. "No, their effort (work) is still of a high quality. But there is a nestful of children, young hawks"
357. *many ... goose-quills* – Gentlemen are afraid of being the target of writers for these plays performed by the child actors.
360. *escotted* – provided for
360. *pursue the quality* – continue to be actors

in form and moving how express and admirable, in action how like an angel, in apprehension how like a god, the beauty of the world, the paragon of animals — and yet, to me, what is this quintessence of dust? Man delights not me — nor woman neither, though by your smiling you seem to say so. | 320

ROSENCRANTZ: My lord, there was no such stuff in my thoughts.

HAMLET: Why did you laugh then, when I said man delights not me?

ROSENCRANTZ: To think, my lord, if you delight not in man, what Lenten entertainment the players shall receive from you. We coted them on the way, and hither are they coming to offer you service. | 330

HAMLET: He that plays the king shall be welcome. His Majesty shall have tribute on me, the adventurous knight shall use his foil and target, the lover shall not sigh gratis, the humorous man shall end his part in peace, the clown shall make those laugh whose lungs are tickled a the sere, and the lady shall say her mind freely, or the blank verse shall halt for it. What players are they? | 340

ROSENCRANTZ: Even those you were wont to take delight in, the tragedians of the city.

HAMLET: How chances it they travel? Their residence, both in reputation and profit, was better both ways.

ROSENCRANTZ: I think their inhibition comes by the means of the late innovation.

HAMLET: Do they hold the same estimation they did when I was in the city? Are they so followed?

ROSENCRANTZ: No, indeed, are they not. | 350

HAMLET: How comes it? Do they grow rusty?

ROSENCRANTZ: Nay, their endeavour keeps in the wonted pace. But there is, sir, an eyrie of children, little eyases, that cry out on the top of question, and are most tyrannically clapped for it. These are now the fashion, and so berattle the common stages — so they call them — that many wearing rapiers are afraid of goose-quills and dare scarce come thither.

HAMLET: What, are they children? Who maintains them? How are they escotted? Will they pursue the quality no longer than they can sing? Will they not say afterwards, if they should grow themselves to common players — as it is most like, if their means are no better — their writers do them wrong to make them exclaim against their own succession? | 360

ROSENCRANTZ: Faith, there has been much to do on both sides, and the nation holds it no sin to tar them to controversy. There was for a while no money bid for argument, unless the poet and the player went to cuffs in the question.

HAMLET: Is it possible? 370

GUILDENSTERN: O, there has been much throwing about of brains.

HAMLET: Do the boys carry it away?

ROSENCRANTZ: Ay, that they do, my lord. Hercules and his load too.

HAMLET: It is not very strange, for mine uncle is King of Denmark, and those that would make mouths at him while my father lived give twenty, forty, fifty, a hundred ducats apiece for his picture in little. 'Sblood, there is something in this more than natural, if philosophy could find it out. 380

Flourish of trumpets for the Players.

GUILDENSTERN: There are the players.

HAMLET: Gentlemen, you are welcome to Elsinore. Your hands, come then. The appurtenance of welcome is fashion and ceremony. Let me comply with you in this garb, lest my extent to the players, which, I tell you, must show fairly outwards, should more appear like entertainment than yours. You are welcome, but my uncle-father and aunt-mother are deceived.

GUILDENSTERN: In what, my dear lord?

HAMLET: I am but mad north-north-west. When the wind 390 is southerly I know a hawk from a handsaw.

Enter Polonius.

POLONIUS: Well be with you, gentlemen!

HAMLET: Hark you, Guildenstern, and you too. At each ear a hearer. That great baby you see there is not yet out of his swaddling-clouts.

ROSENCRANTZ: Happily he's the second time come to them, for they say an old man is twice a child.

HAMLET: I will prophesy he comes to tell me of the players. Mark it — You say right, sir, on Monday morning, 'twas so indeed. 400

POLONIUS: My lord, I have news to tell you.

HAMLET: My lord, I have news to tell you. When Roscius was an actor in Rome, —

367. *tar* – incite
368. *no ... argument* – no money paid by the producers
372. *carry it away* – carry the day; are victorious

373. The sign at the Globe Theatre featured Hercules bearing the world on his shoulders.

376. *mouths* – faces
378. *picture in little* – miniature portrait
383. *appurtenance* – outward show
384 – 387. "Let me compliment you (by shaking hands), lest the welcome I show the players appears more warm than that I have shown you."

390 – 391. Hamlet may be warning his friends that sometimes his powers of discrimination are acute.
395. *clouts* – clothes

399 – 400. When Polonius approaches, Hamlet pretends that he is in the middle of a conversation.

402. *Roscius* – the most famous actor in classical Roman times.

Act Two • Scene 2

410. *tragical historical* – a new form of drama in Shakespeare's day. The first play to be described as such was *Hamlet*.

412. *Seneca* – Roman playwright

413. *Plautus* – Roman comic playwright

415. *Jephthah* – In the Biblical story (Judges 11), Jephthah promises God that if he is successful in battle, he will sacrifice the first thing he meets on returning home. He is victorious. As he approaches his home, his beloved daughter rushes forth to meet him. Jephthah keeps his vow and sacrifices his daughter.

430. *row* – stanza

431. *abridgement* – entertainment that serves to cut short the time

434. *valanced* – adorned (with a beard)

chopine

438. *chopine* – a thick-soled woman's shoe

POLONIUS: The actors are come hither, my lord.

HAMLET: Buzz, buzz!

POLONIUS: Upon mine honour, —

HAMLET: Then came each actor on his ass, —

POLONIUS: The best actors in the world, either for tragedy, comedy, history, pastoral, pastoral-comical, historical-pastoral, tragical-historical, tragical-comical-historical-pastoral, scene individable, orpoem unlimited. Seneca cannot be too heavy, nor Plautus too light. For the law of writ and the liberty, these are the only men.   410

HAMLET: O Jephthah, judge of Israel, what a treasure hadst thou!

POLONIUS: What a treasure had he, my lord?

HAMLET: Why,

'One fair daughter and no more,
The which he loved passing well.'

POLONIUS: *[Aside]* Still on my daughter.   420

HAMLET: Am I not in the right, old Jephthah?

POLONIUS: If you call me Jephthah, my lord, I have a daughter that I love passing well.

HAMLET: Nay, that follows not.

POLONIUS: What follows, then, my lord?

HAMLET: Why,

'As by lot, God wot,'

and then, you know,

'It came to pass, as most like it was,' —
the first row of the pious chanson will show you more. For look, where my abridgement comes.   430

Enter four or five Players.

You are welcome, masters. Welcome, all. I am glad to see thee well. Welcome, good friends. O, my old friend! Thy face is valanced since I saw thee last. Comest thou to beard me in Denmark? What, my young lady and mistress! By our lady, your ladyship is nearer to heaven than when I saw you last, by the altitude of a chopine. Pray God, your voice, like a piece of uncurrent gold, be not cracked within the ring. Masters, you are all welcome. We'll even to it like French falconers, fly at any thing we see. We'll have a speech straight. Come, give us a taste of your quality. Come, a passionate speech.   440

FIRST PLAYER: What speech, my good lord?

HAMLET: I heard thee speak me a speech once, but it was

never acted, or if it was, not above once — for the play, I remember, pleased not the million. 'Twas caviare to the general. But it was — as I received it, and others, whose judgments in such matters cried in the top of mine — an excellent play, well digested in the scenes, set down with as much modesty as cunning. I remember, one said there were no sallets in the lines to make the matter savory, nor no matter in the phrase that might indict the author of affectation, but called it an honest method, as wholesome as sweet, and by very much more handsome than fine. One speech in it I chiefly loved — 'twas Aeneas' tale to Dido, and thereabout of it especially, where he speaks of Priam's slaughter. If it live in your memory, begin at this line, let me see, let me see:

The rugged Pyrrhus, like the Hyrcanian beast,'
'Tis not so. It begins with Pyrrhus:
The rugged Pyrrhus, he whose sable arms,
Black as his purpose, did the night resemble
When he lay couched in the ominous horse,
Hath now this dread and black complexion smeared
With heraldry more dismal. Head to foot
Now is he total gules. Horridly tricked
With blood of fathers, mothers, daughters, sons,
Baked and impasted with the parching streets,
That lend a tyrannous and damned light
To their lord's murder. Roasted in wrath and fire,
And thus over-sized with coagulate gore,
With eyes like carbuncles, the hellish Pyrrhus
Old grandsire Priam seeks.
So, proceed you.

POLONIUS: Before God, my lord, well spoken, with good accent and good discretion.

FIRST PLAYER: *Anon he finds him*
Striking too short at Greeks. His antique sword,
Rebellious to his arm, lies where it falls,
Repugnant to command. Unequal matched,
Pyrrhus at Priam drives. In rage strikes wide,
But with the whiff and wind of his fell sword
The unnerved father falls. Then senseless Ilium,
Seeming to feel this blow, with flaming top
Stoops to his base, and with a hideous crash
Takes prisoner Pyrrhus' ear. For, lo! His sword,
Which was declining on the milky head

450

460

470

480

490

448. *caviare ... general* – too sophisticated for the general public
453. *sallets* – spicy passages

458. *Aeneas* – hero of Virgil's *Aeneid,* an epic poem that tells the story of Aeneas after the fall of Troy. Hamlet has the player recount the murder of King Priam and the mourning of Queen Hecuba's. This speech would contain interesting parallels to what has occurred in the court of Denmark.

466. *ominous horse* – the wooden horse used by the Greeks to enter Troy

469. *total gules* – all red

475. *carbuncles* – precious stones that give off a reddish glow

481. *too short* – ineffectually
483. *repugnant to command* – disobedient
486. *Ilium* – towers
488. *stoops ... base* – collapses
489 – 490. "Forces Pyrrhus to listen. For lo! His sword which was coming down on the white head"

493. *neutral ... will* –
passive and uncertain as to
his next move
501. *Cyclops' hammers* –
Cyclops were one-eyed
giants associated with
Vulcan, blacksmith for the
gods.
506. *synod* – council
507. *fellies* – parts of the
rim
508. *bowl* – roll
512. *He's for* – He must
have
514. *mobled* – muffled,
veiled
518. "With blinding tears, a
cloth upon that head"
520. *over-teemed* – from
having so many children
529. *milch* – milky (because
of the flow of tears)

536. Playwrights and
actors frequently inserted
topical allusions and references to important
personages in their plays,
with the result that plays
were often censored or
banned and writers
imprisoned.

"It has been stated that
Hamlet is the only one of
Shakespeare's characters
who could have written
the plays of his creator."
– Betty Bealey
(b. 1912), American
journalist

Of reverend Priam, seemed in the air to stick.
So, as a painted tyrant, Pyrrhus stood,
And like a neutral to his will and matter,
Did nothing.
But, as we often see, against some storm,
A silence in the heavens, the rack stand still,
The bold winds speechless and the orb below
As hush as death, anon the dreadful thunder
Doth rend the region. So, after Pyrrhus' pause,
Aroused vengeance sets him new a-work. 500
And never did the Cyclops' hammers fall
On Mars's armour forged for proof eterne
With less remorse than Pyrrhus' bleeding sword
Now falls on Priam.
Out, out, thou strumpet, Fortune! All you gods,
In general synod take away her power;
Break all the spokes and fellies from her wheel,
And bowl the round nave down the hill of heaven,
As low as to the fiends!

POLONIUS: This is too long. 510
HAMLET: It shall to the barber's with your beard.
     Prithee, say on. He's for a jig or a tale of bawdry, or
     he sleeps. Say on. Come to Hecuba.
FIRST PLAYER: *But who, O, who had seen the mobled queen —*
HAMLET: 'The mobled queen?'
POLONIUS: That's good; 'mobled queen' is good.
FIRST PLAYER: *Run barefoot up and down, threatening the flames*
     With bisson rheum, a clout upon that head
     Where late the diadem stood, and for a robe,
     About her lank and all over-teemed loins, 520
     A blanket, in the alarm of fear caught up —
     Who this had seen, with tongue in venom steeped,
     'Gainst Fortune's state would treason have pronounced.
     But if the gods themselves did see her then
     When she saw Pyrrhus make malicious sport
     In mincing with his sword her husband's limbs,
     The instant burst of clamour that she made,
     Unless things mortal move them not at all,
     Would have made milch the burning eyes of heaven,
     And passion in the gods. 530
POLONIUS: Look, whether he has not turned his colour
     and has tears in his eyes. Pray you, no more.
HAMLET: 'Tis well. I'll have thee speak out the rest
     soon.Good my lord, will you see the players well
     bestowed? Do you hear, let them be well used, for

they are the abstract and brief chronicles of the time.
After your death you were better have a bad epitaph than
their ill report while you live.

POLONIUS: My lord, I will use them according to their desert.

HAMLET: God's bodkin, man, much better. Use every man   540
after his desert, and who should escape whipping?
Use them after your own honour and dignity. The less
they deserve, the more merit is in your bounty. Take
them in.

POLONIUS: Come, sirs.

HAMLET: Follow him, friends. We'll hear a play to-morrow.

[Exit Polonius with all the Players but the First.]

Dost thou hear me, old friend? Can you play *The
Murder of Gonzago?*

FIRST PLAYER: Ay, my lord.

HAMLET: We'll have it to-morrow night. You could, for a   550
need, study a speech of some dozen or sixteen lines,
which I would set down and insert in it, could you not?

FIRST PLAYER: Ay, my lord.

HAMLET: Very well. Follow that lord, and look you mock him not.

[Exit First Player.]

My good friends, I'll leave you till night. You are
welcome to Elsinore.

ROSENCRANTZ: Good my lord.

HAMLET: Ay, so, God be with ye.

Exeunt Rosencrantz and Guildenstern.

Now I am alone.   560
O, what a rogue and peasant slave am I!
Is it not monstrous that this player here,
But in a fiction, in a dream of passion,
Could force his soul so to his own conceit
That from her working all his visage wanned,
Tears in his eyes, distraction in his aspect,
A broken voice, and his whole function suiting
With forms to his conceit? And all for nothing!
For Hecuba!
What's Hecuba to him, or he to Hecuba,   570
That he should weep for her? What would he do,
Had he the motive and the cue for passion
That I have? He would drown the stage with tears
And cleave the general ear with horrid speech,

Travelling Players

564. *conceit* – that which is conceived
565. *visage wanned* – face grew pale
567–568. "A cracked voice and his actions perfectly corresponding to the role he recreated."

580. *John-a-dreams* – dreamer

580. *unpregnant* – not stirred to act

584. *pate* – top of the head

586–587. "… calls me a liar and makes me swallow this insult to the very core"

591. *kites* – scavenger birds

592. *offal* – putrid flesh

600. *About, my brain* – "Get moving. I must use my head."

604. "They have confessed their evil deeds"

606. *organ* – way

"Yet English Seneca [Shakespeare] read by candlelight yields many good sentences as 'Blood is a beggar,' and so forth, and if you entreat him fair in a frosty morning, he will afford you whole Hamlets, I should say handfuls of tragical speeches."
– Thomas Nashe (1567 – 1601), Elizabethan playwright and essayist

615. *Abuses* – deceives

616. *relative* – substantial, certain

Make mad the guilty and appal the free,
Confound the ignorant, and amaze indeed
The very faculties of eyes and ears.
Yet I,
A dull and muddy-mettled rascal, peak,
Like John-a-dreams, unpregnant of my cause,   580
And can say nothing. No, not for a king,
Upon whose property and most dear life
A damned defeat was made. Am I a coward?
Who calls me villain, breaks my pate across,
Plucks off my beard, and blows it in my face,
Tweaks me by the nose, gives me the lie in the throat,
As deep as to the lungs? Who does me this?
Ha! 'Swounds, I should take it. For it cannot be
But I am pigeon-livered and lack gall
To make oppression bitter, or ere this   590
I should have fatted all the region kites
With this slave's offal. Bloody, bawdy villain!
Remorseless, treacherous, lecherous, kindless villain!
O, vengeance!
Why, what an ass am I! This is most brave,
That I, the son of a dear father murdered,
Prompted to my revenge by heaven and hell,
Must, like a whore, unpack my heart with words,
And fall a-cursing, like a very drab, a scullion!
Fie upon it! Foh! About, my brain! I have heard   600
That guilty creatures sitting at a play
Have by the very cunning of the scene
Been struck so to the soul that presently
They have proclaimed their malefactions.
For murder, though it have no tongue, will speak
With most miraculous organ. I'll have these players
Play something like the murder of my father
Before mine uncle. I'll observe his looks,
I'll tent him to the quick. If he but blench,
I know my course. The spirit that I have seen   610
May be the devil, and the devil hath power
To assume a pleasing shape. Yea, and perhaps
Out of my weakness and my melancholy,
As he is very potent with such spirits,
Abuses me to damn me. I'll have grounds
More relative than this. The play's the thing
Wherein I'll catch the conscience of the King.

Exit.

❧ ❧ ❧

Act Two Considerations

ACT TWO Scene 1

▶ Imagine you are Reynaldo, in Paris, and conversing with a Dane about Laertes' activities. Write a dialogue in which you follow Polonius' instructions.

▶ Ophelia describes in detail Hamlet's appearance and actions. The details in this description would convince an Elizabethan audience that Hamlet is mad. Reword Ophelia's description in such a way as to convince a modern audience that Hamlet is mad.

ACT TWO Scene 2

▶ Claudius, Gertrude, and Polonius all have differing opinions on the source of Hamlet's madness. What are they?

▶ Assume you were present when Polonius presented his theory to the King. How would you describe Polonius' character to a friend or family member?

▶ Read the First Player's speech carefully. Outline what it has in common in terms of characters and situations with what has transpired in the Danish court.

Act Three
Scene 1

A room in the castle.

Enter King, Queen, Polonius, Ophelia,
Rosencrantz, Guildenstern, Lords.

KING: And can you, by no drift of circumstance,
    Get from him why he puts on this confusion,
    Grating so harshly all his days of quiet
    With turbulent and dangerous lunacy?
ROSENCRANTZ: He does confess he feels himself distracted,
    But from what cause he will by no means speak.
GUILDENSTERN: Nor do we find him forward to be sounded,
    But, with a crafty madness, keeps aloof
    When we would bring him on to some confession
    Of his true state.   10
QUEEN: Did he receive you well?
ROSENCRANTZ: Most like a gentleman.
GUILDENSTERN: But with much forcing of his disposition.
ROSENCRANTZ: Niggard of question, but of our demands
    Most free in his reply.
QUEEN: Did you assay him to any pastime?
ROSENCRANTZ: Madam, it so fell out, that certain players
    We over-raught on the way. Of these we told him,
    And there did seem in him a kind of joy
    To hear of it. They are about the court,   20
    And, as I think, they have already order
    This night to play before him.
POLONIUS: 'Tis most true,
    And he beseeched me to entreat your majesties
    To hear and see the matter.
KING: With all my heart, and it doth much content me
    To hear him so inclined.
    Good gentlemen, give him a further edge,
    And drive his purpose on to these delights.

R osencrantz and Guildenstern admit they cannot determine the cause of Hamlet's madness and report that Hamlet would like the King and Queen to attend a play arranged for their entertainment. The King and Polonius, still intent on eavesdropping on Hamlet, ask Ophelia to place herself where Hamlet is accustomed to walking. Hamlet appears and contemplates life in his "To be, or not to be" speech. Ophelia attempts to return Hamlet's gifts. Hamlet berates her and leaves. The King reveals his intention to send Hamlet to England. Polonius receives permission to eavesdrop as the Queen speaks to Hamlet in her private chamber.

1. *drift of circumstance* – course of conversation
7. *forward to be sounded* – eager to be questioned
13. *disposition* – inclination of the moment
16. *assay* – tempt
18. *over-raught* – overtook

28. *give him a further edge* – encourage him

ROSENCRANTZ: We shall, my lord.   30

Exeunt Rosencrantz and Guildenstern.

KING: Sweet Gertrude, leave us too,
　　　　For we have closely sent for Hamlet hither,
　　　　That he, as 'twere by accident, may here
　　　　Affront Ophelia.
　　　　Her father and myself, lawful espials,
　　　　Will so bestow ourselves that, seeing, unseen,
　　　　We may of their encounter frankly judge,
　　　　And gather by him, as he is behaved,
　　　　If it be the affliction of his love or no
　　　　That thus he suffers for.   40
QUEEN: I shall obey you.
　　　　And for your part, Ophelia, I do wish
　　　　That your good beauties be the happy cause
　　　　Of Hamlet's wildness. So shall I hope your virtues
　　　　Will bring him to his wonted way again,
　　　　To both your honours.
OPHELIA: Madam, I wish it may.

[Exit Queen.]

POLONIUS: Ophelia, walk you here. — Gracious, so please you,
　　　　We will bestow ourselves. —
　　　　[To Ophelia.]   Read on this book,   50
　　　　That show of such an exercise may colour
　　　　Your loneliness. — We are oft to blame in this,
　　　　'Tis too much proved, that with devotion's visage
　　　　And pious action we do sugar over
　　　　The devil himself.
KING: *[Aside]* O, 'tis too true!
　　　　How smart a lash that speech doth give my conscience!
　　　　The harlot's cheek, beautied with plastering art,
　　　　Is not more ugly to the thing that helps it
　　　　Than is my deed to my most painted word.   60
　　　　O heavy burden!
POLONIUS: I hear him coming. Let's withdraw, my lord.

Exeunt [King and Polonius.]
Enter Hamlet.

HAMLET: To be, or not to be, that is the question.
　　　　Whether 'tis nobler in the mind to suffer

Margin notes:

32. *closely* – privately

35. *lawful espials* – spies with legal or noble intentions

45. *wonted* – usual

53. *devotion's visage* – appearance of virtue

"Hamlet! Hamlet! When I think of his moving wild speech, in which resounds the groaning of the whole numbed universe, there breaks from my soul not one reproach, not one sigh … That soul is then so utterly oppressed by woe that it fears to grasp the woe entire, lest it lacerate itself."
– Fyodor Dostoevsky (1821 – 1881), Russian novelist

The slings and arrows of outrageous fortune,
Or to take arms against a sea of troubles,
And by opposing end them. To die, to sleep,
No more; and by a sleep to say we end
The heart-ache and the thousand natural shocks
That flesh is heir to. 'Tis a consummation   70
Devoutly to be wished. To die, to sleep;
To sleep, perchance to dream — ay, there's the rub,
For in that sleep of death what dreams may come,
When we have shuffled off this mortal coil,
Must give us pause — there's the respect
That makes calamity of so long life.
For who would bear the whips and scorns of time,
The oppressor's wrong, the proud man's contumely,
The pangs of despised love, the law's delay,
The insolence of office and the spurns   80
That patient merit of the unworthy takes,
When he himself might his quietus make
With a bare bodkin? Who would fardels bear,
To grunt and sweat under a weary life,
But that the dread of something after death,
The undiscovered country from whose bourn
No traveller returns, puzzles the will
And makes us rather bear those ills we have
Than fly to others that we know not of?
Thus conscience does make cowards of us all,   90
And thus the native hue of resolution
Is sicklied over with the pale cast of thought,
And enterprises of great pith and moment
With this regard their currents turn awry,
And lose the name of action.
[Notices Ophelia] Soft you now!
The fair Ophelia! Nymph, in thy orisons
Be all my sins remembered.

OPHELIA: Good my lord,
How does your honour for this many a day?   100

HAMLET: I humbly thank you. Well, well, well.

OPHELIA: My lord, I have remembrances of yours,
That I have longed long to re-deliver.
I pray you, now receive them.

HAMLET: No, not I.
I never gave you aught.

OPHELIA: My honoured lord, you know right well you did,
And, with them, words of so sweet breath composed
As made the things more rich. Their perfume lost,

70. *consummation* – final ending
72. *rub* – obstacle
74. *coil* – life, with all its turmoil and activity
78. *contumely* – humiliations
79. *law's delay* – the slow process of the law
80. *office* – officials
80 – 81. *spurns ... takes* – insults inflicted on worthy persons by inferiors with power

bodkin

83. *bodkin* – dagger
83. *fardels* – burdens
86. *bourn* – borders

85 – 87. This comment is rather odd coming from one who has just been visited by his father's ghost.

90. *conscience* – inner voice of moral judgment
91. *native* – natural

RELATED READING

Well, Frankly ... – parody by Charles, Prince of Wales (page 160)

97. *orisons* – prayers

111. *wax* – become

113. *honest* – truthful, chaste

115. *fair* – beautiful

118. *admit no discourse* – allow no conversation with
119. *commerce* – dealings
121 – 124. "... the power of beauty will transform chastity into something degenerate sooner than chastity will purify beauty."

128. *inoculate our old stock* – be grafted onto our original sinful nature

131. *nunnery* – Perhaps a pun. Besides meaning a convent, nunnery was slang for a brothel.

135 – 136. *at my beck* – ready to be committed

148. *calumny* – slander

150. *monsters* – cuckolds (men with horns)

154. *paintings* – application of makeup

Take these again, for to the noble mind   110
Rich gifts wax poor when givers prove unkind.
There, my lord.

HAMLET: Ha, ha! Are you honest?

OPHELIA: My lord?

HAMLET: Are you fair?

OPHELIA: What means your lordship?

HAMLET: That if you be honest and fair, your honesty should admit no discourse to your beauty.

OPHELIA: Could beauty, my lord, have better commerce than with honesty?   120

HAMLET: Ay, truly, for the power of beauty will sooner transform honesty from what it is to a bawd than the force of honesty can translate beauty into his likeness. This was sometime a paradox, but now the time gives it proof. I did love you once.

OPHELIA: Indeed, my lord, you made me believe so.

HAMLET: You should not have believed me, for virtue cannot so inoculate our old stock but we shall relish of it. I loved you not.

OPHELIA: I was the more deceived.   130

HAMLET: Get thee to a nunnery. Why wouldst thou be a breeder of sinners? I am myself indifferent honest, but yet I could accuse me of such things that it were better my mother had not borne me. I am very proud, revengeful, ambitious, with more offences at my beck than I have thoughts to put them in, imagination to give them shape, or time to act them in. What should such fellows as I do crawling between earth and heaven? We are arrant knaves all. Believe none of us. Go thy ways to a nunnery. Where's your   140
father?

OPHELIA: At home, my lord.

HAMLET: Let the doors be shut upon him, that he may play the fool no where but in his own house. Farewell.

OPHELIA: O, help him, you sweet heavens.

HAMLET: If thou dost marry, I'll give thee this plague for thy dowry: Be thou as chaste as ice, as pure as snow, thou shalt not escape calumny. Get thee to a nunnery, farewell. Or, if thou wilt needs marry, marry a fool, for wise men know well enough what monsters you   150
make of them. To a nunnery, go, and quickly too. Farewell.

OPHELIA: O heavenly powers, restore him!

HAMLET: I have heard of your paintings too, well enough.

God hath given you one face, and you make yourselves
another. You jig and amble, and you lisp, and nick-
name God's creatures, and make your wantonness
your ignorance. Go to, I'll no more on it. It hath made
me mad. I say, we will have no more marriages. Those
that are married already, all but one, shall live. The rest   160
shall keep as they are. To a nunnery, go.

Exit.

OPHELIA: O, what a noble mind is here overthrown!
    The courtier's, soldier's, scholar's, eye, tongue, sword,
    The expectancy and rose of the fair state,
    The glass of fashion and the mould of form,
    The observed of all observers, quite, quite down!
    And I, of ladies most deject and wretched,
    That sucked the honey of his music vows,
    Now see that noble and most sovereign reason,
    Like sweet bells jangled, out of tune and harsh,   170
    That unmatched form and feature of blown youth
    Blasted with ecstasy. O, woe is me,
    To have seen what I have seen, see what I see!

Enter King and Polonius.

KING: Love! His affections do not that way tend,
    Nor what he spake, though it lacked form a little,
    Was not like madness. There's something in his soul,
    Over which his melancholy sits on brood,
    And I do doubt the hatch and the disclose
    Will be some danger, which for to prevent,
    I have in quick determination   180
    Thus set it down: he shall with speed to England,
    For the demand of our neglected tribute.
    Haply the seas and countries different
    With variable objects shall expel
    This something settled matter in his heart,
    Whereon his brains still beating puts him thus
    From fashion of himself. What think you on it?
POLONIUS: It shall do well. But yet do I believe
    The origin and commencement of his grief
    Sprung from neglected love. How now, Ophelia!   190
    You need not tell us what Lord Hamlet said.
    We heard it all. My lord, do as you please,
    But, if you hold it fit, after the play

156. *jig and amble* –
   dancing terms
   lisp–talk affectionately
157 – 158. *make ...
ignorance* – contend that
your immoral actions are
caused by your not knowing
any better

164. *expectancy* – Hamlet is
expected to be the next
king.

171. *blown* – in full blossom
172. *ecstasy* – madness

178. "I fear that when
whatever is bothering
Hamlet is found out, it will
pose some danger to me."

182. *neglected tribute* –
topical allusion to the
renewed attempt on the part
of the Danes, during
Elizabeth's reign, to reimpose
the Danegeld. This was a
payment made by the
English kings since the tenth
century to the Danes.
183. *Haply* – perhaps
184. *variable objects* –
different and new sights
185. *something settled* –
somewhat fixed

195. *round* – direct, severe

"Hamlet's will ... is paralyzed. He seeks to move in one direction and is hauled in another. One moment he sinks into the abyss. The next, he rises above the clouds. His feet seek the ground, but find only the air...."
– Stephen Leacock (1869 – 1944), Canadian author and humorist

Let his queen mother all alone entreat him
To show his grief, let her be round with him,
And I'll be placed, so please you, in the ear
Of all their conference. If she find him not,
To England send him, or confine him where
Your wisdom best shall think.

KING: It shall be so.   200
Madness in great ones must not unwatched go.

Exeunt.

Act Three
Scene 2

A hall in the castle.

Enter Hamlet and three of the Players.

HAMLET: Speak the speech, I pray you, as I pronounced it to you, trippingly on the tongue. But if you mouth it, as many of your players do, I had as lief the town-crier spoke my lines. Nor do not saw the air too much with your hand, thus, but use all gently. For in the very torrent, tempest, and, as I may say, the whirlwind of passion, you must acquire and beget a temperance that may give it smoothness. O, it offends me to the soul to hear a robustious periwig-pated fellow tear a passion to tatters, to very rags, to split the ears of the groundlings, who for the most part are capable of nothing but inexplicable dumbshows and noise. I would have such a fellow whipped for overdoing Termagant. It out-Herods Herod. Pray you, avoid it.   10

FIRST PLAYER: I warrant your honour.

HAMLET: Be not too tame neither, but let your own discretion be your tutor. Suit the action to the word, the word to the action, with this special observation, that you overstep not the modesty of nature. For anything so overdone is from the purpose of playing, whose end, both at the first and now, was and is, to hold, as it were, the mirror up to nature, to show virtue her own feature, scorn her own image, and the very age and body of the time his form and pressure. Now this overdone, or come tardy off, though it make the unskilful laugh, cannot but make the judicious grieve, the censure of the which one must in your allowance overweigh a whole theatre of others.   20

3. *had as lief* – would rather
4. *saw the air* – overuse hand gestures
5. *use all gently* – perform everything with moderation
9 – 10. *periwig-pated* – In Shakespeare's day, actors wore wigs.

periwig

12. *inexplicable* – incomprehensible.
14. *Termagant* – stock character in medieval drama; a noisy heathen god
15. *Herod* – violent stock character in melodramas
16. *warrant* – assure
25. *pressure* – shape, as in a wax impression
28. *censure* – judgment

O, there be players that I have seen play, and heard   30
others praise, and that highly, not to speak it
profanely, that, neither having the accent of Christians
nor the gait of Christian, pagan, nor man, have so
strutted and bellowed that I have thought some of
nature's journeymen had made men and not made
them well, they imitated humanity so abominably.

FIRST PLAYER: I hope we have reformed that indifferently
with us, sir.

HAMLET: O, reform it altogether. And let those that play
your clowns speak no more than is set down for them.   40
For there be of them that will themselves laugh, to set
on some quantity of barren spectators to laugh too,
though, in the mean time, some necessary question of
the play be then to be considered. That's villainous,
and shows a most pitiful ambition in the fool that uses
it. Go, make you ready.

[Exeunt Players.] Enter Polonius, Guildenstern, and Rosencrantz.

How now, my lord! Will the king hear this piece of work?
POLONIUS: And the queen too, and that presently.
HAMLET: Bid the players make haste.

Exit Polonius.

Will you two help to hasten them?   50

37. *indifferently* – moderately well

44. *villainous* –
contemptible

"Hamlet is loathsome
and repugnant. The fact
that he is eloquent has
nothing to do with him
being obnoxious. He's an
aging playboy. The only
time he gets animated is
when he bosses around
the players, telling them
how to do their own
business."
– Charles Marowitz
(b. 1934), American
director, playwright, and
critic

ROSENCRANTZ:
GUILDENSTERN: } We will, my lord.

Exeunt Rosencrantz and Guildenstern.

HAMLET: What ho! Horatio!

Enter Horatio.

HORATIO: Here, sweet lord, at your service.
HAMLET: Horatio, thou art even as just a man
    As ever my conversation coped withal.
HORATIO: O, my dear lord —
HAMLET: Nay, do not think I flatter,
    For what advancement may I hope from thee
    That no revenue hast but thy good spirits,
    To feed and clothe thee? Why should the poor be
      flattered?   60
    No, let the candied tongue lick absurd pomp,
    And crook the pregnant hinges of the knee
    Where thrift may follow fawning. Dost thou hear?

54 – 55. "You are as close to being what an ideal person should be as anyone I have ever met."

61. *candied* – fawning
62. *pregnant* – ready (to kneel)

64. *was ... choice* – had the ability to make choices
65. *election* – choice
68. *buffets* – blows
70. "Whose passions and reason are in balance"

75. "... I have said too much on this subject."

80. *very comment* – closest attention possible
81. *occulted* – secret
82. *unkennel* – reveal to open view (as when a fox is driven from its hole)
85. *Vulcan's stithy* – forge belonging to Vulcan, the blacksmith of the gods
87 – 88. *both ... seeming* – compare our opinions of his appearance
90. *steal aught* – manages to get away with anything
92. *idle* – act foolish or mad

95 – 96. When chameleons eat, they flick their tongues faster than the human eye can see. This led to the belief that chameleons feed off the air. *Promise-crammed* may refer to Claudius' announcement that Hamlet is his heir to the throne.

Since my dear soul was mistress of her choice
And could of men distinguish, her election
Hath sealed thee for herself. For thou hast been
As one, in suffering all, that suffers nothing,
A man that fortune's buffets and rewards
Hast taken with equal thanks. And blest are those
Whose blood and judgment are so well commingled,   70
That they are not a pipe for fortune's finger
To sound what stop she please. Give me that man
That is not passion's slave, and I will wear him
In my heart's core, ay, in my heart of heart,
As I do thee. Something too much of this.
There is a play to-night before the king,
One scene of it comes near the circumstance
Which I have told thee of my father's death.
I prithee, when thou seest that act afoot,
Even with the very comment of thy soul   80
Observe mine uncle. If his occulted guilt
Do not itself unkennel in one speech,
It is a damned ghost that we have seen,
And my imaginations are as foul
As Vulcan's stithy. Give him heedful note,
For I mine eyes will rivet to his face,
And after we will both our judgments join
In censure of his seeming.

HORATIO: Well, my lord.
If he steal aught the whilst this play is playing,   90
And escape detecting, I will pay the theft.

Enter King, Queen, Polonius, Ophelia, Rosencrantz, Guildenstern, and other Lords attendant with his guards carrying Torches. Danish March. Sound a flourish.

HAMLET: They are coming to the play. I must be idle.
Get you a place.
KING: How fares our cousin Hamlet?
HAMLET: Excellent, in faith, of the chameleon's dish. I eat the air, promise-crammed. You cannot feed capons so.
KING: I have nothing with this answer, Hamlet. These words are not mine.
HAMLET: No, nor mine now.   *[To Polonius.]*
My lord, you played once in the university, you say?   100
POLONIUS: That did I, my lord, and was accounted a good actor.
HAMLET: What did you enact?
POLONIUS: I did enact Julius Caesar. I was killed in the Capitol. Brutus killed me.

HAMLET: It was a brute part of him to kill so capital a calf there. Be the players ready?

ROSENCRANTZ: Ay, my lord. They stay upon your patience.

QUEEN: Come hither, my dear Hamlet, sit by me.

HAMLET: No, good mother, here's metal more attractive.

POLONIUS: *[To King]* O, ho! Do you mark that?　　　　110

HAMLET: Lady, shall I lie in your lap?

OPHELIA: No, my lord.

HAMLET: I mean, my head upon your lap?

OPHELIA: Ay, my lord.

HAMLET: Do you think I meant country matters?

OPHELIA: I think nothing, my lord.

HAMLET: That's a fair thought to lie between maids' legs.

OPHELIA: What is, my lord?

HAMLET: Nothing.

OPHELIA: You are merry, my lord.　　　　120

HAMLET: Who, I?

OPHELIA: Ay, my lord.

HAMLET: O God, your only jig-maker. What should a man do but be merry, for, look you, how cheerfully my mother looks, and my father died within these two hours.

OPHELIA: Nay, 'tis twice two months, my lord.

HAMLET: So long? Nay then, let the devil wear black, for I'll have a suit of sables. O heavens! Die two months ago, and not forgotten yet? Then there's hope a great man's memory may outlive his life half a year. But, by　　130 our lady, he must build churches, then, or else shall he suffer not thinking on, with the hobby-horse, whose epitaph is 'For O, for O, the hobby-horse is forgot.'

The Trumpets sound. Dumb-show enters.

Enter a King and a Queen very lovingly, the Queen embracing him, and he her. She kneels, and makes show of protestation unto him. He takes her up, and declines his head upon her neck. He lays him down upon a bank of flowers. She, seeing him asleep, leaves him. Anon comes in a fellow, takes off his crown, kisses it, and pours poison in the King's ears, and exits. The Queen returns, finds the King dead, and makes passionate action. The Poisoner, with some two or three Mutes, comes in again, seeming to lament with her. The dead body is carried away. The Poisoner woos the Queen with gifts. She seems loath and unwilling awhile, but in the end accepts his love.

Exeunt.

"Despite the initial view we get of Hamlet's abhorrence of deception, he tries to dupe everyone else in the play."
– Michael M. Cohen (b. 1943), British Shakespeare critic

107. *stay* – wait
109. *metal* – material

115. *country matters* – physical lovemaking

123. *jig-maker* – maker of merriment; writer of comic songs

128. *sables* – luxurious furs, worn at funerals by those who could afford them

132. *suffer ... on* – resign oneself not to be thought about
133. *hobby-horse* – dancer dressed as a horse in the traditional morris dance

Stage Direction – It is not clear whether Shakespeare intended the dumb show to be seen by Claudius. If Claudius does see it, why does he not stop the play or protest at once?

136. miching malicho –
sneaky wrongdoing
137. argument – plot
139. counsel – secret

OPHELIA: What means this, my lord?
HAMLET: Marry, this is miching malicho. It means mischief.
OPHELIA: Belike this show imports the argument of the play.

Enter Prologue.

HAMLET: We shall know by this fellow.
        The players cannot keep counsel. They'll tell all.
OPHELIA: Will he tell us what this show meant?   140
HAMLET: Ay, or any show that you'll show him. Be not
        you ashamed to show, he'll not shame to tell you what
        it means.
OPHELIA: You are naught, you are naught. I'll mark the play.
PROLOGUE: *For us, and for our tragedy,*
            Here stooping to your clemency,
              We beg your hearing patiently.
HAMLET: Is this a prologue, or the posy of a ring?
OPHELIA: 'Tis brief, my lord.
HAMLET: As woman's love.   150

146. clemency – kindness
148. posy of a ring – short,
simple poem inscribed on
the inside of a ring
151. Phoebus' cart – the
sun

Phoebus' cart

152. salt ... ground –
oceans and earth; Tellus was
the Roman goddess of the
earth
161. distrust – fear for
163. holds quantity – are in
balance

Enter two Players, King and Queen.

PLAYER KING: *Full thirty times hath Phoebus' cart gone round*
        Neptune's salt wash and Tellus' orbed ground,
        And thirty dozen moons with borrowed sheen
        About the world have times twelve thirties been,
        Since love our hearts and Hymen did our hands
        Unite commutual in most sacred bands.
PLAYER QUEEN: *So many journeys may the sun and moon*
        Make us again count over ere love be done!
        But, woe is me, you are so sick of late,
        So far from cheer and from your former state,   160
        That I distrust you. Yet, though I distrust,
        Discomfort you, my lord, it nothing must.
        For women's fear and love holds quantity.
        In neither aught, or in extremity.
        Now, what my love is, proof hath made you know,
        And as my love is sized, my fear is so.
        Where love is great, the littlest doubts are fear;
        Where little fears grow great, great love grows there.
PLAYER KING: *Faith, I must leave thee, love, and shortly too.*

170. operant powers –
faculties

        My operant powers their functions leave to do,   170
        And thou shalt live in this fair world behind,
        Honoured, beloved; and haply one as kind
        For husband shalt thou —

PLAYER QUEEN: *O, confound the rest!*
Such love must needs be treason in my breast.
In second husband let me be accurst!
None wed the second but who killed the first.

HAMLET: *[Aside]* Wormwood, wormwood.

PLAYER QUEEN: *The instances that second marriage move*
Are base respects of thrift, but none of love.　　　180
A second time I kill my husband dead,
When second husband kisses me in bed.

PLAYER KING: *I do believe you think what now you speak,*
But what we do determine oft we break.
Purpose is but the slave to memory,
Of violent birth, but poor validity,
Which now, like fruit unripe, sticks on the tree,
But fall, unshaken, when they mellow be.
Most necessary 'tis that we forget
To pay ourselves what to ourselves is debt,　　　190
What to ourselves in passion we propose,
The passion ending, doth the purpose lose.
The violence of either grief or joy
Their own enactures with themselves destroy.
Where joy most revels, grief doth most lament;
Grief joys, joy grieves, on slender accident.
This world is not for aye, nor 'tis not strange
That even our loves should with our fortunes change,
For 'tis a question left us yet to prove,
Whether love lead fortune, or else fortune love.　　　200
The great man down, you mark his favourite flies;
The poor advanced makes friends of enemies.
And hitherto doth love on fortune tend,
For who not needs shall never lack a friend,
And who in want a hollow friend doth try,
Directly seasons him his enemy.
But, orderly to end where I begun,
Our wills and fates do so contrary run
That our devices still are overthrown;
Our thoughts are ours, their ends none of our own.　　　210
So think thou wilt no second husband wed,
But die thy thoughts when thy first lord is dead.

PLAYER QUEEN: *Nor earth to me give food, nor heaven light,*
Sport and repose lock from me day and night,
To desperation turn my trust and hope,
An anchor's cheer in prison be my scope,
Each opposite that blanks the face of joy,
Meet what I would have well and it destroy,

178. *Wormwood* – bitter (reminder)

179. *instances* – causes

180. *base ... thrift* – thoughts of material benefits and advantage

186. "Strong at first but made weak with time"

194. *enactures* – plans, fulfillments

197. *aye* – ever

204. *who not needs* – one who has no need
206. *seasons* – makes

209. *devices* – designs, plans

216. *anchor* – hermit ... *be my scope* – lifestyle
217. "Each terrible thing that turns the face of joy"

221. *break* – As well as its conventional meaning, *break* also means to reveal. Is Hamlet here referring to the Player Queen's breaking her word or to his mother's revealing her guilt?

228. *protest* – vow, swear

234. *tropically* – metaphorically. A trope is a figure of speech.

239. *galled jade* – old horse (jade) injured by the rubbing of the harness

239. *withers* – shoulders (of a horse) … *unwrung* – uninjured

243. *interpret between* – provide the commentary, as does a puppet master during a performance

247. *better, and worse* – keen (sharper) but more objectionable

249. *Leave* – stop making

251 – 256. Many scholars believe this speech is the one written by Hamlet for the player to insert into the play.

252. *Confederate season* – It is as though time is a confederate with the crime being committed.

Both here and hence pursue me lasting strife,
If, once a widow, ever I be a wife.   220
HAMLET: If she should break it now.
PLAYER KING: *'Tis deeply sworn. Sweet, leave me here awhile.*
My spirits grow dull, and fain I would beguile
The tedious day with sleep.

Sleeps.

PLAYER QUEEN: *Sleep rock thy brain,*
And never come mischance between us twain!

Exit.

HAMLET: Madam, how like you this play?
QUEEN: The lady doth protest too much, methinks.
HAMLET: O, but she'll keep her word.
KING: Have you heard the argument? Is there no
offence in it?   230
HAMLET: No, no, they do but jest, poison in jest.
No offence in the world.
KING: What do you call the play?
HAMLET: *The Mouse-trap.* Marry, how, tropically. This
play is the image of a murder done in Vienna.
Gonzago is the duke's name, his wife, Baptista. You
shall see anon. 'Tis a knavish piece of work. But what
of that? Your majesty and we that have free souls, it
touches us not. Let the galled jade wince, our withers
are unwrung.   240

Enter Lucianus.

This is one Lucianus, nephew to the king.
OPHELIA: You are as good as a chorus, my lord.
HAMLET: I could interpret between you and your love, if I
could see the puppets dallying.
OPHELIA: You are keen, my lord, you are keen.
HAMLET: It would cost you a groaning to take off my
edge.
OPHELIA: Still better, and worse.
HAMLET: So you must take your husbands. Begin,
murderer. Leave thy damnable faces, and begin.
Come: 'the croaking raven doth bellow for revenge.'   250
LUCIANUS: *Thoughts black, hands apt, drugs fit, and time*
agreeing,
Confederate season else no creature seeing,

Thou mixture rank, of midnight weeds collected,
With Hecate's ban thrice blasted, thrice infected,
Thy natural magic and dire property,
On wholesome life usurp immediately.

Pours the poison into the sleeper's ears.

HAMLET: He poisons him in the garden for his estate.
His name's Gonzago. The story is extant, and writ in
choice Italian. You shall see anon how the murderer
gets the love of Gonzago's wife.   260
OPHELIA: The king rises.
HAMLET: What, frighted with false fire!
QUEEN: How fares my lord?
POLONIUS: Give over the play.
KING: Give me some light. Away!
ALL: Lights, lights, lights!

Exeunt all but Hamlet and Horatio.

HAMLET: Why, let the stricken deer go weep,
                        The hart ungalled play;
            For some must watch, while some must sleep:
                        Thus runs the world away.   270
Would not this, sir, and a forest of feathers, if
the rest of my fortunes turn Turk with me, with two
Provincial roses on my razed shoes, get me a
fellowship in a cry of players, sir?
HORATIO: Half a share.
HAMLET: A whole one, I.
                  For thou dost know, O Damon dear,
                        This realm dismantled was
                  Of Jove himself; and now reigns here
                        A very, very pajock.   280
HORATIO: You might have rhymed.
HAMLET: O good Horatio, I'll take the ghost's word for a
thousand pound. Didst perceive?
HORATIO: Very well, my lord.
HAMLET: Upon the talk of the poisoning?
HORATIO: I did very well note him.
HAMLET: Ah, ha! Come, some music! Come, the recorders!
                  For if the king like not the comedy,
                        Why then, belike, he likes it not, perdy.
Come, some music!   290

254. *Hecate* – goddess of the underworld and queen of witches

258. *extant* – still exists

262. *false fire* – sound made by guns firing blanks; make–believe (as in a play)
268. *ungalled* – uninjured
269. *For some must watch, while some must sleep* – This was used as the motto for the 1992 World Congress of Anesthesiologists.

272. *turn Turk* – go bad
274. *cry* – company

277. *Damon* – a name usually associated with shepherds in pastoral poetry
279. *Jove* – Jupiter, King of the Heavens, perhaps a subtle reference to King Hamlet
280. *pajock* – a contemptible, base person

289. *perdy* – colloquial for par Dieu (by God)

RELATED READING

At the Court of King Claudius – short story by Maurice Baring (page 164)

297. *choler* – Guildenstern uses the word to mean anger. However, Hamlet refers to its medical connotation, bilious attack.

Enter Rosencrantz and Guildenstern.

GUILDENSTERN: Good my lord, vouchsafe me a word with you.

HAMLET: Sir, a whole history.

GUILDENSTERN: The king, sir —

HAMLET: Ay, sir, what of him?

GUILDENSTERN: Is in his retirement marvellous distempered.

HAMLET: With drink, sir?

GUILDENSTERN: No, my lord, rather with choler.

HAMLET: Your wisdom should show itself more richer to signify this to his doctor, for, for me to put him to his purgation would perhaps plunge him into far more choler.   300

GUILDENSTERN: Good my lord, put your discourse into some frame and start not so wildly from my affair.

HAMLET: I am tame, sir. Pronounce.

GUILDENSTERN: The queen, your mother, in most great affliction of spirit, hath sent me to you.

HAMLET: You are welcome.

GUILDENSTERN: Nay, good my lord, this courtesy is not of the right breed. If it shall please you to make me a wholesome answer, I will do your mother's commandment. If not, your pardon and my return shall be the end of my business.   310

HAMLET: Sir, I cannot.

GUILDENSTERN: What, my lord?

HAMLET: Make you a wholesome answer. My wit's diseased. But, sir, such answer as I can make, you shall command, or, rather, as you say, my mother. Therefore no more, but to the matter. My mother, you say, —

ROSENCRANTZ: Then thus she says; your behaviour hath struck her into amazement and admiration.   320

HAMLET: O wonderful son, that can so astonish a mother! But is there no sequel at the heels of this mother's admiration? Impart.

ROSENCRANTZ: She desires to speak with you in her closet, ere you go to bed.

HAMLET: We shall obey, were she ten times our mother. Have you any further trade with us?

ROSENCRANTZ: My lord, you once did love me.

HAMLET: So I do still, by these pickers and stealers.

ROSENCRANTZ: Good my lord, what is your cause of distemper? You do, surely, bar the door upon your own liberty, if you deny your griefs to your friend.   330

HAMLET: Sir, I lack advancement.

325. *closet* – her private chamber

329. *pickers and stealers* – hands

332. *deny* – conceal, refuse to tell

ROSENCRANTZ: How can that be, when you have the voice of the king himself for your succession in Denmark?

HAMLET: Ay, but sir, while the grass grows, — the proverb is something musty.

Enter Players with recorders.

O, the recorders! Let me see one. To withdraw with you, why do you go about to recover the wind of me, as if you would drive me into a toil? 340

GUILDENSTERN: O, my lord, if my duty be too bold, my love is too unmannerly.

HAMLET: I do not well understand that. Will you play upon this pipe?

GUILDENSTERN: My lord, I cannot.

HAMLET: I pray you.

GUILDENSTERN: Believe me, I cannot.

HAMLET: I do beseech you.

GUILDENSTERN: I know no touch of it, my lord.

HAMLET: 'Tis as easy as lying. Govern these ventages with your fingers and thumb, give it breath with your mouth, and it will discourse most eloquent music. Look you, these are the stops. 350

GUILDENSTERN: But these cannot I command to any utterance of harmony. I have not the skill.

HAMLET: Why, look you now, how unworthy a thing you make of me! You would play upon me, you would seem to know my stops, you would pluck out the heart of my mystery, you would sound me from my lowest note to the top of my compass, and there is much music, excellent voice, in this little organ, yet cannot you make it speak. 'Sblood, do you think I am easier to be played on than a pipe? Call me what instrument you will, though you can fret me, yet you cannot play upon me. 360

Enter Polonius.

God bless you, sir!

POLONIUS: My lord, the queen would speak with you, and presently.

HAMLET: Do you see yonder cloud that's almost in shape of a camel? 370

POLONIUS: By the mass, and 'tis like a camel, indeed.

HAMLET: Methinks it is like a weasel.

---

334. *voice* – promise, announcement

336. *proverb* – The musty or stale proverb reads: "While the grass grows, the horse starves." This would suggest that Hamlet is not content to sit around and wait.

338. *withdraw* – speak privately

339. *recover the wind* – manoeuvre into an unfavourable position

340. *toil* – net

350. *ventages* – air holes, stops

361. *organ* – body

364. *fret* – annoy; equip with frets (as in a stringed instrument)

377. *top ... bent* – height of my capacity

386. *nature* – natural feeling of a son for a mother
387. *Nero* – Roman emperor who had his mother killed

391. *shent* – rebuked
392. *give them seals* – confirm (as do seals) words into deeds

POLONIUS: It is backed like a weasel.
HAMLET: Or like a whale?
POLONIUS: Very like a whale.
HAMLET: Then I will come to my mother by and by.
They fool me to the top of my bent. I will come by and by.
POLONIUS: I will say so.

Exit [Polonius].

HAMLET: 'By and by' is easily said.
Leave me, friends.   380

[Exeunt all but Hamlet.]

'Tis now the very witching time of night,
When churchyards yawn and hell itself breathes out
Contagion to this world. Now could I drink hot blood,
And do such bitter business as the day
Would quake to look on. Soft! Now to my mother.
O heart, lose not thy nature. Let not ever
The soul of Nero enter this firm bosom.
Let me be cruel, not unnatural.
I will speak daggers to her, but use none.
My tongue and soul in this be hypocrites.   390
How in my words soever she be shent,
To give them seals never, my soul, consent!

Exit.

Act Three
Scene 3

A room in the castle.

Enter King, Rosencrantz, and Guildenstern.

Fearful for his safety, Claudius instructs Rosencrantz and Guildenstern to escort Hamlet to England. Polonius reminds Claudius that Hamlet is on his way to the Queen's chamber. Polonius intends to eavesdrop on the conversation. Now that Claudius is alone, he attempts to pray for forgiveness. Hamlet, who in the last scene was ready to "drink hot blood," comes upon the King who is kneeling and appears to be praying.

KING: I like him not, nor stands it safe with us
 To let his madness range. Therefore prepare you.
 I your commission will forthwith dispatch,
 And he to England shall along with you.
 The terms of our estate may not endure
 Hazard so near us as doth hourly grow
 Out of his lunacies.
GUILDENSTERN: We will ourselves provide.
 Most holy and religious fear it is
 To keep those many many bodies safe   10
 That live and feed upon your majesty.
ROSENCRANTZ: The single and peculiar life is bound,
 With all the strength and armour of the mind,
 To keep itself from noyance. But much more
 That spirit upon whose weal depend and rest
 The lives of many. The cease of majesty
 Dies not alone, but, like a gulf, doth draw
 What's near it with it. It is a massy wheel,
 Fixed on the summit of the highest mount,
 To whose huge spokes ten thousand lesser things   20
 Are mortised and adjoined, which, when it falls,
 Each small annexment, petty consequence,
 Attends the boisterous ruin. Never alone
 Did the King sigh, but with a general groan.
KING: Arm you, I pray you, to this speedy voyage,
 For we will fetters put upon this fear,
 Which now goes too free-footed.
ROSENCRANTZ:
GUILDENSTERN: } We will haste us.

8. *provide* – make ready

12. *peculiar* – of concern only to the individual
14. *noyance* – harm
15. *weal* – well-being
16. *cease* – cessation, death

22. *annexment* – that which is connected
23. *boisterous* – noisy, tumultuous

Exeunt Rosencrantz and Guildenstern.
Enter Polonius.

30. *arras* – large hanging tapestry
31. *tax him home* – take him to task; scold soundly

35. *of vantage* – in addition

40. *primal eldest curse* – a reference to Cain, who in the Biblical story, murdered his brother and thereby gained the reputation as being the first murderer ever

42. *inclination ... will* – desire is as strong as my determination (to pray)
44. *double business bound* – two tasks to perform

POLONIUS: My lord, he's going to his mother's closet.
Behind the arras I'll convey myself,   30
To hear the process, and warrant she'll tax him home,
And, as you said, and wisely was it said,
'Tis meet that some more audience than a mother,
Since nature makes them partial, should overhear
The speech of vantage. Fare you well, my liege.
I'll call upon you ere you go to bed,
And tell you what I know.
KING: Thanks, dear my lord.

Exit Polonius.

O, my offence is rank, it smells to heaven.
It hath the primal eldest curse upon it,   40
A brother's murder. Pray can I not,
Though inclination be as sharp as will,
My stronger guilt defeats my strong intent,
And, like a man to double business bound,
I stand in pause where I shall first begin,
And both neglect. What if this cursed hand
Were thicker than itself with brother's blood,
Is there not rain enough in the sweet heavens
To wash it white as snow? Whereto serves mercy

But to confront the visage of offence? 50
And what's in prayer but this two-fold force,
To be forestalled ere we come to fall,
Or pardoned being down? Then I'll look up.
My fault is past. But, O, what form of prayer
Can serve my turn? 'Forgive me my foul murder'?
That cannot be, since I am still possessed
Of those effects for which I did the murder,
My crown, mine own ambition and my queen.
May one be pardoned and retain the offence?
In the corrupted currents of this world 60
Offence's gilded hand may shove by justice,
And oft 'tis seen the wicked prize itself
Buys out the law. But 'tis not so above:
There is no shuffling, there the action lies
In his true nature, and we ourselves compelled,
Even to the teeth and forehead of our faults,
To give in evidence. What then? What rests?
Try what repentance can. What can it not?
Yet what can it when one cannot repent?
O wretched state! O bosom black as death! 70
O limed soul, that, struggling to be free,
Art more engaged! Help, angels! Make assay!
Bow, stubborn knees, and, heart with strings of steel,
Be soft as sinews of the newborn babe!
All may be well. *[He kneels.]*

50. *confront the visage* – meet face to face

51–53. *two-fold force* – Claudius reviews the two purposes of prayer, which are to prevent (forestall) us from sinning, and to forgive us our sins once they have been committed.

59. *offence* – the benefits of the offence
60. *currents* – courses of events
61. *gilded* – (bribery) richly rewarded with gold
64. *shuffling* – trickery, sleight of hand
66. *to ... forehead* – face to face

71. *limed* – trapped. Lime, a sticky substance, was used to capture birds.
72. *engaged* – entangled
72. *Make assay* – make an effort; try
73. *strings of steel* – hardened

Enter Hamlet.

HAMLET: Now might I do it pat, now he is praying.
And now I'll do it. And so he goes to heaven.
And so am I revenged. That would be scanned:
A villain kills my father, and for that,
I, his sole son, do this same villain send   80
To heaven.
O, this is hire and salary, not revenge.
He took my father grossly, full of bread.
With all his crimes broad blown, as flush as May,
And how his audit stands who knows save heaven?
But in our circumstance and course of thought,
'Tis heavy with him. And am I then revenged,
To take him in the purging of his soul,
When he is fit and seasoned for his passage?
No!   90
Up, sword, and know thou a more horrid hent:
When he is drunk asleep, or in his rage,
Or in the incestuous pleasure of his bed,
At gaming, swearing, or about some act
That has no relish of salvation in it,
Then trip him, that his heels may kick at heaven,
And that his soul may be as damned and black
As hell, whereto it goes. My mother stays.
This physic but prolongs thy sickly days.

Exit.

KING: My words fly up, my thoughts remain below.   100
Words without thoughts never to heaven go.

Exit.

78. *scanned* – considered carefully

83. *grossly* – unprepared for death

84. *flush* – full of life

85. It is puzzling that Hamlet would suggest that only heaven knows how his father's reckoning turned out. Has he not just received evidence that the spirit is indeed the ghost of his father doomed to spend time in purgatory?

91. *hent* – occasion
99. *physic* – purging, i.e. prayer

RELATED READING

The Imagery of *Hamlet* – essay by Caroline Spurgeon (page 184)

Act Three
Scene 4

The Queen's Bed Chamber.

[Enter Queen and Polonius.]

POLONIUS: He will come straight. Look you lay home to him.
Tell him his pranks have been too broad to bear with,
And that your Grace hath screened and stood between
Much heat and him. I'll silence me even here.
Pray you, be round with him.
HAMLET: *[Within]* Mother, mother, mother!
QUEEN: I'll warrant you,
Fear me not. Withdraw, I hear him coming.

[Polonius hides behind the arras.] Enter Hamlet.

HAMLET: Now, mother, what's the matter?
QUEEN: Hamlet, thou hast thy father much offended.   10
HAMLET: Mother, you have my father much offended.
QUEEN: Come, come, you answer with an idle tongue.
HAMLET: Go, go, you question with a wicked tongue.
QUEEN: Why, how now, Hamlet!
HAMLET: What's the matter now?
QUEEN: Have you forgot me?
HAMLET: No, by the rood, not so.
You are the Queen, your husband's brother's wife,
And, would it were not so, you are my mother.
QUEEN: Nay, then, I'll set those to you that can speak.   20
HAMLET: Come, come, and sit you down. You shall not budge.
You go not till I set you up a glass
Where you may see the inmost part of you.
QUEEN: What wilt thou do? Thou wilt not murder me?
Help, help, ho!
POLONIUS: *[From behind the arras.]* What, ho! Help, help, help!

1. *lay home* – deal directly

12. *idle* – foolish

17. *rood* – holy cross

19. *would* – I wish

22. *glass* – mirror

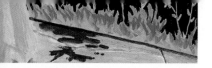

28. *for a ducat* – I'd bet money

HAMLET: *[Drawing a rapier.]* How now! A rat?
    Dead, for a ducat, dead!

Kills Polonius.

POLONIUS: O, I am slain!
QUEEN: O me, what hast thou done?   30
HAMLET: Nay, I know not.
    Is it the king?
QUEEN: O, what a rash and bloody deed is this!
HAMLET: A bloody deed! Almost as bad, good mother,
    As kill a king, and marry with his brother.
QUEEN: As kill a king!
HAMLET: Ay, lady, 'twas my word.

[Lifts up the arras and discovers Polonius.]

40. "You have just learned that to be a busybody can be dangerous."

Thou wretched, rash, intruding fool, farewell!
I took thee for thy better. Take thy fortune.
Thou find'st to be too busy is some danger.   40
Leave wringing of your hands. Peace, sit you down,

44. *custom* – habit ... *brassed* – converted to or covered with brass
45. *proof* – impenetrable
50. *rose* – blush

And let me wring your heart. For so I shall,
If it be made of penetrable stuff,
If damned custom have not brassed it so
That it is proof and bulwark against sense.
QUEEN: What have I done, that thou darest wag thy tongue
    In noise so rude against me?
HAMLET: Such an act

52. *blister* – Prostitutes were sometimes branded on the forehead as punishment.

That blurs the grace and blush of modesty,
Calls virtue hypocrite, takes off the rose   50
From the fair forehead of an innocent love

53. *dicers* – gamblers
54. *body of contraction* – solemn marriage contract
56. *rhapsody* – confused and meaningless string of words
    glow – blush
57. *solidity ... mass* – the earth
59. *thought-sick* – sick at heart
61. *index* – list (of sins)
63. *counterfeit* – imitation. A portrait is an imitation or representation of reality.

And sets a blister there, makes marriage-vows
As false as dicers' oaths — O, such a deed
As from the body of contraction plucks
The very soul, and sweet religion makes
A rhapsody of words. Heaven's face does glow
Over this solidity and compound mass,
With tristful visage, as against the doom,
Is thought-sick at the act.
QUEEN: Ay me, what act   60
    That roars so loud and thunders in the index?
HAMLET: Look here upon this picture, and on this,
    The counterfeit presentment of two brothers.
    See, what a grace was seated on this brow,
    Hyperion's curls, the front of Jove himself,
    An eye like Mars to threaten and command,

A station like the herald Mercury
New-lighted on a heaven-kissing hill,
A combination and a form indeed
Where every god did seem to set his seal   70
To give the world assurance of a man.
This was your husband. Look you now what follows,
Here is your husband, like a mildewed ear
Blasting his wholesome brother. Have you eyes?
Could you on this fair mountain leave to feed
And batten on this moor? Ha, have you eyes?
You cannot call it love, for at your age
The hey-day in the blood is tame, it's humble,
And waits upon the judgment, and what judgment
Would step from this to this? Sense, sure, you have,   80
Else could you not have motion. But sure, that sense
Is apoplexed, for madness would not err
Nor sense to ecstasy was never so thralled
But it reserved some quantity of choice
To serve in such a difference. What devil was it
That thus hath cozened you at hoodman-blind?
Eyes without feeling, feeling without sight,
Ears without hands or eyes, smelling sans all,
Or but a sickly part of one true sense
Could not so mope. O shame, where is thy blush?   90
Rebellious hell,
If thou canst mutine in a matron's bones,
To flaming youth let virtue be as wax
And melt in her own fire. Proclaim no shame
When the compulsive ardour gives the charge,
Since frost itself as actively doth burn
And reason panders will.
QUEEN: O Hamlet, speak no more.
Thou turn'st mine eyes into my very soul,
And there I see such black and grained spots   100
As will not leave their tinct.
HAMLET: Nay, but to live
In the rank sweat of an enseamed bed,
Stewed in corruption, honeying and making love
Over the nasty sty!
QUEEN: O, speak to me no more.
These words, like daggers, enter in mine ears.
No more, sweet Hamlet!
HAMLET: A murderer and a villain.
A slave that is not twentieth part the tithe   110
Of your precedent lord, a vice of kings,

67. "A stance like the winged messenger of the gods, Mercury"
68. *lighted* – alighted
73. *mildewed* – contagiously diseased (as an ear of corn)
74. *Blasting* – infecting
76. *batten* – graze, fatten
78. *hey-day* – sexual passion
82. *apoplexed* – paralyzed
83. *ecstasy* – madness
    thralled – enslaved
85. *difference* – contrast
    cozened – deceived
86. *hoodman-blind* – a child's game
88. *sans* – without
90. *mope* – be unaware
92. *mutine* – mutiny
92 – 94. "If older people cannot control their passions, then virtue in youth is as vulnerable as wax that melts in its own fire."
94. *Proclaim no shame* – Call it not shameful
95. *gives the charge* – orders the attack
96. *frost* – age, supposedly a time of numbed desires
97. *will* – sexual desire

101. "That cannot be erased."
103. *enseamed* – saturated with oils and sweat
104. *Stewed* – play on words: stew is another term for brothel

110. *tithe* – tenth part

113. *diadem* – jewelled crown

diadem

118. *guards* – angels

125. *whet* – sharpen, hone

128. *Conceit* – imagination

132. *vacancy* – nothing
133. *incorporal* – empty, insubstantial
135. "And, as soldiers caught napping when the alarm is sounded"
136. *excrements* – things put out from the body; outgrowths. Hamlet's hair is standing on end.
141 – 142. "Together, his appearance and purpose could preach to stones and make them capable of responding to the words."
144. *effects* – plans
145. *perchance for* – perhaps instead of

152. *habit* – clothes he usually wore

A cutpurse of the empire and the rule,
That from a shelf the precious diadem stole
And put it in his pocket!
QUEEN: No more!
HAMLET: A king of shreds and patches —

Enter Ghost.

Save me and hover over me with your wings,
You heavenly guards! What would your gracious figure?
QUEEN: Alas, he's mad!
HAMLET: Do you not come your tardy son to chide,   120
That, lapsed in time and passion, lets go by
The important acting of your dread command?
O, say!
GHOST: Do not forget. This visitation
Is but to whet thy almost blunted purpose.
But, look, amazement on thy mother sits.
O step between her and her fighting soul,
Conceit in weakest bodies strongest works.
Speak to her, Hamlet.
HAMLET: How is it with you, lady?   130
QUEEN: Alas, how is it with you,
That you do bend your eye on vacancy
And with the incorporal air do hold discourse?
Forth at your eyes your spirits wildly peep,
And, as the sleeping soldiers in the alarm,
Your bedded hair, like life in excrements,
Start up, and stand on end. O gentle son,
Upon the heat and flame of thy distemper
Sprinkle cool patience. Whereon do you look?
HAMLET: On him, on him! Look you how pale he glares!   140
His form and cause conjoined, preaching to stones,
Would make them capable. Do not look upon me,
Lest with this piteous action you convert
My stern effects. Then what I have to do
Will want true colour — tears perchance for blood.
QUEEN: To whom do you speak this?
HAMLET: Do you see nothing there?
QUEEN: Nothing at all; yet all that is I see.
HAMLET: Nor did you nothing hear?
QUEEN: No, nothing but ourselves.   150
HAMLET: Why, look you there! Look how it steals away!
My father, in his habit as he lived!
Look, where he goes even now out at the portal!

Exit Ghost.

QUEEN: This the very coinage of your brain.
This bodiless creation ecstasy
Is very cunning in.

HAMLET: Ecstasy!
My pulse, as yours, doth temperately keep time,
And makes as healthful music. It is not madness
That I have uttered. Bring me to the test,   160
And I the matter will re-word, which madness
Would gambol from. Mother, for love of grace,
Lay not that flattering unction to your soul,
That not your trespass, but my madness speaks.
It will but skin and film the ulcerous place,
Whilst rank corruption, mining all within,
Infects unseen. Confess yourself to heaven,
Repent what's past, avoid what is to come,
And do not spread the compost on the weeds
To make them ranker. Forgive me this my virtue,   170
For in the fatness of these pursy times
Virtue itself of vice must pardon beg,
Yea, curb and woo for leave to do him good.

QUEEN: O Hamlet, thou hast cleft my heart in twain.

HAMLET: O, throw away the worser part of it
And live the purer with the other half.
Good night. But go not to my uncle's bed.
Assume a virtue if you have it not.
That monster, custom, who all sense doth eat
Of habits devil, is angel yet in this,   180
That to the use of actions fair and good
He likewise gives a frock or livery
That aptly is put on. Refrain to-night,
And that shall lend a kind of easiness
To the next abstinence, the next more easy.
For use almost can change the stamp of nature,
And either lodge the devil, or throw him out
With wondrous potency. Once more, good night,
And when you are desirous to be blest,
I'll blessing beg of you. For this same lord,   190
I do repent, but heaven hath pleased it so,
To punish me with this and this with me,
That I must be their scourge and minister.
I will bestow him, and will answer well
The death I gave him. So, again, good night.
I must be cruel only to be kind.

---

156. *cunning in* – skilled at

162. *gambol* – leap wildly
163. *flattering unction* – soothing ointment
164. *trespass* – sin
166. *mining* – spreading

171. *pursy* – puffed up, self-indulgent
173. *curb ... leave* – bow and beg permission
178. *Assume* – adopt, begin to work at having
179 – 183. "Custom is a devilish monster in depriving us of good sense in allowing us to develop bad habits, but it can also be an angel in making it easy to acquire good habits."

186. *use* – practice
191. *pleased it so* – seen fit

192. *this with me* – a reference to Hamlet punishing Polonius for meddling

194. *bestow* – stow away; dispose of

197. "Polonius' death is a bad beginning and worse is yet to come."

203. *reechy* – filthy
204. *paddling in* – caressing
205. *ravel* – reveal, unravel

209. *paddock* – toad
   gib – tomcat
210. *dear concernings* – matters of vital concern
212. *Unpeg the basket* – reveal the secret, as one sets loose the birds. Once the birds are released, it is impossible to get them back into the basket.
214. *try conclusions* – test what will happen

224 – 225. "They have their orders to serve as my escorts and to lead me to some treachery."
226. *enginer* – maker of engines (of warfare)
227. *Hoist ... petard* – blown up by his own bomb
228. *delve* – dig
230. "When in one road, two plots meet head-on."
235. *prating* – babbling, chattering
236. *draw ... end* – finish my business

RELATED READING

Gertrude Talks Back – short story by Margaret Atwood (page 167)

This bad begins and worse remains behind.
One word more, good lady.

QUEEN: What shall I do?

HAMLET: Not this, by no means, that I bid you do: 200
   Let the bloat king tempt you again to bed,
   Pinch wanton on your cheek, call you his mouse,
   And let him, for a pair of reechy kisses,
   Or paddling in your neck with his damned fingers,
   Make you to ravel all this matter out
   That I essentially am not in madness,
   But mad in craft. 'Twere good you let him know,
   For who, that's but a queen, fair, sober, wise,
   Would from a paddock, from a bat, a gib,
   Such dear concernings hide? Who would do so?   210
   No, in despite of sense and secrecy,
   Unpeg the basket on the house's top.
   Let the birds fly, and like the famous ape,
   To try conclusions, in the basket creep,
   And break your own neck down.

QUEEN: Be thou assured, if words be made of breath,
   And breath of life, I have no life to breathe
   What thou hast said to me.

HAMLET: I must to England, you know that?

QUEEN: Alack,   220
   I had forgot. 'Tis so concluded on.

HAMLET: There's letters sealed, and my two schoolfellows,
   Whom I will trust as I will adders fanged —
   They bear the mandate. They must sweep my way
   And marshal me to knavery. Let it work.
   For 'tis the sport to have the enginer
   Hoist with his own petard, and it shall go hard
   But I will delve one yard below their mines
   And blow them at the moon. O, 'tis most sweet
   When in one line two crafts directly meet.   230
   This man shall set me packing.
   I'll lug the guts into the neighbour room.
   Mother, good night indeed. This counsellor
   Is now most still, most secret and most grave,
   Who was in life a foolish prating knave.
   Come, sir, to draw toward an end with you.
   Good night, mother.

[Exeunt, Hamlet dragging in Polonius.]

❧ ❧ ❧

Act Three Considerations

ACT THREE **Scene 1**

▶ Do you think Claudius and Polonius overhear Hamlet's famous soliloquy? What are the advantages and disadvantages of having them hear his speech?

▶ The "To be, or not to be" speech is often parodied. Write your own version of the speech. It can be either a parody or a modern-day translation. Read Prince Charles' attempt at modernizing the speech on page 160 before starting this activity.

ACT THREE **Scene 2**

▶ It has been said that "Hamlet is the only one of Shakespeare's characters who could have written the plays of his creator." What evidence is there in this scene that Hamlet deserves this praise?

▶ According to Hamlet, what are the characteristics of a true friend? To what extent do you agree with him?

▶ Read the short story *At the Court of King Claudius* on page 164. What new insights does this story offer in regard to this scene?

ACT THREE **Scene 3**

▶ Rosencrantz uses a metaphor to express a subject's duty to one's king. Explain the metaphor. Can you think of another metaphor that would work as well in explaining the importance of the king's well-being?

▶ Why exactly does Claudius believe that he cannot be forgiven for his crimes? If you were a counsellor, what advice would you give Claudius?

ACT THREE **Scene 4**

▶ Write Polonius' obituary. Before doing so, read several obituaries from your local newspaper. Can you find a quotation from this scene that would serve as a fitting epitaph for his tombstone?

▶ This scene serves to focus on the relationship between Hamlet and his mother. What is revealed about their relationship?

Act Four
Scene 1

Claudius learns of Polonius' death. He realizes that it could have very easily been himself instead of Polonius hiding behind the arras. He sends Rosencrantz and Guildenstern to fetch Hamlet and to discover the whereabouts of Polonius' body.

A room in the castle.

Enter King, Queen, Rosencrantz, and Guildenstern.

KING: There's matter in these sighs, these profound heaves,
You must translate. 'Tis fit we understand them.
Where is your son?
QUEEN: Bestow this place on us a little while.

[Exeunt Rosencrantz and Guildenstern.]

Ah, my good lord, what have I seen to-night!
KING: What, Gertrude? How does Hamlet?
QUEEN: Mad as the sea and wind when both contend
Which is the mightier. In his lawless fit,
Behind the arras hearing something stir,
Whips out his rapier, cries, 'A rat, a rat!'   10
And in this brainish apprehension kills
The unseen good old man.
KING: O heavy deed!
It had been so with us had we been there.
His liberty is full of threats to all —
To you yourself, to us, to everyone.
Alas, how shall this bloody deed be answered?
It will be laid to us, whose providence
Should have kept short, restrained and out of haunt,
This mad young man. But so much was our love,   20
We would not understand what was most fit,
But like the owner of a foul disease,
To keep it from divulging, let it feed
Even on the pith of life. Where is he gone?
QUEEN: To draw apart the body he hath killed,
Over whom his very madness, like some ore

1. *matter* – matters of significance
2. *translate* – explain the meaning
4. *Bestow* – give us privacy

11. *brainish* – frenzied

18. *providence* – foresight
19. "Should have kept him on a short leash, away from society"

23. *divulging* – becoming known
24. *pith* – most vital part
25. *draw apart* – take away

26 – 28. Hamlet is described as weeping over the body. The *ore* refers to Hamlet's precious nature that enables him to feel remorse.

33. *countenance* – bring forth and explain

37. *fair* – gently, tactfully

41. *haply* – if we are fortunate
43. "As accurate as the cannon is to its target"
45. *woundless* – invulnerable

Among a mineral of metals base,
Shows itself pure. He weeps for what is done.
KING: O Gertrude, come away!
  The sun no sooner shall the mountains touch, 30
  But we will ship him hence, and this vile deed
  We must with all our majesty and skill
  Both countenance and excuse. Ho, Guildenstern!

*   Enter Rosencrantz and Guildenstern.*

  Friends both, go join you with some further aid.
  Hamlet in madness hath Polonius slain,
  And from his mother's closet hath he dragged him.
  Go seek him out, speak fair, and bring the body
  Into the chapel. I pray you, haste in this.

*   Exeunt Rosencrantz and Guildenstern.*

  Come, Gertrude, we'll call up our wisest friends,
  And let them know, both what we mean to do 40
  And what's untimely done. So haply slander,
  Whose whisper over the world's diameter,
  As level as the cannon to his blank,
  Transports his poisoned shot, may miss our name,
  And hit the woundless air. O come away!
  My soul is full of discord and dismay.

*   Exeunt.*

Act Four
Scene 2

Hamlet, having been found by Rosencrantz and Guildenstern, accuses them of being sponges. Hamlet follows them to the King.

Another room in the castle.

Enter Hamlet.

HAMLET: Safely stowed.

ROSENCRANTZ:
GUILDENSTERN: } *[Within]* Hamlet! Lord Hamlet!

HAMLET: But soft, what noise? Who calls on Hamlet? O, here they come.

[Enter Rosencrantz and Guildenstern.]

ROSENCRANTZ: What have you done, my lord, with the dead body?

HAMLET: Compounded it with dust, whereto 'tis kin.

ROSENCRANTZ: Tell us where it is, that we may take it thence and bear it to the chapel.

HAMLET: Do not believe it.

ROSENCRANTZ: Believe what?   10

HAMLET: That I can keep your counsel and not mine own. Besides, to be demanded of a sponge! What replication should be made by the son of a king?

ROSENCRANTZ: Take you me for a sponge, my lord?

HAMLET: Ay, sir, that soaks up the King's countenance, his rewards, his authorities. But such officers do the King best service in the end: he keeps them, like an ape, in the corner of his jaw — first mouthed, to be last swallowed. When he needs what you have gleaned, it is but squeezing you and, sponge, you   20 shall be dry again.

ROSENCRANTZ: I understand you not, my lord.

HAMLET: I am glad of it. A knavish speech sleeps in a foolish ear.

13. *replication* – reply

This is the story of a man who could not make up his mind.
– Sir Laurence Olivier (1907 – 1989), British actor/director

23. *sleeps* – is not understood

ROSENCRANTZ: My lord, you must tell us where the body is and go with us to the King.

HAMLET: The body is with the King, but the King is not with the body. The King is a thing —

GUILDENSTERN: A thing, my lord?

HAMLET: Of nothing. Bring me to him. 30 Hide fox, and all after.

Exeunt.

31. Hamlet's last line is probably a reference to a game such as hide-and-seek.

"Hamlet is like a sponge. If he is not played in stylized or antiquated manner, he immediately soaks up the entire contemporary scene unto himself. It is the most unique of all plays that have ever been written, just because of its porosity."
– Jan Kott (b. 1914), Polish professor of literature and Shakespearean critic

Act Four
Scene 3

Claudius, sensing danger to his own person, is anxious to remove Hamlet from the Danish court. Hamlet reveals the location of Polonius' body and is informed that he must leave for England.

Another room in the castle.

Enter King and two or three [Lords].

KING: I have sent to seek him and to find the body.
How dangerous is it that this man goes loose!
Yet must not we put the strong law on him:
He's loved of the distracted multitude,
Who like not in their judgment but their eyes,
And where tis so, the offender's scourge is weighed,
But never the offence. To bear all smooth and even,
This sudden sending him away must seem
Deliberate pause. Diseases desperate grown
By desperate appliance are relieved,   10
Or not at all.

Enter Rosencrantz and all the rest.

How now, what hath befallen?
ROSENCRANTZ: Where the dead body is bestowed, my lord,
We cannot get from him.
KING: But where is he?
ROSENCRANTZ: Without, my lord, guarded, to know your
pleasure.
KING: Bring him before us.
ROSENCRANTZ: Ho, Guildenstern! Bring in my lord.

Enter Hamlet and Guildenstern.

KING: Now, Hamlet, where's Polonius?
HAMLET: At supper.   20
KING: At supper! Where?
HAMLET: Not where he eats, but where he is eaten.

4. *distracted* – irrational
6. *scourge is weighed* – punishment is considered

9. *Deliberate pause.* – the outcome of careful thought
9 – 10. Common proverb: "Desperate sicknesses … must have desperate remedies."

23. *convocation* – meeting
politic shrewd

"[Shakespeare] wrote of Hamlet as if Hamlet he were; and having, in the first instance, imagined his hero excited to partial insanity by the disclosures of the ghost – he (the poet) felt that it was natural he should be impelled to exaggerate the insanity."
– Edgar Allan Poe (1809 – 1849), American poet, short story writer, and novelist

22 – 24. A clever allusion to the historical event that took place in 1521 at Worms, Germany, in which a council (diet) was presided over by Emperor Charles V. At the Diet of Worms, Martin Luther, leader of the Protestant Reformation, defended his case. The Church ruled against him and pronounced its ban on him and his works.

54. *cherub* – an angel that sees all things. Ezekiel (10:12) describes the cherubim as being "full of eyes."

60. *at foot* – at his heels; closely

A certain convocation of politic worms are even at him. Your worm is your only emperor for diet: we fat all creatures else to fat us, and we fat ourselves for maggots. Your fat king and your lean beggar is but variable service — two dishes, but to one table. That's the end.

KING: Alas, alas.

HAMLET: A man may fish with the worm that hath eat of   30
a king, and eat of the fish that hath fed of that worm.

KING: What dost thou mean by this?

HAMLET: Nothing but to show you how a king may go a progress through the guts of a beggar.

KING: Where is Polonius?

HAMLET: In heaven. Send thither to see. If your messenger find him not there, seek him in the other place yourself. But if indeed you find him not within this month, you shall nose him as you go up the stairs into the lobby.   40

KING: *[To some Attendants.]* Go seek him there.

HAMLET: He will stay till you come.

[Exeunt Attendants.]

KING: Hamlet, this deed, for thine especial safety,
Which we do tender, as we dearly grieve
For that which thou hast done — must send thee hence
With fiery quickness. Therefore prepare thyself.
The bark is ready, and the wind at help,
Thy associates tend, and everything is bent
For England.

HAMLET: For England?   50

KING: Ay, Hamlet.

HAMLET: Good.

KING: So is it, if thou knewest our purposes.

HAMLET: I see a cherub that sees them. But, come,
for England! Farewell, dear mother.

KING: Thy loving father, Hamlet.

HAMLET: My mother. Father and mother is man and wife, man and wife is one flesh, and so, my mother. Come, for England!

Exit.

KING: Follow him at foot. Tempt him with speed aboard,   60
Delay it not. I'll have him hence to-night.

96

Away, for everything is sealed and done
That else leans on the affair. Pray you make haste.

Exeunt all but the King.

And, England, if my love thou holdest at aught —
As my great power thereof may give thee sense,
Since yet thy cicatrice looks raw and red
After the Danish sword, and thy free awe
Pays homage to us — thou mayest not coldly set
Our sovereign process, which imports at full,
By letters congruing to that effect,   70
The present death of Hamlet. Do it, England,
For like the hectic in my blood he rages,
And thou must cure me. Till I know 'tis done,
However my haps, my joys were never begun.

Exit.

63. *leans* – depends, appertains

64. *England* – i.e., the King of England
66. *cicatrice* – scar
67. *free awe* – respect that is freely given
68. *coldly set* – ignore; turn a cold shoulder to
69. *process* – orders
72. *hectic* – fever

Act Four
Scene 4

On their way to England, Hamlet and company come across Fortinbras leading his army toward Poland to fight over a worthless patch of ground. The willingness of Fortinbras and his men to act spurs Hamlet toward exacting his revenge.

A plain in Denmark.

Enter Fortinbras, with his army [marching] over the stage.

FORTINBRAS: Go, captain, from me greet the Danish king.
    Tell him that by his license, Fortinbras
    Craves the conveyance of a promised march
    Over his kingdom. You know the rendezvous.
    If that his majesty would aught with us,
    We shall express our duty in his eye,
    And let him know so.
    Captain: I will do it, my lord.
FORTINBRAS: Go softly on.

[Exeunt Fortinbras and Soldiers.]
Enter Hamlet, Rosencrantz, Guildenstern, and others.

HAMLET: Good sir, whose powers are these? 10
CAPTAIN: They are of Norway, sir.
HAMLET: How purposed, sir, I pray you?
CAPTAIN: Against some part of Poland.
HAMLET: Who commands them, sir?
CAPTAIN: The nephew to old Norway, Fortinbras.
HAMLET: Goes it against the main of Poland, sir,
    Or for some frontier?
CAPTAIN: Truly to speak, and with no addition,
    We go to gain a little patch of ground
    That hath in it no profit but the name. 20
    To pay five ducats, five, I would not farm it.
    Nor will it yield to Norway or the Pole
    A ranker rate should it be sold in fee.
HAMLET: Why, then the Polack never will defend it.
CAPTAIN: Yes, it is already garrisoned.
HAMLET: Two thousand souls and twenty thousand ducats
    Will not debate the question of this straw!

5. *would ... us* – wishes anything of me
6. *in his eye* – in person

9. *softly* – gently, respectfully

18. *addition* – exaggeration

23. *ranker* – richer
23. *in fee* – outright

This is the imposthume of much wealth and peace,
That inward breaks, and shows no cause without
Why the man dies. I humbly thank you, sir.   30
CAPTAIN: God be with you, sir.

[Exit.]

ROSENCRANTZ: Will it please you go, my lord?
HAMLET: I'll be with you straight. Go a little before.

[Exeunt all except Hamlet.]

How all occasions do inform against me,
And spur my dull revenge. What is a man
If his chief good and market of his time
Be but to sleep and feed? A beast, no more.
Sure he that made us with such large discourse,
Looking before and after, gave us not
That capability and god-like reason   40
To fust in us unused. Now, whether it be
Bestial oblivion, or some craven scruple
Of thinking too precisely on the event —
A thought which, quartered, hath but one part wisdom
And ever three parts coward — I do not know
Why yet I live to say this thing's to do,
Sith I have cause and will and strength and means
To do it. Examples gross as earth exhort me,
Witness this army of such mass and charge
Led by a delicate and tender prince,   50
Whose spirit with divine ambition puffed,
Makes mouths at the invisible event,
Exposing what is mortal and unsure
To all that fortune, death and danger dare,
Even for an egg-shell. Rightly to be great
Is not to stir without great argument,
But greatly to find quarrel in a straw
When honour's at the stake. How stand I then,
That have a father killed, a mother stained,
Excitements of my reason and my blood,   60
And let all sleep, while to my shame I see
The imminent death of twenty thousand men
That, for a fantasy and trick of fame,
Go to their graves like beds, fight for a plot
Whereon the numbers cannot try the cause,
Which is not tomb enough and continent
To hide the slain? O, from this time forth
My thoughts be bloody or be nothing worth!

Exit.

28. *imposthume* – abscess; a swelling due to festering
28 – 30. Hamlet comments on how affluent states become corrupted without anyone's noticing until it is too late.

34. *inform against* – denounce
36. *chief ... market* – profit and employment
38. *discourse* – intelligence
41. *fust* – become mouldy
42. *Bestial oblivion* – Animals do not have good memories.
47. *Sith* – Since
48. *gross* – as large
51. *divine ambition puffed* – Fortinbras is described as being one whose spirit is enlarged by his ambition to be immortal.
52. "Mocks the unforeseeable outcome"
56. *argument* – cause
55 – 58. "To be truly great, one must act not solely in response to powerful incentives but also on the basis of slight provocations when one's good name is at stake."
63. *trick of fame* – trifle
64 – 67. "The battleground is not large enough to bury the dead that will result from the fighting."

99

Act Four
Scene 5

The Queen receives a report that Ophelia has gone mad. Horatio convinces the Queen to see Ophelia. The reports soon prove to be true as Ophelia enters singing and dancing. A concerned Claudius orders that she be watched carefully. Laertes, in the meantime, has returned to Denmark and is intent on avenging his father's murder. Laertes believes that Claudius is the guilty party. Ophelia reappears and Laertes is heartbroken by her obvious state of insanity.

Elsinore. A room in the castle.

Enter Queen, Horatio, and a Gentleman.

QUEEN: I will not speak with her.
GENTLEMAN: She is importunate,
    Indeed distract. Her mood will needs be pitied.
QUEEN: What would she have?
GENTLEMAN: She speaks much of her father, says she hears
    There's tricks in the world, and hems, and beats her heart,
    Spurns enviously at straws, speaks things in doubt
    That carry but half sense. Her speech is nothing,
    Yet the unshaped use of it doth move
    The hearers to collection. They aim at it,   10
    And botch the words up fit to their own thoughts,
    Which, as her winks and nods and gestures yield them,
    Indeed would make one think there might be thought,
    Though nothing sure, yet much unhappily.
HORATIO: 'Twere good she were spoken with, for she may strew
    Dangerous conjectures in ill-breeding minds.
QUEEN: Let her come in.

[Exit Horatio.]

To my sick soul, as sin's true nature is,
Each toy seems prologue to some great amiss.
So full of artless jealousy is guilt,   20
It spills itself in fearing to be spilt.

Enter Ophelia distracted.

OPHELIA: Where is the beauteous Majesty of Denmark?
QUEEN: How now, Ophelia!

---

2. *importunate* – insistent
3. *distract* – mad ...
will needs – must
7. *Spurns ... straws* – becomes angry over trivial things
10. *collection* – attempts to make sense of
11. *botch* – patch
16. *ill-breeding* – that think the worse

18. *sin's ... is* – sin is a sickness of the soul
19. *toy* – trifle
20 – 21. "Guilt invariably gives itself away."

OPHELIA: *[She sings.]*
        How should I your true love know
          From another one?
        By his cockle hat and staff,
          And his sandal shoon.

QUEEN: Alas, sweet lady, what imports this song?

OPHELIA: Say you? Nay, pray you, mark.
[Sings.]   *He is dead and gone, lady,*   30
          He is dead and gone;
        At his head a grass-green turf,
          At his heels a stone.

QUEEN: Nay, but, Ophelia —

OPHELIA: Pray you, mark. *[Sings.]*
        White his shroud as the mountain snow, —

Enter King.

QUEEN: Alas, look here, my lord.

OPHELIA: *[Sings.]* *Larded with sweet flowers*
        Which bewept to the grave did go
          With true-love showers.   40

KING: How do you, pretty lady?

OPHELIA: Well, good dild you! They say the owl was a baker's daughter. Lord, we know what we are, but know not what we may be. God be at your table!

KING: Conceit upon her father.

OPHELIA: Pray you, let's have no words of this, but when they ask you what it means, say you this:
[Sings.]   *To-morrow is Saint Valentine's day,*
        All in the morning betime,
        And I a maid at your window,   50
          To be your Valentine.
        Then up he rose, and donned his clothes,
        And dupped the chamber-door,
        Let in the maid, that out a maid
          Never departed more.

KING: Pretty Ophelia!

OPHELIA: Indeed, without an oath, I'll make an end on it.
        By Gis and by Saint Charity,
          Alack, and fie for shame!
        Young men will do it, if they come to it —   60
          By cock, they are to blame.
        Quoth she, before you tumbled me,
          You promised me to wed.
     He answers,

cockle hat

26. *cockle hat* – hat adorned with a cockleshell
27. *shoon* – shoes

38. *Larded* – strewn

42. *good dild you!* – may God reward you

42. *owl* – According to legend, a baker's daughter was turned into an owl for refusing to give bread to Jesus.

45. *Conceit* – she thinks/broods

48 – 65. Ophelia's songs suggest that her madness may have been caused by more than just grief for her father's death. Hamlet's departure may also have played its part. The bawdy nature of her songs can also be seen to suggest that she and Hamlet were lovers.

49. *betime* – early
53. *dupped* – opened
58. *Gis* – Jesus

Act Four • Scene 5

> *So would I a done, by yonder sun,*
> *An thou hadst not come to my bed.*

KING: How long hath she been thus?

OPHELIA: I hope all will be well. We must be patient. But
I cannot choose but weep to think they should lay him
in the cold ground. My brother shall know of it. And
so I thank you for your good counsel. Come, my   70
coach! Good night, ladies, good night. Sweet ladies,
good night, good night.

Exit.

KING: Follow her close. Give her good watch, I pray you.

[Exit Horatio.]

O, this is the poison of deep grief. It springs
All from her father's death. And now behold —
O Gertrude, Gertrude,
When sorrows come, they come not single spies
But in battalions. First, her father slain;
Next, your son gone, and he most violent author
Of his own just remove; the people muddied,   80
Thick and unwholesome in their thoughts and whispers
For good Polonius' death; and we have done but greenly
In hugger-mugger to inter him. Poor Ophelia
Divided from herself and her fair judgment,
Without the which we are pictures, or mere beasts.
Last, and as much containing as all these,

65. *An* – if

77. *spies* – scouts

80. *remove* – exile
   muddied – confused
82. *greenly* – foolishly
83. *hugger-mugger* – secret

85. *pictures* – poor reflec-
tions of our true selves

Her brother is in secret come from France,
Feeds on his wonder, keeps himself in clouds,
And wants not buzzers to infect his ear
With pestilent speeches of his father's death,   90
Wherein necessity, of matter beggared,
Will nothing stick our person to arraign
In ear and ear. O my dear Gertrude, this,
Like to a murdering-piece, in many places
Gives me superfluous death.

A noise within.

Attend!
QUEEN: Alack, what noise is this?
KING: Where are my Switzers? Let them guard the door.

Enter a Messenger.

What is the matter?
MESSENGER: Save yourself, my lord.
The ocean, overpeering of his list,   100
Eats not the flats with more impetuous haste
Than young Laertes, in a riotous head,
Overbears your officers. The rabble call him lord,
And, as the world were now but to begin,
Antiquity forgot, custom not known —
The ratifiers and props of every word,
They cry 'Choose we! Laertes shall be king.'

88 – 93. "Laertes lives off his suspicions, indulges himself in fancies rather than facts, and lacks not rumour-mongers who fill his ears with foul accounts of his father's death, and by necessity, because they lack facts, they do not hesitate to accuse me to anyone who will listen."

94. *murdering–piece* – cannon that when fired scatters fragments of metal over a wide area
95. *superfluous death* – death resulting from more than one fatal wound
97. *Switzers* – royal bodyguards

100. *overpeering ... list* – rising above its shores
101. *flats* – lowlands
102. *head* – band of rebels
103. *Overbears* – overcomes
104. *as* – as if
105. "Disregarding and ignoring long-established traditions"

106. The ratifiers and props refer to the aforementioned *antiquity* and *custom*.

Caps, hands, and tongues, applaud it to the clouds,
'Laertes shall be king, Laertes king!'

QUEEN: How cheerfully on the false trail they cry!　　　110
O, this is counter, you false Danish dogs!

A noise within.

KING: The doors are broke.

Enter Laertes with others.

LAERTES: Where is this king? Sirs, stand you all without.
ALL: No, let's come in.
LAERTES: I pray you, give me leave.
ALL: We will, we will.
LAERTES: I thank you. Keep the door.

[Exeunt Followers.]

O thou vile king,
Give me my father!
QUEEN: Calmly, good Laertes.
LAERTES: That drop of blood that's calm proclaims me　　　120
bastard,
Cries cuckold to my father, brands the harlot
Even here, between the chaste unsmirched brow
Of my true mother.
KING: What is the cause, Laertes,
That thy rebellion looks so giant-like?—
Let him go, Gertrude. Do not fear our person.
There's such divinity doth hedge a king
That treason can but peep to what it would,
Acts little of his will.—Tell me, Laertes,
Why thou art thus incensed.—Let him go, Gertrude.—　　130
Speak, man.
LAERTES: Where is my father?
KING: Dead.
QUEEN: But not by him.
KING: Let him demand his fill.
LAERTES: How came he dead? I'll not be juggled with.
To hell, allegiance! Vows, to the blackest devil!
Conscience and grace, to the profoundest pit!
I dare damnation. To this point I stand,
That both the worlds I give to negligence,　　　140
Let come what comes, only I'll be revenged

---

111. *counter* – following the wrong trail
113. *without* – outside

122. *unsmirched* – unstained

125. *giant-like* – violent

127 – 129. The Elizabethans believed that royalty was established and protected by divine right, and thus treason can but catch a glimpse of what it would like to accomplish but cannot.

136. *juggled with* – deceived

140. *give to negligence* – care nothing for

Most thoroughly for my father.

KING: Who shall stay you?

LAERTES: My will, not all the world's.
And for my means, I'll husband them so well,
They shall go far with little.

KING: Good Laertes,
If you desire to know the certainty
Of your dear father's death, is it writ in your revenge
That, swoopstake, you will draw both friend and foe,   150
Winner and loser?

LAERTES: None but his enemies.

KING: Will you know them then?

LAERTES: To his good friends thus wide I'll ope my arms,
And, like the kind life-rendering pelican,
Repast them with my blood.

KING: Why, now you speak
Like a good child and a true gentleman.
That I am guiltless of your father's death
And am most sensibly in grief for it,   160
It shall as level to your judgment 'pear
As day does to your eye.

ALL: [Within] Let her come in.

LAERTES: How now! What noise is that?

Enter Ophelia.

O heat, dry up my brains! Tears seven times salt
Burn out the sense and virtue of mine eye.
By heaven, thy madness shall be paid by weight
Till our scale turn the beam. O rose of May!
Dear maid, kind sister, sweet Ophelia!
O heavens, is it possible, a young maid's wits   170
Should be as mortal as an old man's life?
Nature is fine in love, and where 'tis fine,
It sends some precious instance of itself
After the thing it loves.

OPHELIA: [Sings.] *They bore him barefaced on the bier,*
Hey non nonny, nonny, hey nonny:
And in his grave rained many a tear,
Fare you well, my dove!

LAERTES: Hadst thou thy wits, and didst persuade revenge,
It could not move thus.   180

OPHELIA: You must sing *A-down a-down*, and you *Call*
him a-down-a. O, how the wheel becomes it! It is
the false steward, that stole his master's daughter.

---

143. *stay* – hinder, prevent
144. "Nothing in the world, short of my will."
145. *husband* – manage

150. *swoopstake* – indiscriminately
150. *draw* – rake in

155. *pelican* – It was believed that the pelican opened up its own breast to feed its young.

156. *repast* – feed

160. *sensibly* – deeply
161. *level* – clearly
        'pear – appear

168. *turn the beam* – tilt the bar that balances the two sides of a scale

172. *Nature ... love* – human nature is refined by love
173. *instance* – token

179 – 180. "If you were sane and attempted to incite me to revenge, you could not do so as well as the sight of you like this."
182. *wheel* – refrain

Act Four • Scene 5

184. "This nonsense conveys more than matters of common sense do."

188. *fitted* – appropriately bestowed

189 – 193. Each of the flowers proffered by Ophelia has symbolic value:
fennel – flattery
columbine – ingratitude
rue – sorrow, repentance
daisy – infidelity
violet – faithfulness

197. *Thought* – melancholy contemplation
197. *passion* – suffering
198. *favour* – charm

212. *commune with* – share
216. *collateral* – indirect

LAERTES: This nothing's more than matter.

OPHELIA: There's rosemary, that's for remembrance — pray you love, remember. And there is pansies. That's for thoughts.

LAERTES: A document in madness: thoughts and remembrance fitted.

OPHELIA: There's fennel for you, and columbines. There's rue for you. And here's some for me. 190 We may call it herb of grace a Sundays. O you must wear your rue with a difference. There's a daisy. I would give you some violets, but they withered all when my father died. They say he made a good end.

[Sings.] For bonny sweet Robin is all my joy.

LAERTES: Thought and affliction, passion, hell itself, She turns to favour and to prettiness.

OPHELIA: *[Sings.]*

> *And will he not come again?*
> *And will he not come again?* 200
> *No, no, he is dead,*
> *Go to thy death-bed,*
> *He never will come again.*
>
> *His beard was as white as snow,*
> *All flaxen was his poll.*
> *He is gone, he is gone,*
> *And we cast away moan.*
> *God have mercy on his soul!*

And of all Christian souls, I pray God.
God be with ye. 210

Exit.

LAERTES: Do you see this, O God?

KING: Laertes, I must commune with your grief, Or you deny me right. Go but apart, Make choice of whom your wisest friends you will, And they shall hear and judge 'twixt you and me. If by direct or by collateral hand They find us touched, we will our kingdom give, Our crown, our life, and all that we call ours To you in satisfaction; but if not, Be you content to lend your patience to us, 220 And we shall jointly labour with your soul To give it due content.

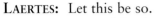

LAERTES: Let this be so.
His means of death, his obscure funeral —
No trophy, sword, nor hatchment over his bones,
No noble rite, nor formal ostentation —
Cry to be heard, as 'twere from heaven to earth,
That I must call it in question.

KING: So you shall.
And where the offence is, let the great axe fall.
I pray you, go with me.   230

Exeunt.

224 – 226. To cover up for Hamlet's actions, Polonius must have been buried secretly and without the ostentation usually associated with the funeral of such a high-ranking minister.

Horatio receives news that Hamlet has returned to Denmark.

Act Four
Scene 6

Another room in the castle.

Enter Horatio and a Servant.

HORATIO: What are they that would speak with me?
SERVANT: Seafaring men, sir. They say they have letters for you.
HORATIO: Let them come in.

[Exit Servant.]

I do not know from what part of the world
I should be greeted, if not from Lord Hamlet.

Enter Sailors.

FIRST SAILOR: God bless you, sir.
HORATIO: Let him bless thee too.
FIRST SAILOR: He shall, sir, and please him. There's a letter
for you, sir. It comes from the ambassador that was
bound for England, if your name be Horatio, as I am   10
let to know it is.
HORATIO: *[Reads the letter.]* 'Horatio, when thou shalt
have overlooked this, give these fellows some means
to the King. They have letters for him. Ere we were
two days old at sea, a pirate of very warlike
appointment gave us chase. Finding ourselves
too slow of sail, we put on a compelled valour, and in
the grapple I boarded them. On the instant they got
clear of our ship, so I alone became their prisoner.
They have dealt with me like thieves of mercy. But   20
they knew what they did: I am to do a good turn for
them. Let the King have the letters I have sent, and
repair thou to me with as much speed as thou*

13. *overlooked* – looked over; read

16. *appointment* – equipment

18. *grapple* – fastening together of the two ships

wouldst fly death. I have words to speak in thine ear
will make thee dumb, yet are they much too light for
the bore of the matter. These good fellows will bring
thee where I am. Rosencrantz and Guildenstern hold
their course for England. Of them I have much to tell
thee. Farewell.

'*He that thou knowest thine,*   30
Hamlet.'

Come, I will give you way for these your letters,
And do it the speedier that you may direct me
To him from whom you brought them.

Exeunt.

26. *bore* – bore of a gun.
Hamlet's words cannot
adequately express the
enormity of what has
occurred to him recently.

Act Four
Scene 7

Another room in the castle.

Enter King and Laertes.

Claudius clarifies for Laertes why he did not deal with Hamlet more directly. Their conversation is interrupted with news that Hamlet has returned and will soon arrive at the court. Claudius and Laertes plot to kill Hamlet. Gertrude brings word that Ophelia has drowned.

KING: Now must your conscience my acquaintance seal,
And you must put me in your heart for friend,
Sith you have heard, and with a knowing ear,
That he which hath your noble father slain
Pursued my life.
LAERTES: It well appears. But tell me
Why you proceeded not against these feats,
So crimeful and so capital in nature,
As by your safety, wisdom, all things else,
You mainly were stirred up.   10
KING: O, for two special reasons,
Which may to you perhaps seem much unsinewed,
But yet to me they are strong. The Queen his mother
Lives almost by his looks, and for myself —
My virtue or my plague, be it either which —
She is so conjunctive to my life and soul,
That, as the star moves not but in his sphere,
I could not but by her. The other motive
Why to a public count I might not go,
Is the great love the general gender bear him,   20
Who, dipping all his faults in their affection,
Work like the spring that turneth wood to stone,
Convert his gyves to graces; so that my arrows,
Too slightly timbered for so loud a wind,
Would have reverted to my bow again,
And not where I had aimed them.
LAERTES: And so have I a noble father lost,
A sister driven into desperate terms,
Whose worth, if praises may go back again,

1. *my ... seal* – my innocence accept

8. *capital* – crimes punishable by death

12. *unsinewed* – weak
16. *conjunctive* – closely linked
18. *I ... her* – I could not act without considering her

19. *count* – reckoning, trial
20. *general gender* – common people

23. *gyves* – deformities. Pronounced with a hard *g* to be alliterative with "graces."
24. *wind* – i.e., popular opinion
29 – 31. "Her perfection was unequalled in her time."

Stood challenger on mount of all the age   30
        For her perfections. But my revenge will come.
KING: Break not your sleeps for that. You must not think
        That we are made of stuff so flat and dull
        That we can let our beard be shook with danger
        And think it pastime. You shortly shall hear more.
        I loved your father, and we love ourself,
        And that, I hope, will teach you to imagine —

                Enter a Messenger with letters.

        How now! what news?
MESSENGER: Letters, my lord, from Hamlet. This to your
        Majesty, this to the Queen.   40
KING: From Hamlet! Who brought them?
MESSENGER: Sailors, my lord, they say. I saw them not.
        They were given me by Claudio. He received them
        Of him that brought them.
KING: Laertes, you shall hear them. Leave us.

                Exit Messenger.

        *[Reads.] High and mighty, You shall know I am set
        naked on your kingdom. Tomorrow shall I beg leave
        to see your kingly eyes, when I shall, first asking your
        pardon, thereunto recount the occasion of my sudden
        and more strange return.*   50
                                                Hamlet.

        What should this mean? Are all the rest come back?
        Or is it some abuse, and no such thing?
LAERTES: Know you the hand?
KING: 'Tis Hamlet's character. 'Naked!
        And in a postscript here, he says 'Alone.'
        Can you advise me?
LAERTES: I'm lost in it, my lord. But let him come.
        It warms the very sickness in my heart,
        That I shall live and tell him to his teeth,
        'Thus diest thou.'   60
KING: If it be so, Laertes —
        As how should it be so, how otherwise? —
        Will you be ruled by me?
LAERTES: Ay, my lord,
        So you will not overrule me to a peace.
KING: To thine own peace. If he be now returned,

33 – 34. "That I can tolerate insults because of danger"

47. *naked* – stripped of possessions

52. *abuse* – trick, joke

54. *character* – handwriting

67. *checking at* – shying away from (completing)
69. *ripe ... device* – fully developed in my devising

72. *uncharge the practice* – not suspect a trick

75. *The rather* – more readily

80. *sum of parts* – qualities and accomplishments combined
83. *unworthiest siege* – lowest order
86 – 89. "It is just as fitting for youths to wear their light and fanciful clothing as it is for the older generation to wear furs and clothing that project concern for their health and their maturity."
95 – 96. *incorpsed ... beast* – made into one body with and become half horse
96 – 98. "So far did he surpass my expectations that in imagining feats of skill and horsemanship, I fell short of what he actually did."

105. *confession of you* – acknowledged your superiority
107. *art and exercise* – theory and practice
110. *scrimers* – fencers
111. *motion ... eye* – fencing movements, parry, nor sharpness of the eye

---

As checking at his voyage, and that he means
No more to undertake it, I will work him
To an exploit, now ripe in my device,
Under the which he shall not choose but fall. 70
And for his death no wind of blame shall breathe,
But even his mother shall uncharge the practice
And call it accident.

LAERTES: My lord, I will be ruled,
The rather, if you could devise it so
That I might be the organ.

KING: It falls right.
You have been talked of since your travel much,
And that in Hamlet's hearing, for a quality
Wherein, they say, you shine. Your sum of parts 80
Did not together pluck such envy from him
As did that one, and that, in my regard,
Of the unworthiest siege.

LAERTES: What part is that, my lord?

KING: A very ribbon in the cap of youth,
Yet needful too, for youth no less becomes
The light and careless livery that it wears
Than settled age his sables and his weeds
Importing health and graveness. Two months since
Here was a gentleman of Normandy — 90
I have seen myself, and served against, the French,
And they can well on horseback, but this gallant
Had witchcraft in it. He grew unto his seat,
And to such wondrous doing brought his horse,
As he had been incorpsed and demi-natured
With the brave beast. So far he topped my thought,
That I, in forgery of shapes and tricks,
Come short of what he did.

LAERTES: A Norman was it?

KING: A Norman. 100

LAERTES: Upon my life, Lamord.

KING: The very same.

LAERTES: I know him well. He is the brooch indeed
And gem of all the nation.

KING: He made confession of you,
And gave you such a masterly report
For art and exercise in your defence
And for your rapier most especial,
That he cried out, it would be a sight indeed,
If one could match you. The scrimers of their nation, 110
He swore, had had neither motion, guard, nor eye,

If you opposed them. Sir, this report of his
Did Hamlet so envenom with his envy
That he could nothing do but wish and beg
Your sudden coming over to play with him.
Now, out of this —
LAERTES: What out of this, my lord?
KING: Laertes, was your father dear to you?
    Or are you like the painting of a sorrow,
    A face without a heart?   120
LAERTES: Why ask you this?
KING: Not that I think you did not love your father,
    But that I know love is begun by time,
    And that I see, in passages of proof,
    Time qualifies the spark and fire of it.
    There lives within the very flame of love
    A kind of wick or snuff that will abate it;
    And nothing is at a like goodness still,
    For goodness, growing to a pleurisy,
    Dies in his own too–much. That we would do   130
    We should do when we would: for this 'would' changes
    And hath abatements and delays as many
    As there are tongues, are hands, are accidents,
    And then this 'should' is like a spendthrift sigh
    That hurts by easing. But, to the quick of the ulcer:
    Hamlet comes back. What would you undertake
    To show yourself your father's son in deed
    More than in words?
LAERTES: To cut his throat in the church.
KING: No place, indeed, should murder sanctuarize.   140
    Revenge should have no bounds. But, good Laertes,
    Will you do this, keep close within your chamber.
    Hamlet returned shall know you are come home.
    We'll put on those shall praise your excellence
    And set a double varnish on the fame
    The Frenchman gave you, bring you in fine together
    And wager over your heads. He, being remiss,
    Most generous and free from all contriving,
    Will not peruse the foils, so that, with ease,
    Or with a little shuffling, you may choose   150
    A sword unbated, and in a pass of practice
    Requite him for your father.
LAERTES: I will do it.
    And, for that purpose, I'll anoint my sword.
    I bought an unction of a mountebank
    So mortal that but dip a knife in it,

124. *passages of proof* – incidents that prove a point
125. *qualifies* – weakens
127. *abate* – lessen
128. "Nothing remains at the same level of goodness always."
129. *pleurisy* – excess

132. *abatements* – reductions in intensity
135. *quick ... ulcer* – core of the problem

139. Laertes' resolve to avenge his father's death contrasts strongly with Hamlet's reluctance to kill the praying Claudius.

140. *sanctuarize* – provide sanctuary for
142. *keep close* – stay
145. *set ... varnish* – add to the glossy finish
146. *in fine* – finally
147. *remiss* – careless, unsuspecting
151. *unbated* – unblunted
152. *Requite* – repay
155. *unction* – ointment ... *mountebank* – a travelling quack doctor

157. *cataplasm* – plaster, poultice
158. *simples* – herbs with medicinal properties
161. *gall* – graze

164 – 167. "Consider what time and place would best suit our plan. If it should fail and if our scheme becomes known through carelessness, it would be better not attempted at all."
169. *blast in proof* – blow up in our faces

173. *As make* – and you should make
175. *nonce* – occasion

181. *askant* – slanting out over
182. *hoary* – greyish

186. *cold* – chaste
187. *coronet* – in the shape of a crown
188. *envious* – malicious

193. *incapable* – unable to comprehend
194. *native and indued* – born to and adapted

197. *lay* – song

RELATED READING

198. *Ophelia's Song* – poem by Marya Zaturenska (page 170)

Where it draws blood no cataplasm so rare,
Collected from all simples that have virtue
Under the moon, can save the thing from death
That is but scratched withal. I'll touch my point   160
With this contagion, that if I gall him slightly,
It may be death.

KING: Let's further think of this,
Weigh what convenience both of time and means
May fit us to our shape. If this should fail,
And that our drift look through our bad performance,
'Twere better not essayed. Therefore this project
Should have a back or second, that might hold
If this should blast in proof. Soft, let me see.
We'll make a solemn wager on your cunnings —   170
I have it!
When in your motion you are hot and dry —
As make your bouts more violent to that end —
And that he calls for drink, I'll have prepared him
A chalice for the nonce, whereon but sipping,
If he by chance escape your venomed stuck,
Our purpose may hold there. But stay what noise?

Enter Queen.

QUEEN: One woe doth tread upon another's heel,
So fast they follow. Your sister's drowned, Laertes.
LAERTES: Drowned! O, where?   180
QUEEN: There is a willow grows askant the brook
That shows his hoary leaves in the glassy stream.
Therewith fantastic garlands did she make
Of crow-flowers, nettles, daisies, and long purples
That liberal shepherds give a grosser name,
But our cold maids do dead men's fingers call them.
There, on the pendent boughs her coronet weeds
Clambering to hang, an envious sliver broke,
When down her weedy trophies and herself
Fell in the weeping brook. Her clothes spread wide,   190
And, mermaid-like, awhile they bore her up,
Which time she chanted snatches of old tunes,
As one incapable of her own distress,
Or like a creature native and indued
Unto that element. But long it could not be
Till that her garments, heavy with their drink,
Pulled the poor wretch from her melodious lay
To muddy death.

LAERTES: Alas, then, she is drowned?

QUEEN: Drowned, drowned.   200

LAERTES: Too much of water hast thou, poor Ophelia,
And therefore I forbid my tears. But yet
It is our trick. Nature her custom holds,
Let shame say what it will. When these are gone,
The woman will be out. Adieu, my lord,
I have a speech of fire, that fain would blaze,
But that this folly douts it.

Exit.

KING: Let's follow, Gertrude.
How much I had to do to calm his rage.
Now fear I this will give it start again.   210
Therefore let's follow.

Exeunt.

ða   ða   ða

203. *our trick* – a natural response; our way

204 – 205. "When these tears are gone, there will be no further sign of weakness in me."

206. *fain would* – is eager to

207. "But these foolish tears extinguish it."

Act Four Considerations

ACT FOUR Scene 1

▶ What evidence is there in this scene that Hamlet's advice has had an effect on Gertrude?

▶ In regard to Polonius' murder, what seem to be Claudius' major concerns?

ACT FOUR Scene 2

▶ Why does Hamlet not cooperate with Rosencrantz and Guildenstern?

ACT FOUR Scene 3

▶ Hamlet, in outlining how a king can "go a progress through the guts of a beggar" is in effect describing a food chain. Draw a diagram in which you illustrate this food chain. Create a similar food chain using details from today's society.

▶ Why does Hamlet not object to his being sent to England? Does this not delay, if not make impossible, his revenge? Create a dialogue with Horatio in which Hamlet explains his reasons for not protesting the King's decision.

ACT FOUR Scene 4

▶ Imagine you are directing this play and would like to cut this scene from the performance. The author, of course, objects. Write a dialogue between you and the author in which you discuss the purpose(s) served by this scene.

ACT FOUR Scene 5

▶ In what significant ways does Ophelia's real madness differ from Hamlet's feigned madness? What different themes do her songs deal with?

▶ Claudius puts on a good show of bravado in this scene. What other aspects of his character are emphasized here?

▶ Like Hamlet, Laertes has had his father killed. However, that is where the similarity ends. Using magazine illustrations and/or original artwork, develop a contrast between Hamlet and Laertes.

ACT FOUR Scene 6

▶ The episode with the pirates seems all too convenient. Do you think it possible that Hamlet planned the encounter with the pirates before leaving for England? Why or why not?

ACT FOUR Scene 7

▶ We learn the contents of the letter Hamlet sends to the King but not of the letter he sends to the Queen. Write the letter that Hamlet would send his mother. It need not be much longer than the one he sends Claudius.

▶ This scene continues to develop a contrast between Hamlet and Laertes. What positive characteristics of Hamlet's are indirectly emphasized in this scene?

▶ Gertrude, in describing Ophelia's death, provides some very specific details. It is as if there were an eyewitness to the event. How would she have been able to acquire this information?

Act Five
Scene 1

A churchyard.

Enter two Clowns, [the Grave-digger and Another.]

GRAVE-DIGGER: Is she to be buried in Christian burial that wilfully seeks her own salvation?

OTHER: I tell thee she is, and therefore make her grave straight. The crowner hath sat on her and finds it Christian burial.

GRAVE-DIGGER: How can that be, unless she drowned herself in her own defence?

OTHER: Why, 'tis found so.

GRAVE-DIGGER: It must be *se offendendo*, it cannot be else. For here lies the point: if I drown myself wittingly, it argues an act, and an act hath three branches — it is, to act, to do, to perform. Argal, she drowned herself wittingly.   10

OTHER: Nay, but hear you, Goodman Delver —

GRAVE-DIGGER: Give me leave. Here lies the water — good. Here stands the man — good. If the man go to this water and drown himself, it is, will he, nill he, he goes, mark you that. But if the water come to him and drown him, he drowns not himself. Argal, he that is not guilty of his own death shortens not his own life.   20

OTHER: But is this law?

GRAVE-DIGGER: Ay, marry is it, crowner's quest law.

OTHER: Will you have the truth on it? If this had not been a gentlewoman, she should have been buried out of Christian burial.

GRAVE-DIGGER: Why, there thou sayest. And the more pity that great folk should have countenance in this world to drown or hang themselves, more than their even

A Grave-digger banters with his companion. Hamlet and Horatio appear and Hamlet exchanges wit with the Grave-digger until Ophelia's funeral procession arrives. Hamlet declares his love for Ophelia but also becomes involved in an altercation with Laertes. When Hamlet leaves, the King reminds Laertes of their scheme to kill Hamlet.

1. It was believed that people who committed suicide would go directly to hell, therefore they were denied Christian burial.

2. *salvation* – perhaps an error for "damnation." The Grave-digger believes that Ophelia should not be granted the same privilege as those who died not of their own accord.

4. *crowner hath sat* – the coroner decided

9. *se offendendo* – a mistaken version of the legal term se defendendo, which means "self–defence"

12. *argal* – mispronunciation of the Latin *ergo*, "therefore"

23. *quest* – inquest

28. *countenance* – privilege

Christian. Come, my spade. There is no ancient 30
gentleman but gardeners, ditchers, and grave-makers
— they hold up Adam's profession.

OTHER: Was he a gentleman?

GRAVE-DIGGER: He was the first that ever bore arms.

OTHER: Why, he had none.

GRAVE-DIGGER: What, art a heathen? How dost thou
understand the Scripture? The Scripture says Adam
digged. Could he dig without arms? I'll put another
question to thee. If thou answerest me not to the
purpose, confess thyself— 40

OTHER: Go to.

GRAVE-DIGGER: What is he that builds stronger than
either the mason, the shipwright, or the carpenter?

OTHER: The gallows-maker, for that frame outlives a
thousand tenants.

GRAVE-DIGGER: I like thy wit well, in good faith. The
gallows does well. But how does it well? It does well
to those that do ill. Now thou dost ill to say the
gallows is built stronger than the church. Argal, the
gallows may do well to thee. To it again, come. 50

OTHER: Who builds stronger than a mason, a shipwright,
or a carpenter?

GRAVE-DIGGER: Ay, tell me that, and unyoke.

OTHER: Marry, now I can tell.

GRAVE-DIGGER: To it.

OTHER: Mass, I cannot tell.

Enter Hamlet and Horatio, afar off.

GRAVE-DIGGER: Cudgel thy brains no more about it, for
your dull ass will not mend his pace with beating.
And when you are asked this question next, say 'A
grave-maker.' The houses he makes last till 60
doomsday. Go, get thee to Yaughan. Fetch me a
stoup of liquor.

[Exit Other. Grave-digger continues to dig and sing.]

In youth, when I did love, did love,
Methought it was very sweet,
To contract—O—the time for— a—my behove,
O, methought there—a—was nothing—a—meet.

HAMLET: Has this fellow no feeling of his business,
that he sings at grave-making?

32. *Adam's profession* – out of necessity, Adam became a farmer or gardener, one who digs the earth

34. *bore arms* – pun on the coat of arms that gentlemen were entitled to bear

53. *unyoke* – have done with it, as when an ox is finished with its toil

58. *mend his pace* – go faster

61. *Yaughan* – perhaps the name of a local innkeeper

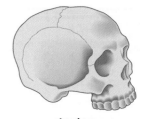

HORATIO: Custom hath made it in him a property of easiness.

HAMLET: 'Tis even so, the hand of little employment hath   70
the daintier sense.

GRAVE-DIGGER: *[Sings.] But age, with his stealing steps,*
Hath clawed me in his clutch,
And hath shipped me intil the land,
As if I had never been such.

[Grave-digger throws up a skull.]

HAMLET: That skull had a tongue in it, and could sing
once. How the knave jowls it to the ground, as if it
were Cain's jawbone, that did the first murder. This
might be the pate of a politician, which this ass now
over-offices, one that would circumvent God, might it   80
not?

HORATIO: It might, my lord.

HAMLET: Or of a courtier, which could say 'Good morrow,
sweet lord! How dost thou, good lord?' This might
be my Lord Such-a-one, that praised my Lord
Such-a-one's horse when he meant to beg it, might
it not?

HORATIO: Ay, my lord.

HAMLET: Why, even so, and now my Lady Worm's,
chopless, and knocked about the mazard with a   90
sexton's spade. Here's fine revolution, if we had the
trick to see it. Did these bones cost no more the
breeding but to play at loggets with them? Mine ache
to think on it.

GRAVE-DIGGER: *[Sings.] A pick-axe, and a spade, a spade,*
For and a shrouding sheet:
O, a pit of clay for to be made
For such a guest is meet.

[Throws up another skull.]

HAMLET: There's another. Why may not that be the skull
of a lawyer? Where be his quiddities now, his   100
quillities, his cases, his tenures, and his tricks? Why
does he suffer this rude knave now to knock him
about the sconce with a dirty shovel, and will not tell
him of his action of battery? Hum, this fellow might
be in his time a great buyer of land, with his statutes,
his recognizances, his fines, his double vouchers, his

69. "He has grown in time to feel comfortable with his profession."

74. *intil* – to

77. *jowls* – throws. There is also a play on jowl, or jawbone.

78. *Cain's jawbone* – Cain killed his brother with the jawbone of an ass.

79. *pate* – head

chopless

90. *chopless* – without a jaw

90. *mazard* – head

91. *revolution* – turn of events

93. *loggets* – tossing game, the object of which is to throw pieces of wood closest to the target

100 – 101. *quiddities ... quillities* – quibbling arguments

103. *sconce* – head

104. *action of battery* – assault case

104 – 114. The legal terms used in this speech and elsewhere have led many to believe that Shakespeare had some form of legal training.

106. *fine* – the end, the finish. Hamlet puns using four different meanings of the word "fine."

119. *assurance* – security

129. *quick* – the living

140. *absolute* – exact
141. *equivocation* – relying upon the ambiguous nature of certain words, frequently with the intention of deceiving others or acting above the law
143. *picked* – refined or overly concerned with what is fashionable

142 – 145. Hamlet complains that the commoners have become so fashion conscious that they follow courtiers close enough to rub sore (gall) the courtier's heel (kibe).

recoveries. Is this the fine of his fines, and the recovery of his recoveries, to have his fine pate full of fine dirt? Will his vouchers vouch him no more of his purchases, and double ones too, than the length and breadth of a pair of indentures? The very conveyances of his lands will scarcely lie in this box, and must the inheritor himself have no more, ha?   110

HORATIO: Not a jot more, my lord.

HAMLET: Is not parchment made of sheepskins?

HORATIO: Ay, my lord, and of calveskins too.

HAMLET: They are sheep and calves which seek out assurance in that. I will speak to this fellow.— Whose grave's this, sirrah?   120

GRAVE-DIGGER: Mine, sir.

[Sings.]   *O, a pit of clay for to be made*
                        For such a guest is meet.

HAMLET: I think it be thine, indeed, for thou liest in it.

GRAVE-DIGGER: You lie out on it, sir, and therefore it is not yours. For my part, I do not lie in it, and yet it is mine.

HAMLET: Thou dost lie in it, to be in it and say it is thine. 'Tis for the dead, not for the quick. Therefore thou liest.   130

GRAVE-DIGGER: 'Tis a quick lie, sir, it will away again, from me to you.

HAMLET: What man dost thou dig it for?

GRAVE-DIGGER: For no man, sir.

HAMLET: What woman, then?

GRAVE-DIGGER: For none, neither.

HAMLET: Who is to be buried in it?

GRAVE-DIGGER: One that was a woman, sir, but, rest her soul, she's dead.

HAMLET: How absolute the knave is! We must speak by the card, or equivocation will undo us. By the Lord, Horatio, these three years I have taken a note of it, the age is grown so picked that the toe of the peasant comes so near the heel of the courtier, he galls his kibe. How long hast thou been a grave-maker?   140

GRAVE-DIGGER: Of all the days in the year, I came to it that day that our last King Hamlet overcame Fortinbras.

HAMLET: How long is that since?

GRAVE-DIGGER: Cannot you tell that? Every fool can tell that. It was the very day that young Hamlet was born —   150 he that is mad, and sent into England.

HAMLET: Ay, marry. Why was he sent into England?

GRAVE-DIGGER: Why, because he was mad. He shall recover his wits there. Or if he do not, it's no great matter there.

HAMLET: Why?

GRAVE-DIGGER: 'Twill, not be seen in him there. There the men are as mad as he.

HAMLET: How came he mad?

GRAVE-DIGGER: Very strangely, they say.   160

HAMLET: How strangely?

GRAVE-DIGGER: Faith, even with losing his wits.

HAMLET: Upon what ground?

GRAVE-DIGGER: Why, here in Denmark. I have been sexton here, man and boy, thirty years.

HAMLET: How long will a man lie in the earth ere he rot?

GRAVE-DIGGER: Faith, if he be not rotten before he die — as we have many pocky corses nowadays, that will scarce hold the laying in — he will last you some eight year or nine year. A tanner will last you nine year.   170

HAMLET: Why he more than another?

GRAVE-DIGGER: Why, sir, his hide is so tanned with his trade, that he will keep out water a great while, and your water is a sore decayer of your whoreson dead body. Here's a skull now has lain in the earth three and twenty years.

HAMLET: Whose was it?

GRAVE-DIGGER: A whoreson mad fellow's it was. Whose do you think it was?

HAMLET: Nay, I know not.   180

GRAVE-DIGGER: A pestilence on him for a mad rogue! He poured a flagon of Rhenish on my head once. This same skull, sir, was Yorick's skull, the King's jester.

HAMLET: This?

GRAVE-DIGGER: Even that.

HAMLET: Let me see.

[Takes the skull.]

Alas, poor Yorick. I knew him, Horatio, a fellow of infinite jest, of most excellent fancy. He hath bore me on his back a thousand times, and now — how abhorred in my imagination it is. My gorge rises at   190
it. Here hung those lips that I have kissed I know not how oft. Where be your gibes now, your gambols, your songs, your flashes of merriment, that were

RELATED READING

Intimations – poem by Robert Currie (page 174) and *They All Want to Play Hamlet* – poem by Carl Sandburg (page 169)

168. *pocky corses* – diseased corpses that fell apart before they could be buried

182. *flagon of Rhenish* – bottle of Rhine wine

RELATED READING

187. *Alas, Poor Bauer* – poem by Richard Woollatt (page 172)

192. *gibes* – jests
192. *gambols* – dances

Act Five • Scene 1

195. *chop-fallen* – lacking a
lower jaw; sad
197. *favour* – appearance

201. *Alexander* – the Great
(356 – 323 B.C.); Greek
conqueror who succeeded in
amassing the greatest
empire in the Western world
until the time of Caesar

208. *stopping a bung-hole* –
corking a beer barrel
209. *curiously* – minutely

219. *flaw* – squall; wind

222. *maimed* – falling far
short of a full ceremony
224. *estate* – high standing
or position in society

229. *obsequies* – funeral
230.*warranty* – authority
doubtful – suspicious

RELATED READING

230. *Remembering
Ophelia* – poem by Diane
Fahey (page 171)

wont to set the table on a roar? Not one now to
mock your own grinning? Quite chop-fallen? Now
get you to my lady's chamber and tell her, let her
paint an inch thick, to this favour she must come.
Make her laugh at that. Prithee, Horatio, tell me one
thing.

HORATIO: What's that, my lord? 200

HAMLET: Dost thou think Alexander looked of this
fashion in the earth?

HORATIO: Even so.

HAMLET: And smelt so? Pah!

[Puts down the skull.]

HORATIO: Even so, my lord.

HAMLET: To what base uses we may return, Horatio! Why
may not imagination trace the noble dust of
Alexander, till he find it stopping a bung-hole?

HORATIO: 'Twere to consider too curiously, to consider so.

HAMLET: No, faith, not a jot, but to follow him thither 210
with modesty enough, and likelihood to lead it.
Alexander died, Alexander was buried, Alexander
returneth into dust, the dust is earth, of earth we make
loam, and why of that loam, whereto he was
converted, might they not stop a beer-barrel?
Imperious Caesar, dead and turned to clay,
Might stop a hole to keep the wind away.
O, that that earth, which kept the world in awe,
Should patch a wall to expel the winter's flaw!
But soft, but soft awhile. Here comes the King. 220

*Enter [Priest], King, Queen, Laertes, and a Coffin,
with Lords Attendant.*

The Queen, the courtiers. Who is this they follow?
And with such maimed rites? This doth betoken
The corse they follow did with desperate hand
Fordo its own life. 'Twas of some estate.
Couch we awhile, and mark.

LAERTES: What ceremony else?

HAMLET: That is Laertes, a very noble youth. Mark.

LAERTES: What ceremony else?

PRIEST: Her obsequies have been as far enlarged
As we have warranty. Her death was doubtful, 230
And, but that great command oversways the order,

She should in ground unsanctified been lodged
Till the last trumpet. For charitable prayers
Shards, flints and pebbles should be thrown on her.
Yet here she is allowed her virgin crants,
Her maiden strewments and the bringing home
Of bell and burial.

LAERTES: Must there no more be done?

PRIEST: No more be done.
We should profane the service of the dead   240
To sing a requiem and such rest to her
As to peace-parted souls.

LAERTES: Lay her in the earth,
And from her fair and unpolluted flesh
May violets spring. I tell thee, churlish priest,
A ministering angel shall my sister be
When thou liest howling.

HAMLET: What, the fair Ophelia!

QUEEN: *[Scattering flowers.]* Sweets to the sweet. Farewell.
I hoped thou shouldst have been my Hamlet's wife.   250
I thought thy bride-bed to have decked, sweet maid,
And not have strewed thy grave.

LAERTES: O, treble woe
Fall ten times treble on that cursed head
Whose wicked deed thy most ingenious sense
Deprived thee of! Hold off the earth awhile,
Till I have caught her once more in mine arms.

Leaps into the grave.

Now pile your dust upon the quick and dead,
Till of this flat a mountain you have made,
To overtop old Pelion, or the skyish head   260
Of blue Olympus.

HAMLET: What is he whose grief
Bears such an emphasis, whose phrase of sorrow
Conjures the wandering stars and makes them stand
Like wonder-wounded hearers? This is I,
Hamlet the Dane.

LAERTES: The devil take thy soul!

[Grappling with him.]

HAMLET: Thou prayest not well.
I prithee take thy fingers from my throat,
For though I am not splenitive and rash,   270

235. *crants* – garlands; funeral wreaths for maidens

234 – 237. Ophelia's trip to her final resting place (bringing home) has been accompanied by the ringing of the church bell and some funeral rites, despite the suspicious circumstances of her death.

245. *churlish* – unkind; rude

251. *decked* – strewn with flowers

255. *ingenious* – lively

260. *Pelion* – high mountain in Greece used by the giants in their war with the gods in Olympus. In their attempt to scale Olympus, the giants piled Pelion on the top of Mount Ossa.

264. *Conjures* – casts a hypnotic spell on

265. *wonder-wounded* – struck by wonder or amazement

266. In referring to himself as Hamlet the Dane, he is in effect asserting his right to the throne.

270. *splenitive* – hot tempered

Act Five • Scene 1

Yet have I something in me dangerous,
Which let thy wiseness fear. Hold off thy hand.

KING: Pluck them asunder.

QUEEN: Hamlet! Hamlet!

ALL: Gentlemen!

HORATIO: Good my lord, be quiet.

HAMLET: Why, I will fight with him upon this theme
Until my eyelids will no longer wag.

QUEEN: O my son, what theme?

HAMLET: I loved Ophelia. Forty thousand brothers   280
Could not with all their quantity of love
Make up my sum. What wilt thou do for her?

KING: O, he is mad, Laertes.

QUEEN: For love of God, forbear him.

HAMLET: 'Swounds, show me what thou wilt do.
Woo't weep, woo't fight, woo't fast, woo't tear thyself,
Woo't drink up eisel, eat a crocodile?
I'll do it. Dost thou come here to whine,
To outface me with leaping in her grave?
Be buried quick with her, and so will I.   290
And, if thou prate of mountains, let them throw
Millions of acres on us, till our ground,
Singeing his pate against the burning zone,
Make Ossa like a wart. Nay, and thou'lt mouth,
I'll rant as well as thou.

QUEEN: This is mere madness,
And thus awhile the fit will work on him.
Anon, as patient as the female dove,
When that her golden couplets are disclosed,
His silence will sit drooping.   300

HAMLET: Hear you, sir,
What is the reason that you use me thus?
I loved you ever. But it is no matter.
Let Hercules himself do what he may,
The cat will mew and dog will have his day.

Exit.

KING: I pray you, good Horatio, wait upon him.

Exit Horatio.

[To Laertes.]
Strengthen your patience in our last night's speech.
We'll put the matter to the present push. —

282. *sum* – total quantity

284. *forbear him* – leave him alone

286. *Woo't* – variant form of wilt – will you?

287. *eisel* – vinegar

291. *And ... prate* – if you talk, chatter

291 – 294. Hamlet outdoes Laertes in his talk of mountains. Hamlet's hyperbole features creating a mountain so high that its top is singed by the sun.

294. *mouth* – speak with passion

299. "When her two eggs are hatched"

308. *present push* – immediate action

Good Gertrude, set some watch over your son.
This grave shall have a living monument. 310
An hour of quiet shortly shall we see.
Till then, in patience our proceeding be.

Exeunt.

310. *living* – enduring

'Character,' ... 'is destiny.' But not the whole of our destiny. Hamlet ... was speculative and irresolute and we have a great tragedy in consequence. But if his father had lived to a good old age and his uncle had died an early death, we can conceive Hamlet having married Ophelia and got through life with a reputation of sanity, notwithstanding many soliloquies and some moody sarcasm towards the fair daughter of Polonius, to say nothing of the frankest incivility to his father-in-law.
– George Eliot (1819 – 1880), British novelist

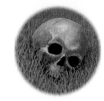

Act Five
Scene 2

A hall in the castle.

Enter Hamlet and Horatio.

HAMLET: So much for this, sir. Now shall you see the other.
    You do remember all the circumstance?
HORATIO: Remember it, my lord?
HAMLET: Sir, in my heart there was a kind of fighting
    That would not let me sleep. Methought I lay
    Worse than the mutines in the bilboes. Rashly —
    And praised be rashness for it, let us know
    Our indiscretion sometimes serves us well
    When our deep plots do pall. And that should learn us
    There's a divinity that shapes our ends,   10
    Rough-hew them how we will —
HORATIO: That is most certain.
HAMLET: Up from my cabin,
    My sea-gown scarfed about me, in the dark
    Groped I to find out them, had my desire,
    Fingered their packet, and in fine withdrew
    To mine own room again, making so bold,
    My fears forgetting manners, to unseal
    Their grand commission. Where I found, Horatio —
    Oh royal knavery — an exact command,   20
    Larded with many several sorts of reasons
    Importing Denmark's health and England's too,
    With ho, such bugs and goblins in my life,
    That, on the supervise, no leisure bated,
    No, not to stay the grinding of the axe,
    My head should be struck off.
HORATIO: Is it possible?
HAMLET: Here's the commission, read it at more leisure.
    But wilt thou hear now how I did proceed?

Hamlet relates to Horatio what transpired during his absence and how he found his way back to Denmark. Osric informs Hamlet that Claudius has wagered that Laertes can best Hamlet at a fencing match. Hamlet accepts the challenge. The match begins with Hamlet scoring the first two hits. In the ensuing action, Gertrude, Claudius, Laertes, and Hamlet are killed. Fortinbras appears and claims the throne of Denmark.

bilboes

6. *mutines in the bilboes* – mutineers in ankle irons

9. *pall* – fail

21. *Larded* – garnished

23 – 24. "With such imaginary dangers if I were to live, that, on the reading of the mandate, with no time lost"

HORATIO: I beseech you.   30
HAMLET: Being thus benetted round with villainies —
    Ere I could make a prologue to my brains,
    They had begun the play — I sat me down,
    Devised a new commission, wrote it fair —
    I once did hold it, as our statists do,
    A baseness to write fair, and laboured much
    How to forget that learning, but, sir, now
    It did me yeoman's service. Wilt thou know
    The effect of what I wrote?
HORATIO: Ay, good my lord.   40
HAMLET: An earnest conjuration from the King,
    As England was his faithful tributary,
    As love between them like the palm might flourish,
    As peace should stiff her wheaten garland wear
    And stand a comma 'tween their amities,
    And many such-like 'as'es of great charge,
    That, on the view and knowing of these contents,
    Without debatement further more or less,
    He should those bearers put to sudden death,
    Not shriving-time allowed.   50
HORATIO: How was this sealed?
HAMLET: Why, even in that was heaven ordinant.
    I had my father's signet in my purse,
    Which was the model of that Danish seal,
    Folded the writ up in form of the other,
    Subscribed it, gave it the impression, placed it safely,
    The changeling never known. Now, the next day
    Was our sea-fight, and what to this was sequent
    Thou knowest already.
HORATIO: So Guildenstern and Rosencrantz go to it.   60
HAMLET: Why, man, they did make love to this employment.
    They are not near my conscience. Their defeat
    Does by their own insinuation grow.
    'Tis dangerous when the baser nature comes
    Between the pass and fell incensed points
    Of mighty opposites.
HORATIO: Why, what a king is this!
HAMLET: Does it not, think thee, stand me now upon —
    He that hath killed my king and whored my mother,
    Popped in between the election and my hopes,   70
    Thrown out his angle for my proper life
    And with such cozenage — is it not perfect conscience
    To quit him with this arm? And is it not to be damned
    To let this canker of our nature come

32 – 33. "Without a plan, my brain began to work immediately on what to do."
35. *statists* – politicians
36. *baseness* – vulgar achievement

41. *conjuration* – order
44. *wheaten garland* – symbol of peace and prosperity
45. *comma* – a pause or interval
46. *'as'es* – legal-sounding clauses beginning with "as"
48. *debatement* – discussion, debate
50. "Without granting time for them to make confession."
52. *ordinant* – operating in my behalf
56. *Subscribed* – signed
    impression – official seal
58. *was sequent* – followed

63. *insinuation* – meddling
64. *baser nature* – commoner (as opposed to a nobleman)
65. *pass and fell* – (sword) thrust and fierce
66. *opposites* – opponents

70. *election* – kingship
71. *angle* – fishing hook
72. *cozenage* – deception
74. *canker* – spreading ulcerous sore; cancer

79. "A man can be killed in the time it takes to count to one."

82 – 83. "In thinking about my reasons for revenge, I see a similar picture in his situation."

84. *bravery* – brave show

> "Hamlet has not a tear for Ophelia: her death moves him to fierce disgust for the sentimentality of Laertes by her grave; and when he discusses the scene with Horatio immediately after, he utterly forgets her though he is sorry he forgot himself with Laertes, and jumps at the proposal for a fencing match to finish the day with."
> – George Bernard Shaw (1856 – 1950), British playwright and essayist

88. *water-fly* – insect, perhaps a dragonfly

91 – 93. Osric is allowed at court because he is rich, but according to Hamlet, he is no better than the animals he owns.

92. *crib* – food trough

93. *mess* – table

93. *chough* – noisy chattering bird; jackdaw

94. "owning much land"

102. *indifferent* – somewhat

In further evil?

HORATIO: It must be shortly known to him from England
What is the issue of the business there.

HAMLET: It will be short. The interim is mine.
And a man's life's no more than to say 'one.'
But I am very sorry, good Horatio,   80
That to Laertes I forgot myself,
For, by the image of my cause I see
The portraiture of his. I'll court his favours.
But, sure, the bravery of his grief did put me
Into a towering passion.

HORATIO: Peace! who comes here?

Enter young Osric, a Courtier.

OSRIC: Your lordship is right welcome back to Denmark.

HAMLET: I humbly thank you sir. — Dost know this water-fly?

HORATIO: No, my good lord.

HAMLET: Thy state is the more gracious, for 'tis a vice to   90
know him. He hath much land and fertile. Let a beast
be lord of beasts and his crib shall stand at the king's
mess. 'Tis a chough, but, as I say, spacious in the
possession of dirt.

OSRIC: Sweet lord, if your lordship were at leisure, I
should impart a thing to you from his majesty.

HAMLET: I will receive it, sir, with all diligence of
spirit. Put your bonnet to his right use: 'tis for the
head.

OSRIC: I thank your lordship, it is very hot.   100

HAMLET: No, believe me, 'tis very cold. The wind is northerly.

OSRIC: It is indifferent cold, my lord, indeed.

HAMLET: But yet methinks it is very sultry and hot for my
complexion.

OSRIC: Exceedingly, my lord, it is very sultry — as it were
— I cannot tell how. But, my lord, his Majesty bade
me signify to you that he has laid a great wager on
your head. Sir, this is the matter —

HAMLET: I beseech you, remember —

[Hamlet motions to Osric to put on his hat.]

OSRIC: Nay, good my lord, for mine ease, in good faith.   110
Sir, here is newly come to court Laertes — believe me,
an absolute gentleman, full of most excellent differences, of very soft society and great showing. Indeed,

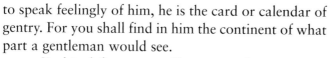

to speak feelingly of him, he is the card or calendar of gentry. For you shall find in him the continent of what part a gentleman would see.

HAMLET: Sir, his definement suffers no perdition in you, though, I know, to divide him inventorially would dozy the arithmetic of memory, and yet but yaw neither, in respect of his quick sail. But, in the verity of extolment, I take him to be a soul of great article and his infusion of such dearth and rareness as, to make true diction of him, his semblable is his mirror and who else would trace him his umbrage, nothing more.

OSRIC: Your lordship speaks most infallibly of him.

HAMLET: The concernancy, sir? Why do we wrap the gentleman in our more rawer breath?

OSRIC: Sir?

HORATIO: Is it not possible to understand in another tongue? You will to it, sir, really.

HAMLET: What imports the nomination of this gentleman?

OSRIC: Of Laertes?

HORATIO: His purse is empty already, all his golden words are spent.

HAMLET: Of him, sir.

OSRIC: I know you are not ignorant —

HAMLET: I would you did, sir. Yet, in faith, if you did, it would not much approve me. Well, sir?

OSRIC: You are not ignorant of what excellence Laertes is —

HAMLET: I dare not confess that, lest I should compare with him in excellence. But, to know a man well, were to know himself.

OSRIC: I mean, sir, for his weapon. But in the imputation laid on him by them, in his meed he's unfellowed.

HAMLET: What's his weapon?

OSRIC: Rapier and dagger.

HAMLET: That's two of his weapons. But, well.

OSRIC: The King, sir, hath wagered with him six Barbary horses, against the which he has impawned, as I take it, six French rapiers and poniards, with their assigns, as girdle, hangers, and so. Three of the carriages, in faith, are very dear to fancy, very responsive to the hilts, most delicate carriages, and of very liberal conceit.

HAMLET: What call you the carriages?

HORATIO: I knew you must be edified by the margin ere you had done.

120

130

140

150

113. *differences* – distinctions

114. *card or calendar* – perfect model

115. *continent* – totality

117. *perdition* – loss

118 – 125. " ... to make a list of his individual qualities would confuse the arithmetic of memory, and yet any attempt to list his fine qualities would fail to keep up to his quick sail. I consider Laertes to be one of a kind and his only likeness is to be seen in his mirror. If anyone attempts to be like him, he will fall short and appear as a mere shadow of Laertes."

127. *concernancy* – purpose

127 – 128. "Why are we speaking of him at all?

130 – 131. Horatio chastises Osric for his inability to understand Hamlet, who has been speaking Osric's own kind of ornate speech.

132. *nomination* – bringing forward the name of

139. *approve* – flatter

144. *imputation* – estimation; reputation

145. *meed* – area of excellence

150. *impawned* – staked

151. *poniards* – daggers

152. *carriages* – hangers

154 – 155. *liberal conceit* – ornately adorned

157. *edified by the margin* – instructed by the explanatory notes (as in the margins of a book)

Act Five • Scene 2

167 – 169. In a bout consisting of a dozen passes, Laertes must win by a margin of three hits.

171. *vouchsafe the answer* – accept the wager

176. *breathing time* – exercise period

184 – 185. "He does well to praise his duty to me. No one else would praise him."

186. *lapwing* – This foolish bird leaves the nest shortly after it is hatched, hence with the shell still on its head.

187. *did ... dug* – paid courtesies to his mother's breast

189. *drossy* – worthless, shoddy

191 – 193. "frothy accumulation of empty phrases that carries them through the most sifted and refined opinions, but the least blowing on the bubbles (superficial phrases) and they will burst"

OSRIC: The carriages, sir, are the hangers.

HAMLET: The phrase would be more german to the matter if we could carry a cannon by our sides — I would it might be hangers till then. But on. Six Barbary horses against six French swords, their assigns, and three liberal-conceited carriages — that's the French bet against the Danish. Why is this — impawned, as you call it? 160

OSRIC: The King, sir, hath laid, sir, that in a dozen passes between yourself and him he shall not exceed you three hits. He hath laid on twelve for nine. And it would come to immediate trial, if your lordship would vouchsafe the answer. 170

HAMLET: How if I answer no?

OSRIC: I mean, my lord, the opposition of your person in trial.

HAMLET: Sir, I will walk here in the hall. If it please his Majesty, it is the breathing time of day with me. Let the foils be brought, the gentleman willing, and the King hold his purpose, I will win for him and I can. If not, I will gain nothing but my shame and the odd hits.

OSRIC: Shall I deliver you even so? 180

HAMLET: To this effect, sir, after what flourish your nature will.

OSRIC: I commend my duty to your lordship.

HAMLET: Yours, yours.

[Exit Osric.]

He does well to commend it himself, there are no tongues else for his turn.

HORATIO: This lapwing runs away with the shell on his head.

HAMLET: He did comply with his dug before he sucked it. Thus has he — and many more of the same bevy that I know the drossy age dotes on — only got the tune of the time and outward habit of encounter, a kind of yeasty collection, which carries them through and through the most fanned and winnowed opinions. And do but blow them to their trial, the bubbles are out. 190

Enter a Lord.

LORD: My lord, his majesty commended him to you by young Osric, who brings back to him that you attend him in the hall. He sends to know if your pleasure hold to play with Laertes, or that you will take longer time.

HAMLET: I am constant to my purpose, they follow the

King's pleasure. If his fitness speaks, mine is ready.
Now or whensoever, provided I be so able as now.   200
LORD: The King and Queen and all are coming down.
HAMLET: In happy time.
LORD: The Queen desires you to use some gentle enter-
tainment to Laertes before you fall to play.
HAMLET: She well instructs me.

[Exit Lord.]

HORATIO: You will lose, my lord.
HAMLET: I do not think so. Since he went into France, I
have been in continual practice. I shall win at the
odds. But thou wouldst not think how ill all's here
about my heart. But it is no matter.   210
HORATIO: Nay, good my lord.
HAMLET: It is but foolery, but it is such a kind of
gaingiving as would perhaps trouble a woman.
HORATIO: If your mind dislike any thing, obey it. I will
forestall their repair hither, and say you are not fit.
HAMLET: Not a whit. We defy augury. There's a special
providence in the fall of a sparrow. If it be now, 'tis
not to come. If it be not to come, it will be now. If it
be not now, yet it will come. The readiness is all. Since
no man knows aught of what he leaves, what is it to   220
leave betimes?

*A table prepared and flagons of wine on it. Trumpets, Drums and
Officers with Cushions. Enter King, Queen, Laertes, and all the
State, and Attendants with foils and daggers.*

KING: Come, Hamlet, come, and take this hand from me.

[King puts Laertes' hand into Hamlet's.]

HAMLET: Give me your pardon, sir. I've done you wrong.
But pardon it as you are a gentleman.
This presence knows, and you must needs have heard,
How I am punished with sore distraction.
What I have done,
That might your nature, honour and exception
Roughly awake, I here proclaim was madness.
Was it Hamlet wronged Laertes? Never Hamlet.   230
If Hamlet from himself be taken away,
And when he's not himself does wrong Laertes,

199 – 200. "I am ready if
he is."
203. *gentle entertainment* –
courteous conversation
213. *gaingiving* – misgiving
214 – 215. Horatio advises
Hamlet to follow his
intuition and will go so far
as to fabricate an excuse for
him to cancel the match.
217. *providence* – divine
plan
220. *knows aught* – is really
aware
221. *leave betimes* – die
early
228. *exception* – disapproval

"The most maligned man
in history, one whose
memory I propose not
only to defend but to
extol, is the man who
complained that *Hamlet*
was a boring play full of
quotations, thereby
proving the soundness of
his literary instinct.
Honour to this
anonymous critic, whose
sensitive though unlet-
tered brain, stunned into
apathy as one well-known
phrase after another
came booming across the
footlights....
– Dame Ethel Smyth
(b. 1921), British critic

Act Five • Scene 2

235. *faction* – party

238 – 239. "Let this declaration that I intended no
wrong release me from any
guilt in your kind thoughts."
242. *in nature* – internally
(as a son and a brother)

255. *foil* – shiny base metal
placed behind a jewel to
make the jewel shine more
brilliantly

Then Hamlet does it not, Hamlet denies it.
Who does it, then? His madness. If it be so,
Hamlet is of the faction that is wronged.
His madness is poor Hamlet's enemy.
Sir, in this audience,
Let my disclaiming from a purposed evil
Free me so far in your most generous thoughts
That I have shot mine arrow over the house   240
And hurt my brother.
LAERTES: I am satisfied in nature,
Whose motive, in this case, should stir me most
To my revenge, but in my terms of honour
I stand aloof, and will no reconcilement
Till by some elder masters of known honour,
I have a voice and precedent of peace,
To keep my name ungored. But till that time
I do receive your offered love like love,
And will not wrong it.   250
HAMLET: I embrace it freely,
And will this brothers' wager frankly play.
Give us the foils. Come on.
LAERTES: Come, one for me.
HAMLET: I'll be your foil, Laertes. In mine ignorance
Your skill shall like a star in the darkest night
Stick fiery off indeed.
LAERTES: You mock me, sir.
HAMLET: No, by this hand.

KING: Give them the foils, young Osric. Cousin Hamlet, 260
    You know the wager?
HAMLET: Very well, my lord.
    Your grace hath laid the odds on the weaker side.
KING: I do not fear it. I have seen you both,
    But since he is bettered, we have therefore odds.
LAERTES: This is too heavy. Let me see another.
HAMLET: This likes me well. These foils have all a length?

267. length – are all the same length

> *They prepare to play.*

OSRIC: Ay, my good lord.
KING: Set me the stoups of wine upon that table.
    If Hamlet give the first or second hit, 270
    Or quit in answer of the third exchange,
    Let all the battlements their ordnance fire:
    The King shall drink to Hamlet's better breath,
    And in the cup an union shall he throw
    Richer than that which four successive kings
    In Denmark's crown have worn. Give me the cups
    And let the kettle to the trumpet speak,
    The trumpet to the cannoneer without,
    The cannons to the heavens, the heaven to earth,
    'Now the King drinks to Hamlet.' Come, begin. 280
    And you, the judges, bear a wary eye.
HAMLET: Come on, sir.

274. union – precious pearl

"*Hamlet* is a great story. It's got some great things in it. I mean there's something like eight violent deaths, there's murder, there's adultery, there's a ghost, a madwoman, poisoning, revenge, sword fights. It's a pretty good story."
– Mel Gibson, Australian actor

287. *palpable* – clear

297. Gertrude's comment that Hamlet is fat can be interpreted as a mother making excuses for her son's perspiration. However, it may also be a clue that the first Hamlet, played by Richard Burbage, was himself overweight. After all, it was also Burbage who played the corpulent Falstaff.

LAERTES: Come, my lord.

They play.

HAMLET: One.
LAERTES: No.
HAMLET: Judgment.
OSRIC: A hit, a very palpable hit.
LAERTES: Well, again.
KING: Stay, give me drink. Hamlet, this pearl is thine.
    Here's to thy health.   290

Drums; trumpets; and shot goes off.

    Give him the cup.
HAMLET: I'll play this bout first. Set it by awhile.
    Come.

They play again.

    Another hit. What say you?
LAERTES: A touch, a touch, I do confess.
KING: Our son shall win.
QUEEN: He's fat, and scant of breath.
    Here, Hamlet, take my napkin, rub thy brows.
    The Queen carouses to thy fortune, Hamlet.
HAMLET: Good madam.   300
KING: Gertrude, do not drink.
QUEEN: I will, my lord, I pray you, pardon me.
KING: *[Aside]* It is the poisoned cup. It is too late.
HAMLET: I dare not drink yet, madam — by and by.
QUEEN: Come, let me wipe thy face.
LAERTES: My lord, I'll hit him now.
KING: I do not think it.
LAERTES: *[Aside]* And yet it is almost against my conscience.
HAMLET: Come, for the third, Laertes. You do but dally.
    I pray you, pass with your best violence.   310
    I am afeard you make a wanton of me.
LAERTES: Say you so? Come on.

They play.

OSRIC: Nothing, neither way.
LAERTES: Have at you now!

310. *pass* – thrust
311. *make a wanton* – toying with; holding back

[Laertes wounds Hamlet; then] In scuffling, they change rapiers,
[and Hamlet wounds Laertes.]

KING: Part them; they are incensed.
HAMLET: Nay, come, again.

[Queen falls.]

OSRIC: Look to the Queen there, ho!
HORATIO: They bleed on both sides. How is it, my lord?
OSRIC: How is it, Laertes?
LAERTES: Why, as a woodcock to mine own springe, Osric.   320
    I am justly killed with mine own treachery.
HAMLET: How does the Queen?
KING: She swoons to see them bleed.
QUEEN: No, no, the drink, the drink! O my dear Hamlet!
    The drink, the drink! I am poisoned.

Dies.

HAMLET: O villainy! Ho! let the door be locked!
    Treachery! Seek it out.
LAERTES: It is here, Hamlet. Hamlet, thou art slain.
    No medicine in the world can do thee good.
    In thee there is not half an hour of life.   330
    The treacherous instrument is in thy hand,
    Unbated and envenomed. The foul practice
    Hath turned itself on me. Lo, here I lie,
    Never to rise again. Thy mother's poisoned.
    I can no more. The King — the King's to blame.
HAMLET: The point envenomed too! Then, venom, to thy work.

Wounds the King.

ALL: Treason! Treason!
KING: O, yet defend me, friends. I am but hurt.
HAMLET: Here, thou incestuous, murderous, damned Dane,
    Drink off this potion. Is thy union here?   340
    Follow my mother.

King dies.

LAERTES: He is justly served.
    It is a poison tempered by himself.
    Exchange forgiveness with me, noble Hamlet.

320. "Why, as a foolish game bird caught in its own snare"

343. *tempered* – concocted, mixed

Act Five • Scene 2

349. *chance* – this chain of events

351. *fell* – cruel

355. *unsatisfied* – those still in the dark; unknowing

357. *antique Roman* – one who prefers death to an unhappy life

364. "Postpone seeking the peace and happiness of death"

The name Horatio comes from the Latin *oratio*, which means "to narrate." It is appropriate that Hamlet asks Horatio to tell his story.

370. *volley* – salute

372. *over-crows* – triumphs over

374 – 375. Hamlet foresees that Fortinbras will be chosen the next king of Denmark, and he approves of the choice.

376. *occurrents* – occurrences

377. *solicited* – persuaded me to support his claim to the throne

RELATED READING

378. *Meditation at Elsinore* – poem by Elizabeth Coatsworth (page 175)

> Mine and my father's death come not upon thee,
> Nor thine on me.

[Laertes] Dies.

HAMLET: Heaven make thee free of it. I follow thee.
I am dead, Horatio. Wretched queen, adieu.
You that look pale and tremble at this chance,
That are but mutes or audience to this act,   350
Had I but time — as this fell sergeant, Death,
Is strict in his arrest — O, I could tell you —
But let it be. Horatio, I am dead,
Thou livest. Report me and my cause aright
To the unsatisfied.
HORATIO: Never believe it.
I am more an antique Roman than a Dane.
Here's yet some liquor left.
HAMLET: As thou art a man,
Give me the cup. Let go, by heaven I'll have it.   360
O good Horatio, what a wounded name,
Things standing thus unknown, shall I leave behind me.
If thou didst ever hold me in thy heart,
Absent thee from felicity awhile,
And in this harsh world draw thy breath in pain
To tell my story.

A march afar off and shot within.

What warlike noise is this?

Enter Osric.

OSRIC: Young Fortinbras, with conquest come from Poland,
To the ambassadors of England gives
This warlike volley.   370
HAMLET: O, I die, Horatio.
The potent poison quite over-crows my spirit.
I cannot live to hear the news from England,
But I do prophesy the election lights
On Fortinbras. He has my dying voice.
So tell him, with the occurrents more and less
Which have solicited. The rest is silence.

[Hamlet] Dies.

HORATIO: Now cracks a noble heart. Good night sweet prince,
And flights of angels sing thee to thy rest.
Why does the drum come hither?   380

Enter Fortinbras, the English Ambassadors,
with Drum, Colours and Attendants.

FORTINBRAS: Where is this sight?
HORATIO: What is it ye would see?
If aught of woe or wonder, cease your search.
FORTINBRAS: This quarry cries on havoc. O proud Death,
What feast is toward in thine eternal cell,
That thou so many princes at a shot
So bloodily hast struck?
FIRST AMBASSADOR: The sight is dismal,
And our affairs from England come too late.
The ears are senseless that should give us hearing   390
To tell him his commandment is fulfilled,
That Rosencrantz and Guildenstern are dead.
Where should we have our thanks?
HORATIO: Not from his mouth,
Had it the ability of life to thank you.
He never gave commandment for their death.
But since, so jump upon this bloody question,
You from the Polack wars and you from England,
Are here arrived, give order that these bodies
High on a stage be placed to the view,   400
And let me speak to the yet unknowing world
How these things came about. So shall you hear
Of carnal, bloody, and unnatural acts,
Of accidental judgments, casual slaughters,
Of deaths put on by cunning and forced cause,
And, in this upshot, purposes mistook
Fallen on the inventors' heads. All this can I
Truly deliver.
FORTINBRAS: Let us haste to hear it,
And call the noblest to the audience.   410
For me, with sorrow I embrace my fortune.
I have some rights of memory in this kingdom,
Which now to claim my vantage doth invite me.
HORATIO: Of that I shall have also cause to speak,
And from his mouth whose voice will draw on more.
But let this same be presently performed
Even while men's minds are wild, lest more mischance
On plots and errors happen.

383. *aught* – anything
384. "This pile of dead bodies shouts out of a slaughter."

397 – 399. "And seeing as you have arrived so immediately after these bloody events"

404. "Of divine acts of justice and deaths due to chance. They may be deemed divine because they appear as accidents."

412. *of memory* – that have not been forgotten
413. *vantage* – opportunity

415. *draw on more* – persuade others

RELATED READING

421. *Elegy of Fortinbras*
– poem by Zbigniew
Herbert (page 205)

426. *Becomes* – is more
appropriate for the battle-
field

"Other works of the
human mind equal
Hamlet; none surpass it.
There is in *Hamlet* all
the majesty of the
mournful. A drama
issuing from an open
sepulchre, – this is
colossal. Hamlet is to our
mind Shakespeare's
capital work."
– Victor Hugo (1802 –
1885), French novelist,
author of *Les Miserables*

FORTINBRAS: Let four captains
    Bear Hamlet like a soldier to the stage,   420
    For he was likely, had he been put on,
    To have proved most royally. And for his passage,
    The soldiers' music and the rites of war
    Speak loudly for him.
    Take up the bodies. Such a sight as this
    Becomes the field but here shows much amiss.
    Go, bid the soldiers shoot.

*Exeunt marching, [bearing off the bodies] after which a peal of
ordnance is shot off.*

FINIS.

    ℀ ℀ ℀

Act Five Considerations

ACT FIVE Scene 1

▶ Why does Shakespeare include the Grave-digger scene? What effect does it have on the reader/audience?

▶ We are told that Hamlet was born on the same day that his father defeated the King of Norway. Write a newspaper account dealing with the events of this auspicious day.

▶ Write an appropriate eulogy for Ophelia's funeral. In doing so, adopt the point of view of a specific character such as Hamlet, Laertes, Gertrude, or Claudius.

▶ Why does Hamlet jump into the grave with Laertes? Write the dialogue for a scene in which Hamlet explains to Horatio his actions at the gravesite.

ACT FIVE Scene 2

▶ Does Hamlet, as he claimed in the previous scene, love Ophelia? What evidence is there in this scene that perhaps he doesn't?

▶ Why is Hamlet so willing to win for Claudius? Why does he trust Claudius and Laertes when he was so careful about not trusting Rosencrantz and Guildenstern?

▶ Write a news report of the events in the second half of this scene.

▶ Write an obituary for at least one of the characters who dies at the end of this scene.

The 10 Most Difficult Questions One Can Ask about *Hamlet*

Shakespeare's works have survived for over 400 years. Is it because of his great stories and characters? Perhaps, but this would also be true of several of his contemporaries, and they haven't fared as well as Shakespeare. There must be something else. Perhaps one reason is his ambiguity. It is ironic that Shakespeare's most frustrating quality could very well be his greatest strength. His classic lines, his unforgettable characters, and his "problem" plays can be interpreted in many different ways. There are so many unanswered and unanswerable questions in the plays that generations of readers and critics to come will continue to ask questions and pore over his works for as long as literature and poetry are valued.

Hamlet, in particular, abounds with difficult questions. More has been written on the subject of this play than on any other piece of literature. Here are just a few of the more difficult questions to challenge your thinking about the play. The end result of your efforts may take the form of a research essay or a position paper. To attempt to answer these questions you will need to probe the text carefully and consult secondary sources. You must also be prepared to take a stand.

Once you have chosen a question to focus on, you will need to do the following:

- present as effective an argument as you can for the conventional or most straightforward interpretation;
- discuss fully the problems with this interpretation; and
- offer and justify your own interpretation with evidence from the text and/or secondary reading materials.

Here are 10 of the most difficult questions to answer about the play Hamlet:

1. How old is "young Hamlet"? At the beginning of the play, we learn that he is still attending university, and throughout the play he seems to be treated as a petulant young man. And yet the Grave-digger seems to suggest that Hamlet is 30. Or does he? In the First Folio version, the Grave-digger says, in talking about himself, that he has "bin sixteene heere, man and boy thirty years," which can be read as meaning he has worked as a grave-digger for 16 years and he has been a man and boy for a total of 30 years. This would make Hamlet 16! You decide: What makes more sense in the play—a young or an old Hamlet?

2. Does Hamlet really love Ophelia? He says he does and he says he doesn't. What do you think? Before answering, ask yourself if Hamlet ever mentions Ophelia when she is not around. Does he ever refer to her in any soliloquy? Does he mention her after her funeral?

3. Is Hamlet mad? He does say that he will put on an antic disposition, but is that as far as it goes? Some argue that it is more than just an act. What do you think?

4. Does Claudius see the dumb show? If so, why does he not react? Shakespeare does not help us with this question. Directors have handled this scene in quite a few different ways.

5. How old is Hamlet's university friend Horatio? In Act One, scene 1, we are told that he saw Hamlet's father on the day that he defeated King Norway. In Act Five, scene 1, the Grave-digger tells us that this event occurred 30 years previous (or did it? See # 1 above).

6. Why can Hamlet be ruthless with the likes of Polonius, Rosencrantz and Guildenstern, and yet he seems incapable of acting against Claudius?

7. Does Hamlet suffer from an Oedipus complex? Much has been written on this topic, and many stage and film versions of the play capitalize on this theme.

8. Where is the play really set? Is it Denmark or England? Why are there no Danish sounding names in the play? Hamlet says that the players are "the abstract and brief chronicles of the time." If so, what does the play chronicle about English history? Is Polonius, for example, a carica-ture of William Cecil, Lord Burleigh, Queen Elizabeth's chief advisor?

9. The play *Hamlet* takes well over four hours to read straight through with-out intermission. Was the play performed in its entirety during the Elizabethan period? Would the Elizabethans have sat or stood through a complete performance, or were audiences given a shorter version of the play to watch? How long were typical stage plays during the Elizabethan period? Some scholars believe that *Hamlet* as we have it today was intended to be read rather than performed. This may explain the pres-ence of scenes and speeches that some consider unnecessary and undra-matic in the play. In other words, the play is similar in effect to a novel. What do you think? Did Shakespeare intend that the play be presented in its entirety, or did he add scenes and lines for his reading public?

10. When was the play written? A.S. Caircross, in his book *The Problem of Hamlet*, concludes that "it seems impossible to account for the topical allusions ... unless by referring the play ... to a date no later than 1593." Other scholars have placed the composition as early as 1589 and as late as 1601. What do you think?

10 Most Difficult Questions

Hamletology

by Norrie Epstein

*Everyone loves to read statistics. And this article provides some
for* Hamlet *lovers.*

Hamlet is the only play that has inspired its own cult, and there's even a name for it: Hamletology, the study of all things *Hamlet*. Like ardent sports fans, Hamletologists readily cite every record-breaking statistic about the play.

- It's been performed more than any other play in the world, and more has been written about it than any other literary work.

- It's been translated more than any other play and has inspired more spoofs, spin-offs, offshoots, sendups, burlesques, and adaptations, including a spaghetti western called *Johnny Hamlet* and a four-minute cartoon, *Enter Hamlet*, narrated by Maurice Evans. Believe it or not, there's even a Popeye version of the play.

Johnny Hamlet

Related Readings

- There are more than forty-five movie versions of the play, ranging from *Amleto* (Italy) and *Khoon ka Knoon* (India) to *Moi, Hamlet* (France), *Hamile: The Tongo Hamlet* (Ghana), and *Hamlet: The Trouble with Hamlet* (United States).
- The first book written on *Hamlet* — *Some Remarks on the Tragedy of Hamlet* — was published in 1736.
- The line "To be, or not to be" is the most quoted phrase in the English language.
- According to the British critic John Trewin, "There has been a debate on every minute" in the play.
- There have been hippie Hamlets and nude ones, too; the role has been played by dwarfs, fat men, tiny men, women (one with a wooden leg), and twins (to show his divided nature). It's been performed by the five-year-old prodigy hailed as "Master Betty, the Infant Phenomenon of the Regency Period," and by the octogenarian Sir Johnston Forbes-Robertson.
- It has inspired twenty-six ballets, six operas, and dozens of musical works from Tchaikovsky and Liszt to Shostakovich to the contemporary composer David Diamond.
- In 1964, Jan Kott wrote that the bibliography of works on *Hamlet* was longer than the Warsaw telephone directory. Today it's probably twice as large.
- The Hamletologist Ib Melchior notes, "There have been Hamlet cigars, bicycles, beer and laundry mats, Hamlet jewelry, games, paper dolls, and the maps of the world abound with towns, streets, and business establishments called Hamlet."
- Rarely performed in its entirety, *Hamlet* is the longest play Shakespeare wrote. The uncut version, dubbed the "eternity Hamlet" by the critic John Trewin, takes four and a half to five hours to perform.
- According to the novelist Laurens van der Post, the play's first performance outside England occurred in 1607, when a group of sailors enacted it off the Cape of Good Hope. The performance was entered in the ship's log as "this popular play now running in England."

Compile your own set of facts about *Hamlet*. You will need to consult secondary resources for this.

Choose any fact from Epstein's list and research it more fully. Present your findings to the class.

SHAKESPEARE
Changed My Life

by Robert MacNeil

An award-winning television journalist shares how, at the age of 17, his life took a new direction because of the spell of Hamlet.

Tedium often overtook me in my school years; perhaps that's how well-treated slaves feel. Between home and school, life seemed all burdens and no choices. Someone in authority always commanded my attention or presence. The time was so constructively filled, one obligation slid so smoothly into another, that I couldn't escape into my own mind until bedtime. Even what might give pleasure was often covered with a pall of duty.

There was an exception on a winter afternoon in 1948 and it changed my life. I didn't find God but I found William Shakespeare, a piece of God's work so extraordinary that he comes close to divinity itself.

> *How weary, stale, flat, and unprofitable*
> *Seem to me all the uses of this world.*

The words hit me with a flash of recognition. There, exquisitely put, was the enervating mood, the despair so painful-

From the first grinding chords of the opening music over the battlements of Elsinore ... I was bewitched.

ly delicious to seventeen-year-olds that often visited my late adolescence. Never before had there been such instant connection between something I felt and a set of words to describe it — giving me both distance from my feelings and better understanding of them. The words made me two people at once, the person observed and the observer. The ironic cast of Shakespeare's words released me a little from the prison of my self-absorption, and hooked me into a wider, grander scheme of things. They made me larger, freer.

I had received implants of Shakespeare before then, much as an inert doll gets its sawdust stuffing. When no one was looking, gobs of *Henry IV, Part I, The Tempest*, and *Julius Caesar* — previously packed into me — had just trickled out again.

The play set that year for the Ontario senior matriculation was *Hamlet* and the English master, Mr. Belcher, took us to see

147

Laurence Olivier's new film version. From the first grinding chords of the opening music over the battlements of Elsinore, its dark walls washed by the angry sea, I was bewitched.

So perfect was Olivier's diction that you heard every word; you could imagine you heard even the commas. The words made kinds of sense I had never encountered. They carried the plot and character, certainly. They conveyed emotions appropriate to the scenes and a lot of humour — but something more. They lifted me to a not quite earthly plane, transported me for long moments into another realm of time and being; a poetic world, in which the flow of words controlled the weather and the climate, the cast and light of the day, and the mood of the people.

'Tis now the very witching time of night,
When churchyards yawn and hell itself
* breathes out*
Contagion to this world:

The sounds of the words put a precious mist over reality and I was inside the mist. I was excited by the sword-play, titillated by the love scenes, amused by Hamlet's ridicule of the courtiers, but I was enchanted by the words and Olivier's way of speaking the meter so that it sounded both poetic and conversational.

I went back to school in a daze and got out the text of *Hamlet*. Almost without effort, a passage read a few times shifted itself into my memory. I had memorised it without trying to. It was Hamlet's first substantial speech, to his mother, that begins *Seems, madam! Nay, it is; I know not "seems."* Once they were in my memory, the more I said the words to myself and thought

For me at seventeen, Hamlet was the great teller-off, an angry young man for all seasons

about their meaning, the more pleasure they gave me.

There were simple effects, like the three *k* sounds running together in *inky cloak*, arresting because they arrest the tongue. There was the sarcasm in the overblown images he tosses at his mother in exasperation because she reads his grief too lightly.

There was a level on which the late adolescent in me responded to Hamlet, thrilled by the power of words he had to tell the world off: such a quiverful of word weapons with which to flick, or pierce, or smash those who frustrated him because they controlled him.

Bloody, bawdy villain! Remorseless,
treacherous, lecherous, kindless villain!

What ammunition! I felt intuitive kinship with this Prince who wavered between the callow and the manly, petulant and philosophical, self-pitying and self-mocking.

What youth has not felt that *the time is out of joint*? But until he said it, who thought of such a neat and startling image? *The time is out of joint.* No wonder people have used it for four centuries. What late adolescent has not lived weeks when

the native hue of resolution
Is sicklied o'er with the pale cast of
* thought ...*

For me at seventeen, Hamlet was the great teller-off, an angry young man for all seasons; a very young man in spirit, who escapes from action by talking and hates himself for it.

Why, what an ass am I! This is most brave
That I, the son of a dear father murder'd,
Prompted to my revenge by heaven and
* hell,*

Must, like a whore, unpack my heart with
words,
And fall a-cursing, like a very drab,
A scullion!

Yet he goes on *unpacking his heart with words*, with an extraordinary list of things — apart from the murder of his father — that annoy him: drunkenness and debauchery; actors who overact; people who mistreat underlings; proud men contemptuous of others, insolent officeholders, delays of the law, unworthy people who scorn those with merit who don't push themselves; unnecessary pomp, and the foppish affectations of courtiers.

Hamlet is a part of the world mind and part of the common speech of people who speak English all over the world.

Very young men are often vociferous about such things, as older men are more relaxed, resigned to an imperfect world. But they fall a little oddly from the lips of the Crown Prince of an important country who has finished his studies and is waiting to be King. What need had he to catalogue *the law's delay, the insolence of office ... the proud man's contumely*? to consider them grounds for suicide? What officeholder would have dared be insolent to Hamlet, at least before he appeared mad?

Hamlet also dwells with disgust on the carnality of lovemaking, painting gross pictures like *the rank sweat of an enseamed bed* to make his mother ashamed of her behaviour with Claudius, and he lashes out at women generally for frailty, inconstancy, dishonesty, even for using make-up.

T.S. Eliot, who thought *Hamlet* an artistic failure, complained that the Prince is "dominated by an emotion that is ... in *excess* of the facts as they appear." Eliot said the play, "like the Sonnets, is full of some stuff the writer could not drag to light, contemplate, or manipulate into art."

Others have intuited that "stuff" to be the pith of Shakespeare himself, and that Hamlet was the character in which he most revealed it. Before Eliot, Frank Harris argued persuasively that "whenever Shakespeare fell out of a character he was drawing, he unconsciously dropped into the Hamlet vein." In *The Man Shakespeare and His Tragic Life-Story*, Harris finds many of Hamlet's traits — the habit of talking to himself, that pensive sadness and world weariness, the melancholy and contemplative spirit, the loving sympathy, the bookish phrases, the gentle heart, the quick intelligence, the irresolute man driven to violent action, and, above all, the incomparable lyric gift — in Romeo, in Jaques in *As You Like It*, in Macbeth, in the Duke in *Measure for Measure*, in Posthumus, the hero of *Cymbeline*, and in others.

Scholars may argue endlessly about such things, as they do with great passion about the identity of the man who wrote the plays. What cast a spell over me that day in 1948, and has held me ever since, was the Shakespearean sensibility: that mysterious and compelling bitter-sweet attitude to life of which Hamlet is one intoxicating expression.

Sometimes, when young, you have a dream of something you have not yet experienced and on waking feel set ahead, as though the player controlling your life had moved you several spaces on the board. You have a strong feeling of having been advanced in experience. That was my feeling on encountering *Hamlet*. Knowing him, I felt more worldly, advanced a space or two.

Related Readings

Like millions before me, the more I looked, the more I found, and forty years later, the more I look, the more I still find; better recognising that this play has become a thought bank for English, more quoted than anything but the Bible. Think of that: just this one play, only one of thirty-seven, gave such effective voice to so many ideas and feelings human beings encounter that, four hundred years later, Shakespeare's are the words that come to our minds to express them.

Masefield said, "The play is a part of the English mind for ever." He was too insular: Hamlet is a part of the *world* mind and part of the common speech of people who speak English all over the world. Millions who have never read it and never seen it performed yet speak it from day to day in everyday phrases like:

'Tis bitter cold
I am sick at heart
Not a mouse stirring
It started like a guilty thing
So much for him
This too too solid flesh
That it should come to this!
It cannot come to good
In my mind's eye
More in sorrow than in anger
All is not well
Neither a borrower, nor a lender be
To thine own self be true
More honoured in the breach than the
observance
I could a tale unfold
O my prophetic soul!
Leave her to heaven
Brevity is the soul of wit
More matter, with less art
What a piece of work is a man
The play's the thing
To hold the mirror up to nature
The lady doth protest too much
I must be cruel, only to be kind
We know what we are, but know not

what we may be
Rosemary, that's for remembrance
The rest is silence

Those are only the often-used phrases from *Hamlet* that sound most colloquial today, leaving those equally familiar but with a more literary ring:

The bird of dawning singeth all night long
Frailty, thy name is woman!
The primrose path of dalliance treads,
And recks not his own rede
Give thy thoughts no tongue
Something is rotten in the state of
Denmark.
There are more things in heaven and
earth, Horatio,
Than are dreamt of in your philosophy.
'Tis true; 'tis true 'tis pity;
And pity 'tis 'tis true.
Man delights not me; no, nor woman
neither
'Twas caviare to the general
To be, or not to be: that is the question
The slings and arrows of outrageous
fortune
To die: to sleep: No more
To sleep: perchance to dream
Thus conscience does make cowards of
us all
Like sweet bells jangled, out of tune and
harsh
To have seen what I have seen, see what
I see!
Give me that man that is not passion's
slave
O! my offence is rank, it smells to heaven
Lay not that flattering unction to your
soul.
How all occasions do inform against me
When sorrows come, they come not sin-
gle spies,
But in battalions
Sweets to the sweet: farewell!
There's a divinity that shapes our ends

Absent thee from felicity awhile
Now cracks a noble heart. Good-night,
  sweet prince,
And flights of angels sing thee to thy rest!

Obviously, I saw only a fraction of this on first encountering *Hamlet* that winter. I knew how he spoke to me at seventeen. He was intriguingly mysterious and yet perfectly understandable. I understood him, as every sympathetic person does, in my heart, while delighting in the ultimate mystery that has intrigued the world for four centuries. The drug that altered the mind and made me understand was the ceaseless flow of words, so cunningly, so deliciously combined.

How weary, stale, flat, and unprofitable
Seem to me all the uses of this world:

I said that — and said it — and said it, savouring the cadence, the flow of sound, with the *ts* clicking and spitting contempt. In the first line, look at the striking effect of juxtaposing Old English, *weary, stale, flat,* with the French *unprofitable.* It changes the rhythm, colours the tone, and crowns the line emphatically. The same effect comes in the words

O! that this too too solid flesh would
  melt,
Thaw and resolve itself into a dew;

The French, Latinate, words often have more syllables and softer sounds, consonants less clipped than the Teutonic or Scandinavian sounds. Our language marries these spirits of the North and the South; spirits from the realms of dark, cold winters and icy seas, where action makes the blood run hot enough to survive; and those from the South, where nature is kinder, where vines and fruit may flourish. All of us descended from these people carry the opposing strains in us, and all of us who use English can feel them. Unconsciously, as we speak and write, we are blending the two. In what measure we blend them governs the effect we produce.

Hamlet gave me more forcibly the idea of words: he made me aware that I had word-hunger and a strong desire to satisfy it. I craved more of the drug, for myself privately, but also to put some of my own noise upon the world — to show off.

It was a few months before graduation and the impending naval fiasco. I was again a boarder at school, my parents convinced I needed to be freer of home distractions as the final exams approached. In breaks from studying I would roam the halls invading the studies of other seniors and spouting whatever chunks of poetry I had just learned.

Olivier had cut O, *what a rogue and peasant slave am I!* I gobbled that one up with all its ranting curses and made a nuisance of myself declaiming it on the slightest provocation. When the LP recording of selections from *Hamlet* came out, I listened so hard that I memorised every inflection and intonation Olivier used. When I later heard other recordings, John Barrymore's, for example, I thought them greatly inferior. ■

Have you ever been influenced strongly by a book or a movie in the same way as MacNeil? If so, in a journal entry, explore how the work affected you.

According to MacNeil, young people share many of Hamlet's concerns. Which ones in particular did you identify with? Why? Are there any other similarities between Hamlet and young people today that MacNeil does not mention? Explain.

Related Readings

AMLETH'S REVENGE

by Saxo Grammaticus

This, the first recorded version of the Hamlet story, was written by a Danish cleric some four hundred years before Shakespeare.

Feng has murdered his brother, the King of Denmark and the father of Amleth, and has married the queen. Amleth, the heir to the throne, feels that his life is threatened.

Seeing this, but not wanting to arouse his uncle's suspicions by intelligent action, Amleth behaved like a witless fool, pretending to have taken leave of his senses, by which ruse he not only concealed his intelligence but also saved his life. Day in and day out he sat listless at his mother's hearth, covered in dust and dirt, or flung himself on the floor and rolled in all the grime and filth. With befouled face and smeared visage he resembled a grotesque and ridiculous fool. His every word was utter nonsense, and all his actions denoted profound folly. In short, one would scarcely have thought him a man at all, but an absurd freak of some perverse fate. Sometimes he would sit by the hearth, poking the embers with his fingers, and

twisting branches into crooks which he would harden in the fire and furnish with barbs to make them hold tighter. When asked what he was about, he would say that he was making spearheads for his father's revenge. This reply evoked no little amusement, all men deriding such an absurd and idle pursuit, but afterward this very work helped him to carry out his purpose. At the same time, it was his diligence and care that first aroused suspicion that all was a ruse on his part; for his very persistence in such a pastime revealed the hidden skill of the craftsman; and no one could believe that a simpleton would be so nimble-fingered and ingenious. Last, he would lay the hardened stakes in a pile and most carefully hide them.

For this reason, there were some who pronounced him sane enough, and said that he only concealed his intelligence under a show of simplicity, cunningly hiding his real mind beneath a feigned manner. The surest way of detecting his ruse (they said) would be to bring to him at some secluded place a fair woman who might tempt him to lust, for the natural desire for a woman's embrace was so intense that it could not be held back by cunning—the instinct too powerful to be subdued by guile. If then the apathy were feigned, he would forthwith seize the opportunity and yield to his strong desire. So men were commissioned who would ride deep into the forest with the young man, and there tempt him in this manner. Now among them it so happened that there was a foster brother of Amleth, who had not forgotten how they had been brought up together, and who rated the memory of their past fellowship higher than the present command. Thus, in joining the other appointed companions it was his intention to warn Amleth rather than to entrap him, for he had little doubt that certain death awaited him if he betrayed but the slightest sign of sanity, and especially if he embraced a woman in their sight: an outcome of which Amleth himself was well aware. When they bade him mount his horse he therefore deliberately seated himself the wrong way round, turning his back to the horse's head and his face toward its tail, and laying the reins round its tail, as if to check the horse's wild career from there. By this ingenious device he made a mockery of his uncle's trick and frustrated his evil design. Ludicrous it was indeed to see the horse run off unreined, with the rider holding on by its tail.

The company finally set off toward the place they had appointed for the meeting. On their way to that place they came down to the beach and his companions found there the rudder of a ship that had been wrecked, saying what a huge knife it was they had come upon. Amleth replied: "Ah, but that is for carving the biggest ham with," whereby he of course meant the wild ocean that the rudder matched. When they passed the sand dunes, and would have had him believe that the sand was flour, he answered that it had surely been ground by the beating of the surf. When his companions praised his reply, he retorted that he had indeed spoken shrewdly.

They now left him to himself, that he might more easily gain courage for the satisfaction of his lust, and the woman whom his uncle had intended for him came forward to meet him, as if accidentally, at a secluded spot. He would also have enjoyed her, had not his foster brother secretly revealed to him their schemes.

Having been forewarned by his former kinsman, he took the woman in his arms and carried her off to a remote and impassable fen. There he lay with her, and begged her earnestly to reveal it to no one. The young woman was as avid to promise silence as Amleth was to plead for it, for they had been friendly as of old, having been fostered together and brought up in the same charge.

They now accompanied him home again; and when all jestingly inquired if he had controlled his desire, he announced that he had enjoyed the maid.

They then questioned the maid, but she declared that he had done no such thing, and they accepted her denial, especially as the attendants were unaware of what had occurred.

Now all being confounded, and none capable of opening the secret lock of the young man's wisdom, a friend of Feng, one more gifted with assurance than with sagacity, spoke up and said that such unfathomable cunning could not be made to betray itself by ordinary stratagem—the man was too obstinate to be mastered by a common plot, nor would craftiness so versatile be caught in so simple a trap. Therefore, on deeper reflection he thought of a more subtle means, one which would not be difficult to apply, and which would surely discover all they desired to know. Feng was deliberately to absent himself on the pretext of an important errand, and Amleth was to be closeted alone with his mother; but first a man should be stationed in some concealed place, unknown to either of them, so that he might listen closely to what they talked of. For if the son had any wits at all, he would speak freely and openly in his mother's hearing, and would not fear to confide in her. He declared himself ready to do the spying himself, in case he be judged quick to advise but slow to perform. Pleased with this advice, Feng departed, pretending to go on a long journey.

"IT REMAINS MY STEADFAST PURPOSE TO AVENGE MY FATHER; BUT I AWAIT A FAVORABLE OPPORTUNITY…"

Now the man who had given counsel went secretly to the closet where Amleth was admitted to his mother, and hid in the straw on the floor. Amleth, however, was equal to the plot. Suspecting the presence of an eavesdropper, he at first had recourse to his usual folly: crowing like a cock, beating his arms as if flapping wings, treading on the straw, and jumping on it to find out if anyone was hiding there beneath it. Feeling something firm under his feet, he thrust his sword into the spot, struck the eavesdropper who lay hidden there, and dragging him from his concealment slew him. Then he cut the body to pieces, boiled them in hot water, and flung them into the gutter for the pigs to eat, the miserable limbs being fouled in stinking mire.

Having thus frustrated this plot, he returned to the chamber; and when his mother set up a loud wailing and began to lament her son's madness, he cried: "How dare you, infamous woman, make such false complaints, which are no more than a cloak for your own grievous offense? Wanton like a harlot, you consented to a wicked and abominable marriage, incestuously embracing your husband's murderer, and kissing and caressing the man who slew the father of your child. So does the mare join with the stallion that triumphs; only brute beasts couple indiscriminately. And now, like them, you have wiped out the memory of your former mate. It is not without reason that I now behave like a fool, for I have little doubt that he who took his brother's life will proceed just as cruelly with his kindred. Better, therefore, to behave foolishly than to display one's wits, and so to save one's life by posing madness and frenzy. It remains my steadfast purpose to avenge my father; but I await a favorable opportunity and will bide my time. There is a time for all things; against a dark and pitiless heart one must use intelligence and ingenuity. For your part, you have no need to bewail my madness, but ought rather to grieve for your own shame. You certainly have cause to weep — not for others, but because you have suffered harm to your own soul. Now see that you hold your peace!" Thus scornfully did he chide his mother, recalling her to the path of virtue, and urging her to set past love above her present lust.

When Feng returned, he could nowhere find the crafty eavesdropper, though he searched long and diligently for him. No one had seen him anywhere. When Amleth, too, was asked jestingly if he had seen any trace of him, he replied that he had gone to the privy and, falling through the hole, had been smothered in filth, and so had been devoured by the pigs that went there. This statement contained only the bare truth, yet seemed to those who heard it so foolish that they ridiculed it.

Now Feng grew suspicious of his stepson, and being convinced of his guile resolved to make away with him, but dared not for fear of his uncle Rorik, as well as for fear of his wife; for which reason he found it expedient to request the king of Britain to slay Amleth, and by so doing feign innocence himself while another did the deed. Anxious to conceal his own cruelty, he thus chose to sully his friend's reputation rather than to bring disgrace on himself. Amleth, on departing from his mother, secretly charged her to hang the hall with woven tapestries, and in a year falsely to mourn his death, promising that he would return at that time. Two of Feng's retainers went with him, bearing a rod that was engraved with runes that enjoined the king of Britain to slay the youth who had been sent to him. But, while the others lay asleep, Amleth searched their belongings, found there the message, read the instructions, and, erasing the runes that were engraved on the rod, carved other symbols in their place, altering the words of the message so as to transfer the death sentence from himself to his companions. Besides averting his own doom and destruction, and plunging others into the misery intended for himself, he also falsely added, in the name of Feng, a petition to the king of Britain that he should give his daughter in marriage to the intelligent young man he was sending him.

THE KING ESTEEMED

AMLETH'S INTELLIGENCE

LIKE THE WISDOM OF

HEAVEN ITSELF...

Arriving in Britain, the envoys waited on the king and presented to him their letter, which they believed would encompass their companion's death but which contained their own death warrant. Betraying no sign of his intentions, the king hospitably invited them to a banquet. Here Amleth thrust aside everything which was on the king's table, as if the food offered to him were poor, to everyone's surprise abstaining from the rich feast, and touching neither food nor drink. All were amazed by this foreign young man who disdained the sumptuous dishes on the king's table and refused all the delicacies as if they had been poor peasant fare.

When the banquet was over and the king took leave of his companions for the night, he instructed one of them to steal into the bedchamber and secretly listen to the conversation of the foreign guests in the night. Now Amleth, when asked by his companions how it was that the evening before he had left all the feast untouched, as if it had been poison, replied that the bread had been saturated with blood, that the liquor tasted of iron, and that the meat reeked of corpses and had the rotten stench of the grave. Furthermore, he said that the king had the eyes of a slave, and the queen had exhibited three acts of a servant. Thus, it was not so much the banquet as the hosts that he had found fault with. His companions now held his old weakness against him, and taunted him with all manner of abuse for blaming what should be praised, speaking ill of what was good, affronting an excellent king and a gentle lady with shameless talk, and making a laughingstock of those who merited praise.

The king, when he heard this from his

retainer, declared that whoever spoke thus must be either the wisest or most foolish of mortals, when in so few words he could display such perfect acumen. Summoning his steward, he asked where he had got the bread. The steward replying that his own baker had made it, the king asked where the corn had grown from which the flour had been made, and whether there was any sign that anyone had been slain there. He replied that near the king's palace was a field, strewn with the bones of slaughtered men, and bearing traces of former carnage; and that, expecting a specially good harvest from this, compared with the rest, he had sown it in the spring in hopes of a rich crop. Therefore, it might well be that the bread had caught a taint from the congealed blood. Hearing this, and believing that Amleth had spoken the truth, the king next inquired where the pork had come from. The steward replied that by neglect his pigs had escaped from their sty and had eaten the rotten corpse of a robber, and that this might be the reason why the meat had been tainted. Perceiving the truth of Amleth's words in this matter also, the king then asked what he had mixed in the mead. When he heard that it had been brewed from honey and water, he demanded to be shown the spring, and ordered men to dig there, and they found several rusty swords, which could have tainted the water.

Realizing now that Amleth had given good reasons for his fastidiousness, and supposing that in scorning him for the meanness of his eyes he had been alluding to his ignoble birth, the king went secretly to his mother and questioned her about his father. She replied that she had known no man save the king; but on threatening to draw the truth from her by torture, he learnt that he was the son of a slave. By this forced confession his doubts and the slighting of his birth by Amleth were confirmed. Ashamed

at his own fate, but agreeably surprised by the young man's intelligence, he inquired of Amleth why he had imputed to the queen the habits of a slave. Annoyed though he indeed was because his guest, in the night's conversation, had found fault with his wife's courtly behavior, he was now forced to hear that she had been born a thrall. For Amleth said that he had observed three actions of a bondwoman in her. First, she had, like a servant, drawn her mantle over her head. Second, she had lifted up her gown when she walked. Third, she had picked her teeth with a splinter and chewed the scraps of food she dug out. Amleth also said that her mother had been a thrall taken in war, which fact enabled him to tell that she was as much a slave by birth as she was by habit.

The king esteemed Amleth's intelligence like the wisdom of heaven itself; he gave him his daughter in marriage and honored his word as evidence from above. In order to carry out Feng's bidding to the full, the king hanged Amleth's escorts the next day. This service Amleth interpreted as a wrong done to himself, and pretended to be angered by it, whereupon, the king, for blood money, gave him gold, which he melted down in fire and secretly poured into two hollow sticks.

Amleth dwelt with the king for a year, but then begged leave of absence and returned home, taking with him of the king's treasures only the two sticks filled with gold. Going ashore in Jutland, he laid aside his present conduct and resumed all his former habits, deliberately giving a ridiculous air to his manner in place of his normal behavior. Besmirched with filth, he entered the banquet hall, where his funeral celebration was just then taking place. All present were astonished, as his death had been falsely reported. Fear turned gradually to mirth as the guests ridiculed one another because the man whose funeral they were attending had suddenly appeared in the flesh amidst them.

Then they inquired about his companions, and, showing them the two sticks he had brought with him, Amleth said: "They are both here." This observation was true, for although most of the funeral guests thought his words foolish, he showed them, in place of the hanged men, the blood money he had received for them. Later he joined the other cupbearers at table and plied the guests with liquor in order to increase the merriment; and so that his long dress should not hamper his movements, he fastened it round his loins with his sword belt. From time to time he deliberately drew his sword from its scabbard, wounding himself at the finger-tips, whereupon the bystanders had a steel pin driven through the sword and scabbard. In order to carry out his plot in greater safety, he diligently filled the noblemen's cups, making them heavy and stupid with drink, lulling them into such a drowsy intoxication that they could not stand on their legs. They staggered about until they fell to rest in the king's hall, making their beds right in the banquet room. Finding them now in the state that suited his purpose, and so seeing his chance to obtain his revenge, he gathered up the crooks that he had previously made in his robe, and going with them into the banquet hall, where the nobles lay sprawling on the floor, vomiting in their drunkenness, cut the supports of the tapestries that his mother had made and that hung on the walls of the hall. Having cut down the hangings and laid them over the sleepers, he took out the crooked stakes, and fixed the hangings so thoroughly and tightly that none of those who lay beneath them had the strength to get up, struggle as he might. He then set fire to the house; and the fire spread far and wide, the flames leaping hither and thither and enveloping the whole house, so that the royal palace was reduced to ashes and all within perished, whether they lay fast asleep or made fruitless attempts to escape. Next he went to Feng's closet — he had some time before been conducted by his men to bed — and taking Feng's sword, which hung by his bedside, hung up his own in its place. Then, rousing his uncle, he told him that his nobles were perishing in the flames, and that Amleth was there with his old crooks, intending to exact due vengeance for his father's murder. At these words, Feng sprang from his bed, but failing to find his own sword, was cut down as he vainly endeavored to draw the other from its scabbard.

Valiant and of immortal memory was the hero who shrewdly behaved like a fool, and under a guise of madness with wondrous art concealed a superior intelligence; for by his stratagem he not only saved himself but also succeeded in avenging his father. Cunningly he defended himself and manfully he avenged his parent, so that it is hard to say which was the greater: his courage or his wits. ■

One of the earliest versions of the Hamlet story was written by a Danish cleric, Saxo Grammaticus (1150? – 1200). The historical Amleth, however, is quite different from Shakespeare's melancholy Dane. Make a list of all the characters in this story (named and unnamed) and briefly outline their role in the story. As you read Shakespeare's *Hamlet,* consult your lists and keep track of the ways in which Shakespeare adapts Saxo Grammaticus' tale.

Create a poster illustrating a scene or a character in this tale. You may even choose to create a movie poster, assuming that this story has been turned into a major film. Be sure to include your casting choices for the major characters in the story.

the night watch

by James McLean

after doing a graveyard shift

in the rail yards at 40 below

with the steam frozen around my parka

like a second skin

the cold settles in my bones

and chaps my wrists raw

so when the day boys finally start to roll in

I'm grateful almost to the point of weary tears

and I remember from high school how well

Shakespeare made the guard in Hamlet say

For this relief much thanks   'tis bitter cold
and I am sick at heart

What kind of person do you imagine the speaker to be? Why would the speaker feel it appropriate to refer to Francisco's speech from Act One to describe his situation?

Write your own poem similar to McLean's in style and length, using any quotation from Act One as a springboard for your writing.

The *SENIORITIS of a* MODERN HAMLET

by Christopher G. Inoue

Oh, that this too, too difficult homework would burn
Return, and form itself into an "A,"
Or that the Headmaster had not fixed
His rules against self-expulsion. Oh God, God,
How dreary, dull, tedious and uninteresting
Seem to me all the classes of this school!
My mind is a garden of weeds
That grows to seed. Students dull and dead in school
Possess it entirely. That I should come to school!
But two months gone, nay, not so much, not two,
So excellent a summer, that was to this
Sleep to an exhausted body, so restful to my thinking
That I might not beteem the winds of study
Visit my mind too often. Heaven and earth,
Must I remember my facts? Why, I would hang on to it
As if appetite for vacation had grown
By what it fed on; and yet within three months —
Let me not think of it; torture, thy name is school —
A brief vacation, or ere these Nikes were old
With which I cruised the malls and the beaches
Like a vagrant, no cares, why I, even I —
Oh God, a student who possesses more intelligence
Would have vacationed longer — returned to school,
My hated occupation, but no more like the summer
Than I to Einstein. Within a few months,
Ere yet the salt of most righteous tears
Had welled in the pits of my ungrateful eyes,
I enrolled. Oh, most wicked speed, to join
With such dexterity in hateful classes!
It is not, nor it cannot come to good.
But rack my brain, for I must do my homework.

Related Readings

by Charles, Prince
of Wales

Well, Frankly ...

"Well, frankly, the problem as I see it

At this moment in time is whether I

Should just lie down under all this hassle

and let them walk all over me,

Or, whether I should just say, 'OK,

I get the message,' and do myself in.

I mean, let's face it, I'm in a no-win

Situation, and quite honestly,

I'm so stuffed up to here with the whole

Stupid mess that, I can tell you, I've just

Got a good mind to take the quick way out.

That's the bottom line. The only problem is:

What happens if I find out that when I've bumped

Myself off, there's some kind of a, you know,

All that mystical stuff about when you die,

You might find you're still — know what I mean?"

"To be, or not to be" — Shakespeare's most often quoted line has been the subject of numerous parodies. Even England's royal family cannot resist the temptation of having fun with Shakespeare. Try creating your own rewrite of the speech. You may choose to do so as a parody of the original, as a rap song, as a modern translation, or in any other style you feel comfortable with.

ALIVE OR DEAD?

To be, or not to be

from The British Magazine, May and June 1762

This essay first appeared in 1762. Nevertheless, it still has some interesting insights to offer modern readers on the subject of the world's most famous speech.

Hamlet having assumed the disguise of madness, as a cloak under which he might the more effectually revenge his father's death upon the murderer and usurper, appears alone upon the stage in a pensive and melancholy attitude, and communes with himself: To be, or not to be? That is the question.

We have already observed that there is not any apparent circumstance in the fate or situation of Hamlet, that should prompt him to harbour one thought of self-murder; and therefore these expressions of despair imply an impropriety in point of character. But supposing his condition was truly desperate, and he saw no possibility of repose, but in the uncertain harbour of death, let us see in what manner he argues on the subject. The question is, "To be, or not to be"; to die by my own hand, or live and suffer the miseries of life. He proceeds to explain the alternative in these terms, "Whether 'tis nobler in the mind to suffer, or endure the frowns of fortune, or to take arms, and by opposing, end them." Here he deviates from his first proposition, and death is no longer the question. The only doubt is, whether he will stoop to misfortune, or exert his faculties in order to surmount it. This surely is the obvious meaning, and indeed the only meaning that can be implied in these words,

> Whether 'tis nobler in the mind to
> suffer
> The stings and arrows of outrageous
> fortune;
> Or to take arms against a sea of
> troubles,
> And by opposing, end them.

He now drops this idea, and reverts to his reasoning on death, in the course of which he owns himself deterred from suicide, by the thoughts of what may follow death:

> — the dread of something after death,
> (That undiscovered country, from
> whose bourne
> No traveller returns)

This might be a good argument in a Heathen or Pagan, and such indeed Hamlet really was; but Shakespear has already represented him as a good catholic, who must have been acquainted with the truths of revealed religion, and says expressly in this very play,

— had not the Everlasting fix'd
His canon 'gainst self-murder.

Moreover, he had just been conversing with his father's spirit, piping hot from purgatory, which we presume is not within the *bourne* of this world. — The dread of what may happen after death, (says he)

Makes us rather bear those ills we have,
Than fly to others that
we know not of.

This declaration, at least, implies some knowledge of the other world, and expressly asserts, that there must be *ills* in that world, though what kind of *ills* they are, we do not know. The argument, therefore, may be reduced to this lemma. — "This world abounds with *ills* which I feel: the other world abounds with *ills*, the nature of which I do not know: therefore, I will rather bear those *ills* I have, than fly to *others* which I know not of." A deduction amounting to a certainty, with respect to the only circumstance that could create a doubt, namely, whether in death he should rest from his misery; and if he was certain there were evils in the next world, as well as in this, he had no room to reason at all about the matter. What alone could justify his thinking on this subject, would have been the hope of flying from the ills of this world, without encountering any *others* in the next. Nor is Hamlet more accurate in the following reflection.

Thus conscience does make cowards of
us all.

A bad conscience will make us cowards; but a good conscience will make us brave. It does not appear that anything lay heavy on his conscience; and from the premises we cannot help inferring that conscience in this case was entirely out of the question. Hamlet was deterred from suicide, by a full conviction that in flying from one sea of troubles which he did know, he should fall into *another* which he did not know.

His whole chain of reasoning, therefore, seems inconsistent and incongruous. — "I am doubtful whether I should live, or do violence upon my own life: for I know not whether it is more honourable to bear misfortune patiently, than to exert myself in opposing misfortune, and by opposing, end it." Let us throw it into the form of a syllogism, it will stand thus: "I am oppressed with ills: I know not whether it is more honourable to bear those ills patiently, or to end them by taking arms against them; *ergo*, I am doubtful whether I should slay myself or live. — To die, is no more than to sleep; and to *say* that by a sleep we end the heart-ach, &c. 'tis a consummation devoutly to be wish'd." Now, to *say it*, was of no consequence unless it had been true. "I am afraid of the dreams that may happen in that sleep of death; and I choose rather to bear those ills I have in this life, than fly to *other ills* in that undiscovered country from whose bourne no traveller returns. I have ills that are almost insupportable in this life. I know not what is in the next, because it is an undiscovered country: *ergo*, I'd rather bear those ills I have, than fly to others which I know not of." Here the conclusion is by no means warranted by the premises. "I am sore afflicted in this life: but, I will rather bear the afflictions of this life, than plunge myself in the afflictions of another life: *ergo*, conscience makes cowards of us all." But, this conclusion would justify the logician in saying *negatur consequens*; for it is

A bad conscience

will make us cowards;

but a good conscience

will make us brave.

entirely detached both from the major and minor proposition.

This soliloquy is not less unexceptionable in the propriety of expression, than in the chain of argumentation. — "To die, — to sleep — no more," contains an ambiguity which all the art of punctuation cannot remove; for it may signify that "to die, is to sleep no more"; or the expression — "no more," may be considered as an abrupt apostrophe in thinking, as if he meant to say — "no more of that reflection."

"Ay, there's the rub" — is a vulgarism beneath the dignity of Hamlet's character, and the words that follow leave the sense imperfect;

For in that sleep of death, what dreams
* may come,*
When we have shuffled off this mortal
* coil,*
Must give us pause.

Not the dreams that might come, but, the fear of what dreams might come, occasioned the pause or hesitation. *Respect* in the same line, may be allowed to pass for consideration: but,

Th' oppressor's wrong, the proud man's
* contumely,*

According to the invariable acceptation of the words *wrong* and *contumely*, can signify nothing but the wrongs sustained by the oppressor, and the contumely or abuse thrown upon the proud man; though it is plain, that Shakespear used them in a different sense; neither is the word *spurn* a substantive; yet as such he has inserted it in these lines:

The insolence of office, and the spurns
That patient merit of th'unworthy
takes.

If we consider the metaphors of this soliloquy, we shall find them jumbled together in strange confusion.

If the metaphors were reduced to painting, we should find it a very difficult task, if not altogether impracticable, to represent with any propriety, outrageous Fortune using her slings and arrows, between which indeed, there is no sort of analogy in nature. Neither can any figure be more ridiculously absurd than that of a man taking arms against a sea, exclusive of the incongruous medley of slings, arrows, and seas, justled within the compass of one reflection. What follows is a strange rhapsody of broken images, of sleeping, dreaming, and shifting off a *coil*, which last conveys no idea that can be represented on canvas. A man may be exhibited shuffling off his garment or his chains: but how he should shuffle off a *coil*, which is another term for noise and tumult, we cannot comprehend. Then we have long-lived calamity, and time armed with whips and scorns; and patient merit spurned at by unworthiness; and misery with a bare bodkin going to make his own quietus, which at best, is but a mean metaphor. These are followed by figures sweating under fardles of burthens, puzzled with doubts, shaking with fears, and flying from evils. Finally, we see resolution sicklied o'er with pale thought, a conception like that of representing health by sickness, and a current of pith turned away so as to lose the name of action, which is both an error in fancy, and a solicism in sense. ■

What inconsistencies does the author find in Hamlet's reasoning? Do you think these inconsistencies are insurmountable? Can you explain them?

Related Readings

By Maurice Baring

At the COURT of KING CLAUDIUS

Baring describes the evening of the performance of The Murder of Gonzago *from the point of view of the First Player. From a Player's Letter.*

We arrived at Elsinore in the morning. We were at once let into the presence of the Prince. He received us with the courtesy and kindliness which were native to him, and he seemed but little changed since his student days when he was as much our companion as our patron. It is true that his face and his expression

have grown older and more serious, just as his body has grown more portly, but in so far as his conduct and demeanour are concerned he is the same. No words can picture the dreariness and monotony of the life which he leads here in the Court. He is virtually a prisoner, for should he in any way transgress the fixed limits of the tradition and etiquette which govern this place, the courtiers and the officials of the Court do not hesitate to say that he is deranged in his mind. As soon as he greeted us he recalled a thousand memories of those freer and happier days, and he seemed to take as great a delight in our art and our trade as in days gone by. His love for the stage, for well-turned verse, and the nice declamation of noble lines is as ardent as ever, and he bade me recall to him a speech from a

tragedy on which his sure taste had alighted, although it escaped the notice and the applause of the populace.

It was arranged that on the night following the morning of our arrival we should play before the King and the Court. The piece chosen by the Prince was entitled "The Murder of Gonzago," a somewhat old-fashioned bit of fustian, chosen no doubt to suit the taste of the King and his courtiers. The Prince himself wrote a speech of some sixteen lines which he bade me insert in my part. We spent the day in study and rehearsal, which were sorely needed, since we had not played the piece for many years. In the evening a banquet was held in the castle. The King and Queen, the Chamberlain and all the Court dignitaries were present, and the Prince, although he did not grace the feast with his presence, insisted that we, the players, should take part in it. The Court dignitaries were averse to this, but the Prince overruled their objections by saying that unless we took part in the banquet he would not be present at the performance.

The feast was in the banqueting-hall; the

King and the Queen together with all the Court took their places before a high, raised table at the end of the banqueting-hall. We players sat at a separate table at the further end of the hall. The feast began long before sunset and lasted far into the night. There was much deep drinking, but an atmosphere of ceremony and gloom hung over the festivity; the mirth rang hollow and the hilarity was false and strained.

Towards the end of the banquet the King rose to his feet and in pompous phrase spoke of the pleasure that he felt in seeing so many loyal friends gathered about him and that he looked forward to the day when the Prince, his nephew, would once more join heart and soul in the festivities of the Court, and then looking towards us he was pleased to say that he trusted to the skill, the well-known skill, and the widely-famed art of the players who were now visiting his capital to have a salutary influence and to be successful in distracting the mind and in raising the spirits of the Prince, which had been so sadly affected ever since the demise of his much-to-be-regretted brother. These words elicited loud cheers from the assembly, and it was pointed out to us by the Chamberlain that the speech of the King was a further sign of his Majesty's unerring tact and never-failing condescension.

As we left the banqueting-hall, after the King and Queen had retired, I noticed that the Prince was pacing up and down the terrace of the castle, lost as it were in abstraction. During the whole of the next day we were busy in study and rehearsal. The Lord Chamberlain was somewhat concerned as to the nature of the performance we were to give. He desired to be present at a rehearsal, but here again the Prince intervened with impetuous authority. The Lord Chamberlain then sought me out in person and said that he earnestly trusted there would be nothing either in the words of the play or in the manner in which it should be played that would give offence to the illustrious audience. I replied that the play had been chosen by the Prince and that it would be well if he would address any suggestions he had to make directly to His Royal Highness. The Lord Chamberlain said that the Prince was in so irritable a frame of mind that he could ill brook any interference, but that he relied on our good sense and inherent tact to omit any word or phrase which, in the present circumstances (for he pointed out that the Court was in half-mourning) might be likely to give offence. He said that for instance any too exuberant display of buffoonery, any too great an insistence on broad jokes would be out of place at the present time. I assured him that so far from the Prince having instigated us towards clowning he had begged us to suppress all buffoonery of any kind, which had ever been distasteful to him, and this none knew so well as I.

Elsinore, like all courts, was rife with gossip, the common talk being that the Prince was courting the daughter of the Chamberlain, who, owing to the position she occupied, they professed to find beautiful, and who in reality is but an insipid minx and likely to develop on the lines of her doddering old father, while they say that she will not hear of his suit, being secretly but passionately enamoured of one of the minor courtiers, by name Osric.

Others say that the Prince's passion for the Chamberlain's daughter is a mere pretence and that it is his friend Horatio who is in reality plighted to her. But we, who know the Prince well, know that he has no thought of such things. He is an artist, and had he not had the misfortune to be born a Prince he would have been a player of first-rate excellence. Being gifted with the artistic temperament and the histrionic nature, the mode of existence which he is forced to lead amidst the conventions, the formalities, the rules, and the unvarying tediousness of stiff and stately

Court decorum, is to him intolerable. He is thinking the whole time of modes of expression, pictures, phrases, situations, conceits, and his mind lives in the world of dream and holds office at the court of Art. That is why, in this nest of officials, he is like a cuckoo among a brood of respectable blackbirds.

The performance took place after the banquet on the second evening of our stay. The stage was appointed in a long, low room adjoining the banqueting-hall. Slightly raised seats for the King and the Queen were erected in the centre of the room in front of the stage, and the Court were assembled in line with them and behind them. The Chamberlain and his daughter sat in the front row, and the gossip of the place seemed to be in some way substantiated by the fact that she never took her eyes off Osric the courtier (a handsome lad) during the whole of the performance. He was standing next to the Queen's throne.

The Prince, before the trumpets sounded for the performance to begin, came to us and gave us his final instructions which bore, as ever, the stamp of his fine taste and nice discrimination, and he proved to us once more that he was by nature a professional player. When the performance began he strolled into the hall and reclined on the floor at the feet of the Chamberlain's daughter. We played as well as might be expected considering the chilling effect which cannot fail to be produced by the presence of exalted personages, for the Court had their eyes fixed on the throne and only dared to murmur approval when approval had already been expressed from that quarter. During all the first part of the play such moments were rare and indeed the audience seemed to have some difficulty in comprehending the words and the still plainer action

which we suited to the words. But the Prince came to our aid, whispering audibly to his uncle and his mother and elucidating for them the passages which proved perplexing. He also made various comments to the Chamberlain's daughter, and was quick to apprehend the slightest play of feature, gesture, or intonation which struck him as being successful and true.

The Chamberlain's daughter was listless throughout and seemed to take no interest in the play, and her father was too enfeebled in mind to catch the drift of it at all, but the manifest interest which the Prince took in it, seemed, nevertheless, to cause him uneasiness, and he never ceased furtively to glance at the King and the Queen. The Queen, on the other hand, seemed much pleased, and indeed they say that she has ever been fond of spectacles and stage-playing. By the time the play had reached its climax, with the entry of Lucianus who spoke the lines which had been inserted by the Prince, the King, who had been growing more and more fretful (for he has no taste for letters) rose from his seat and gave the signal for departure, and the Chamberlain immediately gave orders that the play should cease. The King remarked that the heat in the hall was oppressive and he withdrew, followed by the Court, and the Prince, who was in an ecstasy of joy at the beautiful performance, clapped his hands loudly and congratulated us warmly, saying that he had seldom enjoyed a play so much.

So tedious is the routine at these courts that this little incident was much discussed and debated, and the Prince's conduct in so loudly applauding a play after His Majesty had signified that the performance was tedious has been severely commented on. Tomorrow we sail for Hamburg. ■

To what extent do you think Baring succeeded in capturing the essence of the character? Retell the events of the evening using the point of view of one of the other characters present, such as Polonius, Ophelia, Gertrude, or Claudius.

GERTRUDE

by Margaret Atwood

TALKS BACK ✠

In this shocker of a short story, Gertrude turns the tables on Hamlet.

I always thought it was a mistake, calling you Hamlet. I mean, what kind of a name is that for a young boy? It was your father's idea. Nothing would do but that you had to be called after him. Selfish. The other kids at school used to tease the life out of you. The nicknames! And those terrible jokes about pork.

I wanted to call you George.

I am *not* wringing my hands. I'm drying my nails.

Darling, please stop fidgeting with my mirror. That'll be the third one you've broken.

Yes, I've seen those pictures, thank you very

> **BY THE WAY, DARLING, I WISH YOU WOULDN'T CALL YOUR STEPDAD THE BLOAT KING.**

much. I *know* your father was handsomer than Claudius. High brow, aquiline nose and so on, looked great in uniform. But handsome isn't everything, especially in a man, and far be it from me to speak ill of the dead, but I think it's about time I pointed out to you that your Dad just wasn't a whole lot of fun. Noble, sure, I grant you. But Claudius, well, he likes a drink now and then. He appreciates a decent meal. He enjoys a laugh, know what I mean? You don't always have to be tiptoeing around because of some holier-than-thou principle or something.

By the way, darling, I wish you wouldn't call your stepdad *the bloat king*. He does have a slight weight-problem, and it hurts his feelings.

Related Readings

The rank sweat of a *what?* My bed is certainly not *enseamed,* whatever that might be! A nasty sty, indeed! Not that it's any of your business, but I change those sheets twice a week, which is more than you do, judging from that student slum pigpen in Wittenberg. I'll certainly never visit you *there* again without prior warning! I see that laundry of yours when you bring it home, and not often enough either, by a long shot! Only when you run out of black socks.

And let me tell you, everyone sweats at a time like that, as you'd find out very soon if you ever gave it a try. A real girlfriend would do you a heap of good. Not like that pasty-faced what's-her-name, all trussed up like a prize turkey in those touch-me-not corsets of hers. If you ask me, there's something off about that girl. Borderline. Any little shock could push her right over the edge.

Go get yourself someone more down-to-earth. Have a nice roll in the hay. Then you can talk to me about nasty sties.

No, darling, I am not *mad* at you. But I must say you're an awful prig sometimes. Just like your Dad. *The Flesh,* he'd say. You'd think it was dog dirt. You can excuse that in a young person, they are always so intolerant, but in someone his age it was getting, well, very hard to live with, and that's the understatement of the year.

Some days I think it would have been better for both of us if you hadn't been an only child. But you realize who you have to thank for *that.* You have no idea what I used to put up with. And every time I felt like a little, you know, just to warm up my ageing bones, it was like I'd suggested murder.

Oh! You think *what?* You think Claudius murdered your Dad? Well, no wonder you've been so rude to him at the dinner table!

If I'd known *that,* I could have put you straight in no time flat.

It wasn't Claudius, darling.

It was me. ■

What does Hamlet do next? Continue the story using Atwood's as a basis. What other new revelations are in store for young Hamlet?

They All Want to Play *Hamlet*

by Carl Sandburg

They all want to play Hamlet.

They have not exactly seen their fathers killed

Nor their mothers in a frame-up to kill,

Nor an Ophelia dying with a dust gagging the heart,

Not exactly the spinning circles of singing golden spiders,

Not exactly this have they got at nor the meaning of flowers — O
    flowers, flowers slung by a dancing girl — in the saddest play
    the inkfish, Shakespeare, ever wrote;

Yet they all want to play Hamlet because it is sad like all actors
    are sad and to stand by an open grave with a joker's skull in
    the hand and then to say over slow and say over slow wise,
    keen, beautiful words masking a heart that's breaking, break-
    ing,

This is something that calls and calls to their blood.

They are acting when they talk about it and they know it is acting
    to be particular about it and yet: They all want to play
    Hamlet.

Ask actors and they will tell you that the crowning achievement in their careers would be to play Hamlet. Why does this role hold such a fascination for actors?

Every community has actors living in it. Invite an actor to visit your class to discuss his or her experiences with the play *Hamlet*.

As a project, contact a number of actors, male and female, and ask them a series of questions related to playing the role of Hamlet. Present your findings to the class.

Related Readings

Ophelia's Song

by Marya Zaturenska

Eyes of despair, eyes of fire,
Watchful terror, warlike peace.
Quenched is the star of all desire:
It sings the song of my release.
I throw fresh garlands, white and red,
Into the devouring river bed.

The willows shiver as I pass.
I feel the trembling of the grass.
As the waves rise, and slide, and fall,
I sink through islands of dark water.

None shall remember, few recall
The early Spring's unhappy daughter
Whom amorous Death found loveliest.

No Prince can claim me, and no charm

Scoop from the waters my small flowers.
They drown in running wave and stream —
Pale Undines of some idle hours —
Lost in the willows' drowning gleam.

My floating, underwater bed,
My little garland, white and red,
Will know my name. The willows shed
Familiar shadows on my head.

As the flowers and the stream
Sink deep in elemental calm —
And the song, and the dream …

I shall not come to harm.

Imagine that the title of this poem is also the title of a compilation CD. Choose at least ten titles of songs and music that would be appropriate for such a compilation. Be prepared to play at least one song for the class.

170

Remembering
OPHELIA

by Diane Fahey

Blood trickles down from the castle,
filling the flowers that fill her eyes.

2

Confused, and the victim of confusion . . .
How water clarifies the mind.

3

As they lay, littering the hall, in their blood,
she lingered in crumbling masonry and pillars,
in weeds and flowers intermarrying outside the walls.

4

Centuries later, she returned with a film crew.
She was wearing jeans, an Indian shirt
embroidered with flowers, and a headscarf . . .
He was still lying there among the others
with their sprawling limbs and broken swords.

After the filming, she took off her badge
and pinned it to his chest—TAKE THE TOYS
FROM THE BOYS, it read—then left without
a farewell kiss, though she was compassionate,
and over the bitterness by now.

Write a poem about Ophelia or about your feelings about Ophelia. Create a graphic to
accompany your poem. You could use magazine illustrations or an original piece.

Related Readings

by Richard Woollatt

Alas, Poor Bauer

Horatio was right
Hamlet's graveyard scene
should be staged outdoors
where our players are poised
under May leaves
on springy turf where
dandelions outnumber students
beside a brook on which Ophelia
might float past mermaid-like
bedecked with "fantastic garlands."

But to the live action:
enter the gravediggers
shovel in one hand
    text in the other
(mayhap they'll do
some digging in the play?)
Enter Horatio & the Prince
also text in hand
    but when Hamlet reaches
        for Yorick's skull
(borrowed from biology

in period one)

off the playing field

parallel the brook &

above our heads

into the mad maid's grave

rolls a soccer ball …

the prince picks it up — hesitates —

I want to prompt him

feed him a line or two:

"Alas, poor Bauer

I toed him, well!"

and at this green moment

as two worlds commingle

there's so much advice

I'd give Polonius-like:

"O soon my prince

you'll have to throw away the text

learn to adlib

to improvise

for after this green May

of dandelions &

sweet-lipped Ophelias

come the autumns of crafty Claudius &

those Gertrude-winters so willingly corrupt.

This poem dramatizes what happens when reality interferes with a reading of *Hamlet*. Assume that a day has passed since the events related in this poem. Write a short story or a play in which the students ask the teacher if they can carry on with the performance outdoors.

Related Readings

by Robert Currie

Intimations

Striving to make them sense

their own mortality

I gripped the shrunken head,

a rubber toy but grisly,

addressed it as Yorick,

and no gorge rose.

But after class

one boy shied towards me:

"I was just wonderin if ... well ...

Howdja like a real skull for that part?"

Trying not to think

of what was left headless

I seized upon his offer.

Now when Hamlet holds

the jester's skull,

the classroom grows

quiet as the grave.

They see the end,

and cannot laugh at that.

An intimation is a clue or an indirect suggestion. When the students see the real skull, what intimations do you think they get that make them grow quiet?

Imagine you are in a class where the teacher passes around a real skull. Write a journal response or short poem describing why the classroom grows "quiet as the grave."

Meditation AT Elsinore

by Elizabeth Coatsworth

"Good night, sweet prince"—
That is the tragedy,
not blood, not poison,
not even the reedy stream
where flowers and little bawdy ditties ended.
The tragedy was love.
Love was the chord to which the young prince moved,
and one by one his loves betrayed his love:
his father's ghost was harsh and stank of Hell;
his mother's love was coupled with the siren's;
while young Ophelia spoke, her father listened;
his boon companions came as spies;
on every hand
his love turned sword and twisted in his grasp,
piercing his side. But others died as well.
Despite this heaped-up death, these corpses strewn
as thick as daisies in a meadow, hate
was never victor. All was done for love;
not hate, but love speaks last —
"Good night, sweet prince."

Write your own "meditation" at Elsinore. You may choose to do this as a poem or as a
journal entry.

Spring

by Charlotte E. Reedy

It was not easy that year
to teach *Hamlet*;
for whenever we talked
of Ophelia,
blank-eyed and staring,
singing snatches of songs,
there was the vision of Mary's mother,
lost in a religion of her own,
laughing to herself
and smiling
and really seeing no one.
It was hard to talk
of "incestial sheets"
when Helen's own cousin had raped her,
and she, only seventeen,
had been too scared to share the horror
until an abortion
was out of the question.
And while the kids pondered
if Hamlet really loved Ophelia
and if she really loved him,
I, alone,
faced the dissolution of my own marriage
and frequently contemplated suicide,
were it not for my own daughters.

Life parallels literature
too often,
and often
life is much crueller
than any made-up play.

Do you agree with the statement made in the last five lines of the poem? Explain.
Can you think of any incident in your own experience that has a parallel in literature,
a television program, or a feature film?

Hamlet

(for Jo Nacola)
by Albert Wendt

This short story from Samoa illustrates how deeply we can be affected by the stories we read — sometimes with serious consequences.

Most of us (unfortunately) never discover the passions, obsessions and talents which we possess. The fortunate (among us) sometimes discover them accidentally.

Though Iosua was, physically, very thick-set, with a large head and exceptionally large hands and feet, he was most inconspicuous in class,

withdrawn, offering mumbled replies when I asked him questions; he always sat at the back, the true plodder who had studied extra hard to come from the village primary school to Samoa College and who, after two tries at School Certificate, qualified for the sixth form; a solid citizen who would have maintained his inconspicuousness if I hadn't introduced *Hamlet* (the play, that is) to his class.

I've never been one for Shakespeare: my high-school teachers had ruined him for me, and I've always found the language of the plays extremely difficult. But for that fateful year, *Hamlet* was the set play for the University Entrance Exam, and I *had* to teach it. Just imagine: *Hamlet* in the sweltering tropics in a language foreign to students who know little of Europe and castles

in Denmark! So I decided I'd just try and teach them enough about the play to get them through the exam. For me also, the always intellectual, perpetually self-questioning Hamlet was a slightly ridiculous, sometimes silly, self-indulgent adolescent constantly picking at his deformed navel unable to break out of the cerebral. …

Most of the students groaned (not too audibly though) when, one humid sweaty afternoon I announced we were going to study *Hamlet*, starting the next day. I gave out copies of the play and told them to read them. I described the plot briefly, and tried to get them interested by announcing that Laurence Olivier, "the greatest of all Shakespearean actors," had recorded the play and we would listen to that performance.

The next morning at the start of the period, I put on the first of the long-playing records. The students settled down quickly. I withdrew to the back and, pretending to be following my script and listening to the record, sank into the fuzzy, pleasant world of daydreams. (My usual escape from the

Related Readings

boredom of teaching!) The rhythmic flow of the performance, of poetry and sound effects, the attentive silence of the students, became a barely audible tide surging dully at the edge of my hearing. Throughout the years since then, I've kept remembering the faint but annoying smell of fresh dung wafting in from the paddocks only a short distance away. Why has that memory persisted? It's extraneous to this tale. Life is not art, I must remember that. Chaos is more usual than order, the Principle of Uncertainty is built into the cosmos, Pita would say. The smell of fresh dung was there and had nothing to do with *Hamlet*, but it happened! It wasn't an evil omen, the Apparition come to Elsinore Castle! The fact of it was that I was in the belly of a mellow day-dream — probably a lustful one (I was then a very fit, very hedonistic twenty-four-year-old) — while my poor, bored students were trying to cope with the golden Prince who was trying to cope with his golden navel. (Perhaps the mixed-up Prince should've been contemplating his most central organ only a short distance below his navel!) The smell of dung intruded, a coincidence.

I surfaced when the bell rang to end the period. The students started packing their books. One of them turned off the record-player. "You may leave!" I told the class.

Three boys passed me as I walked up to my desk at the front of the classroom "... *Not so, my lord; I am too much in the sun.*" For a moment, I couldn't believe I'd heard it: it was an almost perfect imitation of Olivier, so English and perfect an utterance couldn't have come from any of my students! I recognized Iosua as the middle of the three. No, he would be the last one capable of such mimicry!

Next day I walked into a noisy English class, put on the next record, and the students quietened down at once. As I went to sit at the back, I saw the sentence in red

chalk on the back blackboard: "I AM TOO MUCH IN THE SUN, signed Hamlet." I didn't say anything about it to the class.

Once, during the next thirty or so minutes of my usual day-dreaming, I noticed the girl next to me nodding to sleep. I coughed. She woke up and smiled. Just beyond her, Iosua was upright with intense attention, his eyes riveted on his script, his lips mouthing the text in time with the actors. At least one of them was excited by the Prince's ordeal, I thought, and then returned to my day-dreaming.

Fifteen minutes before the end of our period the next day, I stopped the record and asked them if they wanted me to explain anything. No requests. (Inwardly, I was relieved because, as yet, I hadn't prepared any detailed explanations.)

"Well, can anyone quote any lines from the play?" (I had to fill in ten minutes, but what a stupid request to make, I thought.) For a short while, there were no offers. Then a thick but timid arm began to rise at the back just under the red sentence, the quotation, on the blackboard. I was reminded of a frightened sunflower, in the morning, unfolding and rising (compelled by its nature) to know the sunlight. "Yes?" I asked the now upright arm. It was Iosua, eyes still focused on his desk top, the top of his thickly haired head pointing at me. Some girls giggled. "Yes, Iosua," I encouraged him.

"I say something from the play?" (Atrocious English!) More giggling. His friends were squirming with him, praying he wasn't going to make a fool of himself.

"Go ahead. You don't have to stand up," I said. With his head lowered, his face hidden from me, he spoke into his desktop, almost inaudibly. "A bit louder," I said. He raised his head slightly and spoke into the back of the student in front of him. "Very good!" I said, even though I hadn't heard him clearly. He raised his face towards me at last. Suddenly I remembered a calf being born, breaking out of the slickly wet caul, stretching its limbs, testing them hesitantly, afraid at first, then gaining confidence with each unimpeded stretch.

> *"... O, that this too too solid flesh would melt.*
> *Thaw, and resolve itself into a dew.*
> *Or that the everlasting had not fix'd ..."*

At first it was broken, barely intelligible. A ripple of mirth fluttered through the class.

"That was very good," I congratulated him, realizing that he had just committed a very courageous act: his peers frowned upon any student who paraded his knowledge or ability in front of a teacher; it wasn't Samoan, it was blatantly papalagi to "show off" one's individual talents. "Do you know any more?" I asked. He shook his head.

That evening while I was drinking with friends at the R.S.A. Club, I unexpectedly thought of him and how he had tried so hard to rise above his insignificance, his timidity and fear. For him, the lines had been more than memorized ones, they had been a magical fish-hook fishing him out of the boundaries of himself. I envied his growing courage.

Abruptly the class stopped laughing when I entered the room. I sensed they were trying to hide something from me. I glanced at Iosua. He looked embarrassed. I put on the next record. "BUT BREAK, MY HEART, FOR I MUST HOLD MY TONGUE signed Hamlet" was scrawled, in bold yellow chalk, across the top of the front blackboard. "At least one person in this class knows *her* Hamlet!" I joked. Some of them laughed. They all tried not to look at Iosua.

Before the end of the period, I tried it out again. He offered to recite. This time none of us laughed. It was an uncanny and astounding performance. Sitting intensely still in his chair, his eyes slits of concentration, his hands gripping the edge of his desk, he cast the miraculous net of his voice over us, trapping us all.

His accent was still noticeably Samoan, yet it was a spell-binding mimicry of the record. This time, the Ghost:

> *"Ay, that incestuous, that adulterate beast,*
> *With witchcraft of his wits, with traitorous gifts —*
> *O wicked wit and gifts that have the power*
> *So to seduce! — won to his shameful lust*
> *The will of my most virtuous queen ..."*

As he recited, I thought: what god was speaking through him? What gift was pulling him above his mediocrity? We clapped when he finished. "Go on, Hamlet!" someone called. He looked at me. I nodded.

> *"... Let not the royal bed of Denmark be*
> *A couch of luxury and damned incest.*
> *But howsoever thou pursuest this act,*
> *Taint not thy mind, nor let ..."*

I sensed then the committed quality of obsession. This wasn't simply a performance: Iosua was discovering his gift for Hamlet, the gift which made him exceptional. How else could you explain his facility to absorb, so easily, uncannily, the record and fury of the Prince's tale?

Some students whistled, we all clapped, he bowed his head once and smiled and was the usual Iosua again, released by the god. "He knows all of Hamlet's lines!" Mamafa, one of his friends, said. "Not possible!" a girl challenged. "Ask him!"

He was soon reciting whole chunks from Hamlet's soliloquies, almost flawlessly. The more he recited, the more confidently he assumed Olivier's voice and delivery. And through his performance and obvious love of Hamlet, I too was, for the first time in my life, falling in love with the play.

That week at the Staff Common Room I asked about him. All his other teachers agreed he wasn't very bright, but worked hard, obeyed his teachers, caused no problems whatsoever, would make a good clerk or civil servant, maybe even a dedicated primary-school teacher. So I kept Iosua's gift to myself.

On Monday morning, I could hear him reciting as I approached the classroom. I entered quietly. He was standing in front of the class. He stopped when he noticed me. I nodded. He continued. I sat down quietly.

He was magnificent. A hypnotic energy emanated from him. He *was* Hamlet, and possessed. Though he did not act, his voice, his presence, performed it all. Such intensity was not of us: it was a terrible beauty.

Later as the class was leaving, I asked him, "Do you remember other plays as well?" He shook his head. "Just *Hamlet?*" He nodded. "Why?"

"I don't know," he mumbled. "Hamlet was a great hero." He was again empty of the god.

Could I have stopped Hamlet from possessing him totally, then? (Or was it the reverse, was he taking possession of Hamlet?) Without Hamlet he would probably have been safe, secure, protected from, unaware of his only gift. (I'm getting carried away again. I'm sure that at that time all I cared about was his miraculous transformation and gift, and about encouraging him to use it. It wasn't until later that I became aware of the danger.)

In our next English lessons, I got other students to read the other roles to his Hamlet.

"Do you understand what you're reciting?" I asked him after the other students had gone.

"A little," he replied. He looked up at me. In his eyes was a brilliant dazzle: he was high, high on Hamlet.

A day later a science teacher asked me if I was teaching *Hamlet* to the sixth form. That explains it, he laughed when I said yes.

"What?" I asked.

"Our Sixth Form now has a *real* Hamlet. They even get him to perform in my class. He signs all his assignments, Hamlet."

"I'm sure he's just joking."

"I hope he is," he said.

In the Staff Common Room some teachers started joking about our College acquiring "a very gifted Hamlet who isn't particularly good at anything else." Fatally flawed! one of them quipped. They laughed. I was annoyed but said nothing.

I began to fear for him.

"Where is Iosua?" I asked at our next English period. Nobody seemed to know. I started the record.

"He has gone home," Mamafa said. "He's not well." I tried to ignore the suppressed wave of laughter which surged through the class.

During that period while *Hamlet* played on, as it were, I couldn't escape my deepening anxiety about Iosua. At the end of the period, Mamafa waited until the other students had left and then told me,

"He is not well. He is afraid."

"Of what?"

"Of him — Hamlet!"

"But why?"

"He says, Hamlet won't leave him alone." Mamafa paused and added,

"Miss Monroe, you must help him. The students and teachers are starting to poke fun at him!"

"I'll try," I promised, though I was heavy with a feeling of helplessness.

"It is as if he is two people. Every time he is Hamlet, which is happening more and more often, he finds it difficult to be himself again ... What is happening to him?"

"Tell him to come and see me!"

I hardly slept that night, refusing to admit to myself that I had been responsible for

Iosua's discovery of his gift, obsession, madness. How was I going to help him? I had to confront that too.

He was away from school for over a week but Mamafa assured me he was well. My anxiety lessened. The day after we finished studying *Hamlet*, the students having completed their notes about the play, and I had told them we were moving into a study of modern poetry, he returned.

While the others were settling down, I asked him if he was all right. He grinned and took his usual seat at the back.

And for a couple of weeks, while we struggled through some modern poetry, he was again his usual withdrawn self, empty of the gift, offering little to our understanding of the poetry

and understanding little of it. He even massacred a poem I got him to read aloud to the class. Further proof, to me, of his dull normality. I was elated he was safe, but I sensed in the class a feeling of disappointment that Hamlet had left us and we were again mired in our uninspired, boring normality without vision or daring, trapped in our perpetually deadening sanity. Better a plodding, normal Iosua though than an insane Hamlet, I persuaded myself! (I wasn't going to be responsible for a kid going crackers!)

Once again we forgot him in his inconspicuousness.

"WITHOUT HIM I AM NOBODY" in red chalk on the front blackboard when I walked into my classroom before school started. Momentarily I was puzzled. A Jesus freak, I concluded. Lines from a hymn. I rubbed it off, sat down at my desk, and started working.

Next morning the same lines appeared in

exactly the same place. A very persistent Jesus freak! Again, I erased it.

"WITHOUT
WITHOUT THE
WITHOUT THE PRINCE
WITHOUT THE PRINCE I
WITHOUT THE PRINCE I AM
WITHOUT THE PRINCE I AM NOBODY"

Good poem, I thought when I saw it, the following morning. I erased it, and before I left school that day wrote in the same place:

"YOU ARE NOT NOBODY
YOU ARE A POET
AND DON'T KNOW IT"

I went straight to my classroom the next morning.

"MISS MONROE
LOVES THE PRINCE
BUT THE PRINCE WENT
MAD"

Annoyed. Puzzled. My anxiety jabbing at me again, I found myself rubbing that off quickly, unwilling and afraid to explore the extraordinary.

"Have any of you poets in this class been writing their brilliant verse on my blackboard?" I asked my sixth form that afternoon. They all looked puzzled.

The next morning — and I still remember the persistent light rain sweeping across the classroom windows — I immediately identified, with erupting fear, my mysterious poet when I read this on the blackboard:

"TO
TO BE
TO BE OR
TO BE OR NOT
TO BE OR NOT TO
TO BE OR NOT TO BE."

I didn't see him that day because I didn't have his class. My fear, tinged with guilt, became disturbingly persistent. At the same time, I began to experience an irrepressible curiosity to penetrate more into that terrible beauty and discover where he was at. Was he still possessed? Beyond the ordinary, touched by the gods? So before going home that day I wrote:

"THAT
THAT IS
THAT IS THE
THAT IS THE QUESTION"

His reply was simple (and really frightened me!).

"THE CHOICE IS NOT TO BE"

I kept imagining him using all sorts of violent methods to commit suicide, as I waited for his class to appear. My other classes passed in a frantic daze and I made frequent trips to the toilet to relieve my fear. I could've hugged him to death when he came as his usual normal self and grinned at me as he sat down. During the lesson I persuaded myself that my fears were unfounded.

I stayed after school in my small office to do some marking, and forgot about him quickly as I attacked the stack of assignments. 4.00 p.m. I shut the last exercise book and discovered I was uncomfortably sticky with sweat, and thought of a long cold shower. I looked out into the classroom. He was at the blackboard writing. His huge arm danced across its surface, leaving these words behind:

"MISS MONROE
THE PRINCE IS NOT
TO BE"

With intense fascination I observed him, knowing he was unaware of my presence.

Turning dramatically to face his audience of empty desks, he began his performance. The light from the upper louvres was like gold on his face; his eyes blazed with a holy fire, his rhythm and movement were flowing and sure and poetic, as he was transformed into Hamlet contemplating the beauty of the abyss, fascinated by it, vulnerable to it, tempting it. I tried not to watch but even my

guilt tasted brilliantly sweet as I witnessed that magnificent hero making love to his self-indulgent fascination with madness and death, risking all. Strangely, yet not strangely, I discovered that my voyeurism was becoming unashamedly sexual as he courted death unconditionally.

"... To die, to sleep—
No more; and by a sleep to say we end
The heartache and the thousand natural
* shocks*
That flesh is heir to. 'Tis a consummation
Devoutly to be wished.
To die, to sleep;
To sleep, perchance to dream ..."

Suddenly I wanted him to see me and stop (and thus stop me from enjoying his tragic dance), but he continued to advance over the abyss, fingering his own contemplation of his death, picking at it, tempting himself, dancing step by step closer to the eye of the abyss.

I moved forward. Too late. Still unaware of me, he swung towards the front door and, still caught in Hamlet's voice, swept out. *Exit.*

Through my tears, I watched him stride, his head held high, his whole body in command of the world, across the lushly green school grounds descending to the main road. Away, diminishing in size with each brave step, with the palms, flame trees and the sky applauding. Hamlet, Prince. Conqueror of the Abyss!

He didn't return to school ever.

Mamafa told me that Iosua had been sent by his parents to live with relatives in New Zealand and attend school there. That salved my conscience; I didn't even check the truth of Mamafa's information. I didn't want to face the possibility that Iosua was insane and in a hospital! I wanted to live with a sane Iosua, a diligent student, in a prosperous New Zealand!

Good art would have me leave him, in my

tale, suspended in a suspenseful bout of heroic madness, with the awed reader applauding his courage, but, alas, life is more tragic (and dreadful) than that.

Six or so years later when I was holidaying in New Zealand, I visited relatives in Porirua and was waiting at the crowded station for a train into Wellington, when someone tapped me lightly on the shoulder. I ignored it, thinking it was someone trying to pick me up. A more insistent tap. I turned sharply and cringed immediately. He was huge, a bulging-all-over Michelin Man with that unmistakable grin and a little girl sleeping in his arms. He nodded. Automatically I shook his hand and kissed him on the cheek.

"It is you, isn't it?" he asked hesitantly in Samoan.

"Yes. Are you well?" I replied in Samoan.

Nodding his head, he said, "Yes, I am well. And you, Miss Monroe?" He was my student again, even the voice, the respect.

"I am well, thank you. Is that your daughter?" I caressed the girl's back.

"Yes. I have two other children." In his awkward, almost inarticulate way he told me he was a foreman in a factory which manufactured mattresses, and lived with his wife, children and five other relatives, in a low-rent state house. Then wistfully, as if it was too painful to say it, he admitted, "I had a bit of illness."

"Yes, I remember," I joked.

His eyes lit up. "It didn't last long," he chuckled. "I've been well ever since."

"That's good," I heard myself say, with the heroic image of him marching over the school fields caught in the heart of my head.

Hamlet, I yearned to say to him. The magic word could free him once again.

"Are you still teaching?"

"No." I was suddenly lost for anything else to say. The train was pulling into the platform and passengers were surging towards it.

"Would you like to visit our home?" he invited me.

"Thank you, but I have to go back into Wellington. I'm returning to Samoa tomorrow." The lie was automatic, final, I didn't want to see what had become of Hamlet in the suburbs. I bent forward and kissed his daughter on the cheek. "Goodbye!"

"Here," he said, sheathing money in my coat pocket. "Please!" he pleaded when I tried to return it to him.

"Goodbye!" I started hurrying to the open door of the carriage.

"Goodbye. May you have a safe journey!" he called.

The train started moving. I looked back and waved. In the milling crowd, his size, his shape, his aloneness made him look so apart, distinct. He waved slowly as if he was waving a heavy flag. I recalled how, in my class, he had first raised his timid arm and had volunteered to quote from *Hamlet*. I struggled to push the memory out of my heart but couldn't.

I wept silently.

Iosua
Hamlet
Prince for a dazzling day
But better that one passionate day
than never at all ■

At the end of the story, Miss Monroe feels some very mixed emotions. What are they? What advice would you offer her to help deal with these emotions?

Iosua writes poetry on the blackboard using lines from the play *Hamlet*. Choose at least three quotations from the play and write your own poems using a similar style.

by Caroline F.E. Spurgeon

THE IMAGERY
of Hamlet

In this classic study of imagery in Hamlet, *Spurgeon finds "radiant touches of beauty" as well as "much that is sombre and unpleasant."*

In *Hamlet*, naturally, we find ourselves in an entirely different atmosphere. If we look closely we see this is partly due to the number of images of sickness, disease or blemish of the body, in the play, and we discover that the idea of an ulcer or tumour, as descriptive of the un-wholesome condition of Denmark morally, is, on the whole, the dominating one.

Hamlet speaks of his mother's sin as a blister on the "fair forehead of an innocent love," she speaks of her "sick soul," and … the emotion is so strong and the picture so vivid, that the metaphor overflows into the verbs and adjectives: heaven's face, he tells her, is *thought-sick* at the act; her husband is a *mildew'd ear*, *blasting* his *wholesome* brother; to have married him, her sense must be not only *sickly*, but *apoplex'd*. Finally, at the end of that terrific scene (3.4), he implores her not to soothe herself with the belief that his father's apparition is due to her son's madness, and not to her own guilt, for that

> *will but skin and*
> *film the ulcerous place,*

> *Whiles rank corruption,*
>   *mining all within,*
> *Infects unseen.*
>
> (3.4.165–167)

So also, later, he compares the unnecessary fighting between Norway and Poland to a kind of tumour which grows out of too much prosperity. He sees the country and the people in it alike in terms of a sick body needing medicine or the surgeon's knife. When he surprises Claudius at his prayers, he exclaims,

> *This physic but prolongs thy sickly days;*
> (3.3.99)

and he describes the action of conscience in the unforgettable picture of the healthy, ruddy countenance turning pale with sickness. A mote in the eye, a "vicious mole," a galled chilblain, a probed wound and purgation, are also among Hamlet's images; and the mind of Claudius runs equally on the same theme.

When he hears of the murder of Polonius, he declares that his weakness in not sooner having had Hamlet shut up was comparable to the cowardly action of a man with a "foul disease" who

> *To keep it from divulging, let it feed*
> *Even on the pith of life;*
>
> (4.1.23–24)

and later, when arranging to send Hamlet to England and to his death, he justifies it by the proverbial tag:

> *diseases desperate*
> *grown*
> *By desperate appliance*
> *are relieved,*
> *Or not at all;*
>
> (4.3.9–10)

and adjures the English king to carry out his behest, in the words of a fever patient seeking a sedative:

> *For like the hectic in my blood he rages,*
> *And thou must cure me.*
>
> (4.3.72–73)

When working on Laertes, so that he will easily fall in with the same design for the fencing match, his speech is full of the same underlying thought of a body sick, or ill at ease:

> *goodness, growing to a plurisy,*
> *Dies in his own too much;*
>
> (4.7.129–130)

and finally, he sums up the essence of the position and its urgency with lightning vividness in a short medical phrase:

> *But, to the quick o' the ulcer:*
> *Hamlet comes back.*
>
> (4.7.135–136)

... anguish is not the dominating thought, but rottenness, disease, corruption ...

... Though bodily disease is emphasised, bodily action and strain are little drawn upon; indeed, only in Hamlet's great speech are they brought before us at all (*to be shot at* with slings and arrows, *to take arms against* troubles and *oppose* them, *to suffer* shocks, *to bear* the lash of whips, and *endure* pangs, to *grunt* and *sweat* under burdens, and so on), and here ... they serve to intensify the feeling of mental anguish. In *Hamlet* ... anguish is not the dominating thought, but *rottenness*, disease, corruption, the result of *dirt*; the people are "muddied,"

> *Thick and unwholesome*
> *in their thoughts and whispers;*
>
> (4.5.81)

and this corruption is, in the words of Claudius, "rank" and "smells to heaven," so that the state of things in Denmark which shocks, paralyses and finally overwhelms Hamlet, is as the foul tumour breaking inwardly and poisoning the whole body, while showing

> *no cause without*
> *Why the man dies.*
>
> (4.4.29–30)

This image pictures and reflects not only the outward condition which causes Hamlet's spiritual illness, but also his own state. Indeed, the shock of the discovery of his father's murder and the sight of his mother's conduct have been such that when the play opens Hamlet has already begun to die, to die internally; because all the springs of life—love, laughter, joy, hope, belief in others—are becoming frozen at their source, are being gradually infected by the disease of the

Related Readings

spirit which is—unknown to him—killing him.

To Shakespeare's pictorial imagination, therefore, the problem in *Hamlet* is not predominantly that of will and reason, of a mind too philosophic or a nature temperamentally unfitted to act quickly; he sees it pictorially *not as the problem of an individual at all*, but as something greater and even more mysterious, as a *condition* for which the individual himself is apparently not responsible, any more than the sick man is to blame for the infection which strikes and devours him, but which, nevertheless, in its course and development, impartially and relentlessly, annihilates him and others, innocent and guilty alike. That is the tragedy of *Hamlet*, as it is perhaps the chief tragic mystery of life.

It is hardly necessary to point out, in a play so well known, and of such rich imaginative quality, how the ugliness of the dominating image (disease, ulcer) is counteracted, and the whole lighted up by flashes of sheer beauty in the imagery; beauty of picture, of sound and association, more particularly in the classical group and in the personifications. Thus, the tragic, murky atmosphere of Hamlet's interview with his mother, with its ever-repeated insistence on physical sickness and revolting disease, is illumined by the glow of his description of his father's portrait, the associations of beauty called up by Hyperion, Jove and Mars, or the exquisite picture evoked by the contemplation of the grace of his father's poise:

> *like the herald Mercury*
> *New-lighted on a heav-*
>   *en-kissing hill.*

These beauties are specially noticeable in the many personifications, as when, with Horatio, we see "the morn, in russet mantle clad," as she "walks o'er the dew of yon high eastward hill," or, with Hamlet, watch Laertes leaping into Ophelia's grave, and ask,

> *Whose phrase of sorrow*
> *Conjures the wandering stars and makes*
>   *them stand*
> *Like wonder-wounded hearers?*
> (5.1.263–265)

Peace, with her wheaten garland, Niobe all tears, Ophelia's garments "heavy with their drink," which pull her from her "melodious lay" to muddy death, or the magnificent picture of the two sides of the queen's nature at war, as seen by the elder Hamlet:

> *But look, amazement on thy mother sits:*
> *O, step between her and her fighting soul;*
> (3.4.126–127)

these, and many more, are the unforgettable and radiant touches of beauty in a play which has, as images, much that is sombre and unpleasant. ∎

Outline the major categories of images to be found in *Hamlet*. List at least three examples of each kind of image.

Create a collage of words and pictures that focuses on the imagery in the play.

SHAKESPEARE IN THE BUSH

by Laura Bohannan

"Hamlet appeals to all nations, expresses the thought, the yearnings, the dilemmas of all, because Shakespeare deals not with national characteristics, but with universal ideas, struggles and despair common to human nature."
—Frederic Harrison

Just before I left Oxford for the Tiv in West Africa, conversation turned to the season at Stratford. "You Americans," said a friend, "often have difficulty with Shakespeare. He was, after all, a very English poet, and one can easily misinterpret the universal by misunderstanding the particular."

I protested that human nature is pretty much the same the whole world over; at least the general plot and motivation of the greater tragedies would always be clear — everywhere — although some details of custom might have to be explained and difficulties of translation might produce other slight changes. To end an argument we could not conclude, my friend gave me a copy of *Hamlet* to study in the African bush: it would, he hoped, lift my mind above its primitive surroundings, and possibly I might, by prolonged meditation, achieve the grace of correct interpretation.

It was my second field trip to that African tribe, and I thought myself ready to live in one of its remote sections — an area difficult to cross even on foot. I eventually settled on the hillock of a very knowledgeable old man, the head of a homestead of some hundred and forty people, all of whom were either his close relatives or their wives and children. Like the other elders in the vicinity, the old man spent most of his time performing ceremonies seldom seen these days in the more accessible parts of the tribe. I was delighted. Soon there would be three months of enforced isolation and leisure, between the harvest that takes place just before the rising of the swamps and the clearing of new farms when the water goes down. Then, I thought, they would have even more time to perform ceremonies and explain them to me.

I was quite mistaken. Most of the ceremonies demanded the presence of elders from several homesteads. As the swamps rose, the old men found it too difficult to walk from one homestead to the next, and the ceremonies gradually ceased. As the swamps rose even higher, all activities but one came to an end. The women brewed beer from maize and millet. Men, women, and children sat on their hillocks and drank it.

People began to drink at dawn. By mid-morning the whole homestead was singing, dancing, and drumming. When it rained, people had to sit inside their huts: there they drank and sang or they drank and told stories. In any case, by noon or before, I either had to join the party or retire to my own hut and my books. "One does not discuss serious matters when there is beer. Come, drink with us." Since I lacked their capacity for the thick native beer, I spent more and more time with *Hamlet*. Before the end of the second month, grace descended on me. I was quite sure that *Hamlet* had only one possible interpretation, and that one universally obvious.

Early every morning, in the hope of having some serious talk before the beer party, I used to call on the old man at his reception hut — a circle of posts supporting a thatched roof above a low mud wall to keep out wind and rain. One day I crawled through the low doorway and found most of the men of the homestead sitting huddled in their ragged cloths on stools, low plank beds, and reclining chairs, warming themselves against the chill of the rain around a smoky fire. In the centre were three pots of beer. The party had started.

The old man greeted me cordially. "Sit down and drink." I accepted a large calabash full of beer, poured some into a small drinking gourd, and tossed it down. Then I poured some more into the same gourd for the man second in seniority to my host before I handed my calabash over to a young man for further distribution. Important people shouldn't ladle beer themselves.

"It is better like this," the old man said, looking at me approvingly and plucking at the thatch that had caught in my hair. "You should sit and drink with us more often. Your servants tell me that when you are not with us, you sit inside your hut looking at a paper."

The old man was acquainted with four kinds of "papers": tax receipts, bride price receipts, court fee receipts, and letters. The messenger who brought him letters from the chief used them mainly as a badge of office, for he always knew what was in them and told the old man. Personal letters for the few who had relatives in the government or mission stations were kept until someone went to a large market where there was a letter writer and reader. Since my arrival, letters were brought to me to be read. A few men also brought me bride price receipts, privately, with requests to change the figures to a higher sum. I found moral arguments were of no avail, since in-laws are fair game, and the technical hazards of forgery difficult to explain to an illiterate people. I did not wish them to think me silly enough to look at any such papers for days on end, and I hastily explained that my "paper" was one of the "things of long ago" of my country.

"Ah," said the old man. "Tell us."

I protested that I was not a storyteller. Storytelling is a skilled art among them; their standards are high, and the audiences critical — and vocal in their criticism. I protested in vain. This morning they wanted to hear a story while they drank. They threatened to tell me no more stories until I told them one of mine. Finally, the old man promised that no one would criticize my style "for we know you are struggling with our language." "But," put in one of the elders, "you must explain what we do not understand, as we do when we tell you our stories." Realizing that here was my chance to prove *Hamlet* universally intelligible, I agreed.

The old man handed me some more beer to help me on with my storytelling. Men filled their long wooden pipes and knocked coals from the fire to place in the pipe bowls; then, puffing contentedly, they sat back to listen. I began in the proper style, "Not yesterday, not yesterday, but long ago, a thing

occurred. One night three men were keeping watch outside the homestead of the great chief, when suddenly they saw the former chief approach them."

"Why was he no longer their chief?"

"He was dead," I explained. "That is why they were troubled and afraid when they saw him."

"Impossible," began one of the elders, handing his pipe on to his neighbour, who interrupted, "Of course it wasn't the dead chief. It was an omen sent by a witch. Go on."

Slightly shaken, I continued. "One of these three was a man who knew things" — the closest translation for scholar, but unfortunately it also meant witch. The second elder looked triumphantly at the first. "So he spoke to the dead chief saying, 'Tell us what we must do so you may rest in your grave,' but the dead chief did not answer. He vanished, and they could see him no more. Then the man who knew things — his name was Horatio — said this event was the affair of the dead chief's son, Hamlet."

There was a general shaking of heads round the circle. "Had the dead chief no living brothers? Or was this son the chief?"

"No," I replied. "That is, he had one living brother who became the chief when the elder brother died."

The old men muttered: such omens were matters for chiefs and elders, not for youngsters; no good could come of going behind a chief's back; clearly Horatio was not a man who knew things.

"Yes, he was," I insisted, shooing a chicken away from my beer. "In our country the son is next to the father. The dead chief's younger brother had become the great chief.

"… NO GOOD COULD COME OF GOING BEHIND A CHIEF'S BACK; CLEARLY HORATIO WAS NOT A MAN WHO KNEW THINGS."

He had also married his elder brother's widow only about a month after the funeral."

"He did well," the old man beamed and announced to the others, "I told you that if we knew more about Europeans, we would find they really were very like us. In our country also," he added to me, "the younger brother marries the elder brother's widow and becomes the father of his children. Now, if your uncle, who married your widowed mother, is your father's full brother, then he will be a real father to you. Did Hamlet's father and uncle have one mother?"

His question barely penetrated my mind; I was too upset and thrown too far off balance by having one of the most important elements of *Hamlet* knocked straight out of the picture. Rather uncertainly I said that I thought they had the same mother, but I wasn't sure — the story didn't say. The old man told me severely that these genealogical details made all the difference and that when I got home I must ask the elders about it. He shouted out the door to one of his younger wives to bring his goatskin bag.

Determined to save what I could of the other motif, I took a deep breath and began again. "The son Hamlet was very sad because his mother had married again so quickly. There was no need for her to do so, and it is our custom for a widow not to go to her next husband until she has mourned for two years."

"Two years is too long," objected the wife, who had appeared with the old man's battered goatskin bag. "Who will hoe your farms for you while you have no husband?"

"Hamlet," I retorted without thinking, "was old enough to hoe his mother's farms himself. There was no need for her to remarry." No one looked convinced. I gave up. "His mother and the great chief told Hamlet not to be sad, for the great chief himself would be a father to Hamlet. Furthermore, Hamlet would be the next chief: therefore he must stay to learn the things of a chief. Hamlet agreed to remain, and all the rest went off to drink beer."

While I paused, perplexed at how to render Hamlet's disgusted soliloquy to an audience convinced that Claudius and Gertrude had behaved in the best possible manner, one of the younger men asked me who had married the other wives of the dead chief.

"He had no other wives," I told him.

"But a chief must have many wives! How else can he brew beer and prepare food for all his guests?"

I said firmly that in our country even chiefs had only one wife, that they had servants to do their work, and that they paid them from tax money.

It was better, they returned, for a chief to have many wives and sons who would help him hoe his farms and feed his people; then everyone loved the chief who gave much and took nothing — taxes were a bad thing.

I agreed with the last comment, but for the rest fell back on their favourite way of fobbing off my questions: "That is the way it is done, so that is how we do it."

I decided to skip the soliloquy. Even if Claudius was here thought quite right to marry his brother's widow, there remained the poison motif, and I knew they would disapprove of fratricide. More hopefully I resumed, "That night Hamlet kept watch with the three who had seen his dead father. The dead chief again appeared, and although the others were afraid, Hamlet followed his dead father off to one side. When they were alone, Hamlet's dead father spoke."

"Omens can't talk!" The old man was emphatic.

"Hamlet's dead father wasn't an omen. Seeing him might have been an omen, but he was not." My audience looked as confused as I sounded. "It *was* Hamlet's dead father. It was a thing we call a 'ghost.'" I had to use the English word, for unlike many of the neighbouring tribes, these people didn't believe in the survival after death of any individuating part of the personality.

"What is a 'ghost'? An omen?"

"No, a 'ghost' is someone who is dead but who walks around and can talk, and people can hear him and see him but not touch him."

They objected. "One can touch zombis."

"No, no! It was not a dead body the witches had animated to sacrifice and eat. No one else made Hamlet's dead father walk. He did it himself."

"Dead men can't walk," protested my audience as one man.

I was quite willing to compromise. "A 'ghost' is the dead man's shadow."

But again they objected. "Dead men cast no shadows."

"They do in my country," I snapped.

The old man quelled the babble of disbelief that arose immediately and told me with that insincere, but courteous, agreement one extends to the fancies of the young, ignorant, and superstitious, "No doubt in your country the dead can also walk without being zombis." From the depths of his bag he produced a withered fragment of kola nut, bit off one end to show it wasn't poisoned, and handed me the rest as a peace offering.

"Anyhow," I resumed, "Hamlet's dead father said that his own brother, the one who became chief, had poisoned him. He wanted Hamlet to avenge him. Hamlet believed this in his heart, for he did not like his father's brother." I took another swallow of beer. "In the country of the great chief, living in the same homestead, for it was a very large one, was an important elder who was often with the chief to advise and help him. His name was Polonius. Hamlet was courting his daughter, but her father and her brother ... [I cast hastily about for some tribal analogy] warned her not to let Hamlet visit her when she was alone on the farm, for he would be a great chief and so could not marry her."

"Why not?" asked the wife, who had settled down on the edge of the old man's chair. He frowned at her for asking stupid questions and growled, "They lived in the same homestead."

"That was not the reason," I informed them. "Polonius was a stranger who lived in the homestead because he helped the chief, not because he was a relative."

"Then why couldn't Hamlet marry her?"

"He could have," I explained, "but Polonius didn't think he would. After all, Hamlet was a man of great importance who ought to marry a chief's daughter, for in his country a man could have only one wife. Polonius was afraid that if Hamlet made love to his daughter, then no one else would give a high price for her."

"That might be true," remarked one of the shrewder elders, "but a chief's son would give his mistress's father enough presents and patronage to more than make up the difference. Polonius sounds like a fool to me."

"Many people think he was," I agreed. "Meanwhile Polonius sent his son Laertes off to Paris to learn the things of that country, for it was the homestead of a very great chief indeed. Because he was afraid that Laertes might waste a lot of money on beer

THE OLD MAN INTERRUPTED, WITH DEEP CUNNING, "WHY SHOULD A FATHER LIE TO HIS SON?" HE ASKED.

and women and gambling, or get into trouble by fighting, he sent one of his servants to Paris secretly, to spy out what Laertes was doing. One day Hamlet came upon Polonius's daughter Ophelia. He behaved so oddly that he frightened her. Indeed" — I was fumbling for words to express the dubious quality of Hamlet's madness — "the chief and many others had also noticed that when Hamlet talked one could understand the words but not what they meant. Many people thought that he had become mad." My audience suddenly became much more attentive. "The great chief wanted to know what was wrong with Hamlet, so he sent for two of Hamlet's age mates [school friends would have taken long explanation] to talk to Hamlet and find out what troubled his heart. Hamlet, seeing that they had been bribed by the chief to betray him, told them nothing. Polonius, however, insisted that Hamlet was mad because he had been forbidden to see Ophelia, whom he loved."

"Why," inquired a bewildered voice, "should anyone bewitch Hamlet on that account?"

"Bewitch him?"

"Yes, only witchcraft can make anyone mad, unless, of course, one sees the beings that lurk in the forest."

I stopped being a storyteller, took out my notebook and demanded to be told more about these two causes of madness. Even while they spoke and I jotted notes, I tried to calculate the effect of this new factor on the plot. Hamlet had not been exposed to the beings that lurk in the forests. Only his relatives in the male line could bewitch him. Barring relatives not mentioned by

Shakespeare, it had to be Claudius who was attempting to harm him. And, of course, it was.

For the moment I staved off questions by saying that the great chief also refused to believe that Hamlet was mad for the love of Ophelia and nothing else. "He was sure that something much more important was troubling Hamlet's heart."

"Now Hamlet's age mates," I continued, "had brought with them a famous storyteller. Hamlet decided to have this man tell the chief and all his homestead a story about a man who had poisoned his brother because he desired his brother's wife and wished to be chief himself. Hamlet was sure the great chief could not hear the story without making a sign if he was indeed guilty, and then he would discover whether his dead father had told him the truth."

The old man interrupted, with deep cunning, "Why should a father lie to his son?" he asked.

I hedged: "Hamlet wasn't sure that it really was his dead father." It was impossible to say anything, in that language, about devil-inspired visions.

"You mean," he said, "it actually was an omen, and he knew witches sometimes send false ones. Hamlet was a fool not to go to one skilled in reading omens and divining the truth in the first place. A man-who-sees-the-truth could have told him how his father died, if he really had been poisoned, and if there was witchcraft in it; then Hamlet could have called the elders to settle the matter."

The shrewd elder ventured to disagree. "Because his father's brother was a great chief, one-who-sees-the-truth might therefore have been afraid to tell it. I think it was for that reason that a friend of Hamlet's father — a witch and an elder — sent an omen so his friend's son would know. Was the omen true?"

"Yes," I said, abandoning ghosts and the devil; a witch-sent omen it would have to be. "It was true, for when the storyteller was telling his tale before all the homestead, the great chief rose in fear. Afraid that Hamlet knew his secret he planned to have him killed."

The stage set of the next bit presented some difficulties of translation. I began cautiously. "The great chief told Hamlet's mother to find out from her son what he knew. But because a woman's children are always first in her heart, he had the important elder Polonius hide behind a cloth that hung against the wall of Hamlet's mother's sleeping hut. Hamlet started to scold his mother for what she had done."

There was a shocked murmur from everyone. A man should never scold his mother.

"She called out in fear, and Polonius moved behind the cloth. Shouting, 'A rat!' Hamlet took his machete and slashed through the cloth." I paused for dramatic effect. "He had killed Polonius!"

The old men looked at each other in supreme disgust. "That Polonius truly was a fool and a man who knew nothing! What child would not know enough to shout, 'It's me!'" With a pang, I remembered that these people are ardent hunters, always armed with bow, arrow, and machete; at the first rustle in the grass an arrow is aimed and ready, and the hunter shouts "Game!" If no human voice answers immediately, the arrow speeds on its way. Like a good hunter Hamlet had shouted, "A rat!"

I rushed in to save Polonius's reputation. "Polonius did speak. Hamlet heard him. But he thought it was the chief and wished to kill him to avenge his father. He had meant to kill him earlier that evening. ..." I broke down, unable to describe to these pagans, who had no belief in individual afterlife, the difference between dying at one's prayers and dying "unhousell'd, disappointed, unaneled."

This time I had shocked my audience seriously. "For a man to raise his hand against his father's brother and the one who has become his father — that is a terrible thing. The elders ought to let such a man be bewitched."

I nibbled at my kola nut in some perplexity, then pointed out that after all the man had killed Hamlet's father.

"No," pronounced the old man, speaking less to me than to the young men sitting behind the elders. "If your father's brother has killed your father, you must appeal to your father's age mates; *they* may avenge him. No man may use violence against his senior relatives." Another thought struck him. "But if his father's brother had indeed been wicked enough to bewitch Hamlet and make him mad that would be a good story indeed, for it would be his fault that Hamlet, being mad, no longer had any sense and thus was ready to kill his father's brother."

There was a murmur of applause. *Hamlet* was again a good story to them, but it no longer seemed quite the same story to me. As I thought over the coming complications of plot and motive, I lost courage and decided to skim over dangerous ground quickly.

"The great chief," I went on, "was not sorry that Hamlet had killed Polonius. It gave him a reason to send Hamlet away, with his two treacherous age mates, with letters to a chief of a far country, saying that Hamlet should be killed. But Hamlet changed the writing on their papers, so that the chief killed his age mates instead." I encountered a reproachful glare from one of the men whom I had told undetectable forgery was not merely immoral but beyond human skill. I looked the other way.

"Before Hamlet could return, Laertes came back for his father's funeral. The great chief told him Hamlet had killed Polonius. Laertes swore to kill Hamlet because of this, and because his sister Ophelia, hearing her father had been killed by the man she loved, went mad and drowned in the river."

"Have you already forgotten what we told you?" The old man was reproachful. "One cannot take vengeance on a madman; Hamlet killed Polonius in his madness. As for the girl, she not only went mad, she was drowned. Only witches can make people drown. Water itself can't hurt anything. It is merely something one drinks and bathes in."

HAMLET WAS AGAIN A GOOD STORY TO THEM, BUT IT NO LONGER SEEMED QUITE THE SAME STORY TO ME.

I began to get cross. "If you don't like the story, I'll stop."

The old man made soothing noises and himself poured me some more beer. "You tell the story well, and we are listening. But it is clear that the elders of your country have never told you what the story really means. No, don't interrupt! We believe you when you say your marriage customs are different, or your clothes and weapons. But people are the same everywhere; therefore, there are always witches and it is we, the elders, who know how witches work. We told you it was the great chief who wished to kill Hamlet, and now your own words have proved us right. Who were Ophelia's male relatives?"

"There were only her father and her brother." Hamlet was clearly out of my hands.

"There must have been many more; this also you must ask of your elders when you get back to your country. From what you tell us, since Polonius was dead, it must have been Laertes who killed Ophelia, although I do not see the reason for it."

We had emptied one pot of beer, and the old men argued the point with slightly tipsy interest. Finally one of them demanded of me, "What did the servant of Polonius say on his return?"

With difficulty I recollected Reynaldo and his mission. "I don't think he did return before Polonius was killed."

"Listen," said the elder, "and I will tell you how it was and how your story will go, then you may tell me if I am right. Polonius knew his son would get into trouble, and so he did. He had many fines to pay for fighting, and debts from gambling. But he had only two ways of getting money quickly. One was to marry off his sister at once, but it is difficult to find a man who will marry a woman desired by the son of a chief. For if the chief's heir commits adultery with your wife, what can you do? Only a fool calls a case against a man who will someday be his judge. Therefore Laertes had to take the second way: he killed his sister by witchcraft, drowning her so he could secretly sell her body to the witches."

I raised an objection. "They found her body and buried it. Indeed Laertes jumped into the grave to see his sister once more — so, you see, the body was truly there. Hamlet, who had just come back, jumped in after him."

"What did I tell you?" The elder appealed to the others. "Laertes was up to no good with his sister's body. Hamlet prevented him, because the chief's heir, like the chief, does not wish any other man to grow rich and powerful. Laertes would be angry, because he would have killed his sister without benefit to himself. In our country he would try to kill Hamlet for that reason. Is this not what happened?"

"More or less," I admitted. "When the great chief found Hamlet was still alive, he encouraged Laertes to try to kill Hamlet and arranged a fight with machetes between them. In the fight both the young men were wounded to death. Hamlet's mother drank the poisoned beer that the chief meant for Hamlet in case he won the fight. When he saw his mother die of poison, Hamlet, dying, managed to kill his father's brother with his machete."

"You see, I was right!" exclaimed the elder.

"That was a very good story," added the old man, "and you told it with very few mistakes. There was just one more error, at the very end. The poison Hamlet's mother drank was obviously meant for the survivor of the fight, whichever it was. If Laertes had won, the great chief would have poisoned him, for no one would know that he arranged Hamlet's death. Then, too, he need not fear Laertes' witchcraft; it takes a strong heart to kill one's only sister by witchcraft.

"Sometime," concluded the old man, gathering his ragged toga about him, "you must tell us some more stories of your country. We, who are elders, will instruct you in their true meaning, so that when you return to your own land your elders will see that you have not been sitting in the bush, but among those who know things and who have taught you wisdom." ■

Do you agree that "human nature is pretty much the same the whole world over"? Why or why not?

In groups or in your journal, consider some of the major ironies in this story. Would the tribal elders agree with Frederic Harrison's statement?

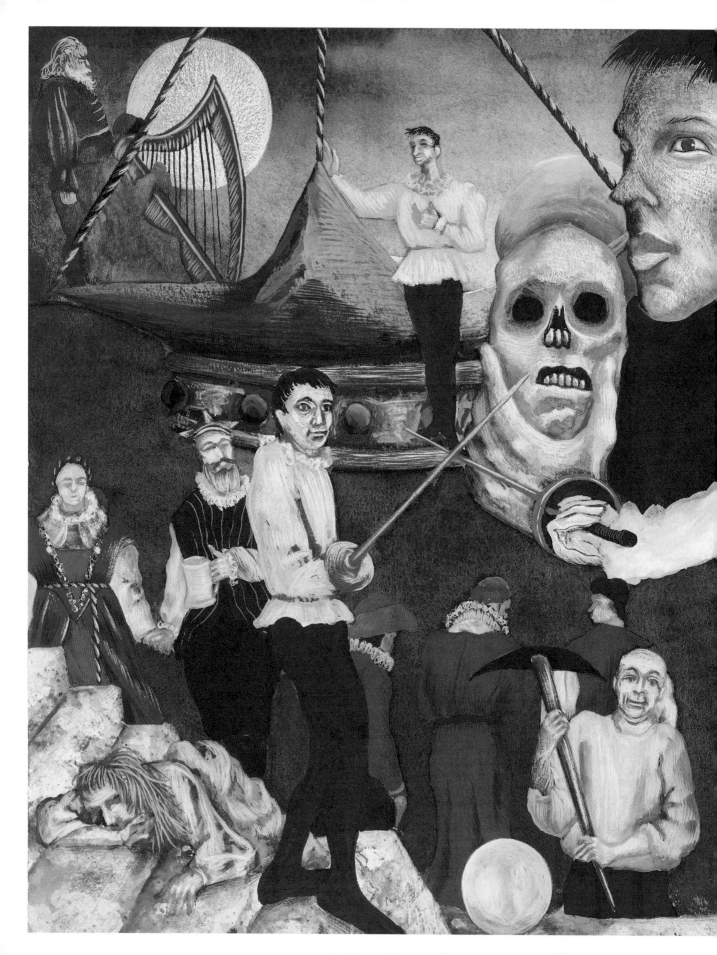

15-Minute HAMLET

by Tom Stoppard

Hamlet *is the longest of Shakespeare's plays. It takes over four hours merely to read the entire text, let alone act it out. Is it possible to compress the action into 15 minutes?*

Prologue

Enter SHAKESPEARE, *bows.*

SHAKESPEARE. For this relief, much thanks.
Though I am native here, and to the manner born,
It is a custom more honoured in the breach
Than in the observance
Well.
Something is rotten in the state of Denmark.
To be, or not to be, that is the question.
There are more things in heaven and earth
Than are dreamt of in your philosophy —

There's a divinity that shapes our ends,
Rough hew them how we will
Though this be madness, yet there is method in it.
I must be cruel only to be kind;
Hold, as t'were, the mirror up to nature.
A countenance more in sorrow than in anger.
      (LADY *in audience shouts "Marmalade."*)
The lady doth protest too much.
Cat will mew, and Dogg will have his day!
      (*Bows and exits. End of prologue.*)

A castle battlement. Thunder and wind. Enter two GUARDS:
BERNARDO / MARCELLUS *and* FRANCISCO / HORATIO.
GUARDS *on the platform.*

BERNARDO. Who's there?

FRANCISCO. Nay, answer me.

BERNARDO. Long live the King. Get thee to bed.

FRANCISCO. For this relief, much thanks.

BERNARDO. What, has this thing appeared again tonight?

FRANCISCO. Peace, break thee off: look where it comes again!

BERNARDO. Looks it not like the King?

FRANCISCO. By heaven, I charge thee, speak!

BERNARDO. (*Points and looks* L.) 'Tis here.

FRANCISCO. (*Points and looks* R.) 'Tis there.

BERNARDO. (*Looks* R.) 'Tis gone.

FRANCISCO. But look, the morn in russet mantle clad
    Walks o'er the dew of yon high eastern hill.

(*On "But look" a cut-out sun shoots up over the stage left screen,
and descends here.*)

BERNARDO. Let us impart what we have seen tonight
    Unto young Hamlet. (*Exeunt. End scene.*)

*A room of state within the castle. A cut-out crown hinges over
stage left screen. Flourish of trumpets. Enter* CLAUDIUS *and*
GERTRUDE.

CLAUDIUS. Though yet of Hamlet our dear brother's death
    The memory be green
                    (*Enter* HAMLET.)
    Our sometime sister, now our Queen
    Have we taken to wife.
    But how, my cousin Hamlet, and my son —

HAMLET. A little more than kin, and less than kind.
                    (*Exit* CLAUDIUS *and* GERTRUDE.)
    O that this too too solid flesh would melt!
    That it should come to this — but two months dead!
    So loving to my mother: Frailty, thy name is woman!
    Married with mine uncle, my father's brother.
    The funeral baked meats did coldly furnish forth
    The marriage tables. (*The crown hinges down.* HORATIO *rush-
    es on.*)

HORATIO. My lord, I think I saw him yesternight —
    The King, your father — upon the platform where we
    watched.

HAMLET. 'Tis very strange.

HORATIO. Armed, my lord —
    A countenance more in sorrow than in anger.

HAMLET. My father's spirit in arms? All is not well.
    Would the night were come! (*The moon hinges up. Exeunt to
    parapet. End scene.*)

198

The castle battlements at night. Noise of carouse, cannon, fireworks. HORATIO *and* HAMLET *appear on platform.*

HAMLET. The King doth wake tonight and takes his rouse,
  Though I am native here and to the manner born,
  It is a custom more honoured in the breach
  Than in the observance. (*Wind noise.*)
HORATIO. Look, my lord, it comes. (*Points.*)
      (*Enter* GHOST *above the wall built of blocks.*)
HAMLET. Angels and ministers of grace defend us!
  Something is rotten in the state of Denmark!
  Alas, poor ghost.
GHOST. I am thy father's spirit.
  Revenge his foul and most unnatural murder.
HAMLET. Murder?
GHOST. The serpent that did sting thy father's life.
  Now wears his crown.
HAMLET. O my prophetic soul? Mine uncle?
          (*Exit* GHOST. *To* HORATIO.)
  There are more things in heaven and earth
  Than are dreamt of in your philosophy.
          (*Exit* HORATIO.)
  Hereafter I shall think meet
  To put an antic disposition on.
  The time is out of joint. O cursed spite
  That ever I was born to set it right! (*Exit* HAMLET. *Moon hinges down. End scene.*)

A room within. Crown hinges up. Flourish of trumpets leading into flute and harpsichord music. Enter POLONIUS; OPHELIA *rushes on.*

POLONIUS. How now Ophelia, what's the matter?
OPHELIA. My lord, as I was sewing in my chamber,
  Lord Hamlet with his doublet all unbraced;
  No hat upon his head, pale as his shirt,
  His knees knocking each other, and with a look so piteous
  He comes before me.
POLONIUS. Mad for thy love?
  I have found the very cause of Hamlet's lunacy.
          (*Enter* HAMLET, *exit* OPHELIA.)
  Look where sadly the poor wretch comes reading
  What do you read, my lord?
HAMLET. Words, words, words.
POLONIUS. Though this be madness, yet there is method in it.
HAMLET. I am but mad north northwest: when the wind is

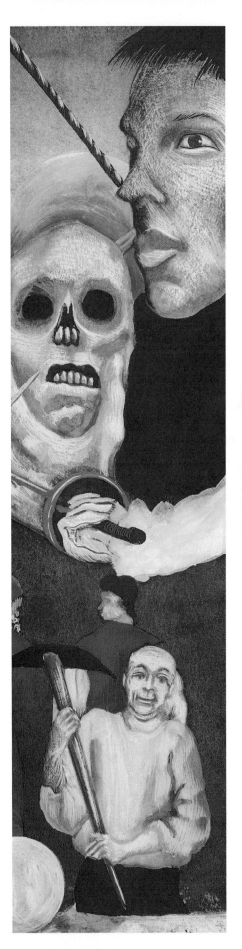

199

southerly I know a hawk from a handsaw.
(*Slams book shut and against* POLONIUS'S *chest.*)
POLONIUS. The actors are come hither, my lord. (*Exits.*)
HAMLET. We'll hear a play tomorrow.
 I have heard that guilty creatures sitting at a play
 Have by the very cunning of the scene
 Been struck so to the soul that presently
 They have proclaimed their malefactions.
 I'll have these players play something
 Like the murder of my father before mine uncle.
 If he but blench, I know my course.
 The play's the thing
 Wherein I'll catch the conscience of the King.
      (*Pause.*)
 To be, or not to be (*Puts dagger, pulled from his sleeve, to heart. Enter* CLAUDIUS *and* OPHELIA.)
 that is the question.
OPHELIA. My lord —
HAMLET. Get thee to a nunnery! (*Exit* OPHELIA *and* HAMLET.)
CLAUDIUS. Love? His affections do not that way tend
 There's something in his soul
 O'er which his melancholy sits on brood.
 He shall with speed to England. (*Exit* CLAUDIUS. *End scene.*)

A hall within the castle. Flourish of trumpets. Enter HAMLET *and*
 OPHELIA, MARCELLUS *and* HORATIO *joking*, CLAUDIUS *and*
 GERTRUDE. *Puppet players appear above stage left screen.*

HAMLET. (*To puppet players.*) Speak the speech, I pray you, as I
 pronounced it to you; trippingly on the tongue.
 Hold, as t'were, the mirror up to nature
(ALL *sit to watch puppet play. Masque music.*) (*To* GERTRUDE.)
 Madam, how like you the play?
GERTRUDE. The lady doth protest too much, methinks.
HAMLET. He poisons him in the garden of his estate. You shall
 see anon how the murderer gets the love of Gonzago's wife.
 (CLAUDIUS *rises.*) The King rises! (*Music stops, hubbub noise
 starts.*) What, frighted with false fire? (*Exit*, CLAUDIUS.)
ALL. Give o'er the play. (*Puppets disappear, crown disappears.*)
HAMLET. Lights! Lights! Lights! I'll take the ghost's word for a
 thousand pounds! (*Exeunt* ALL *except* POLONIUS.)
POLONIUS. (*Standing at side.*) He's going to his mother's closet.
 Behind the arras I'll convey myself to hear the process. (*End
 scene.*)

The Queen's apartment. POLONIUS *stands by stage right screen and hinges a curtain out from behind it. Lute music. Enter* HAMLET *and* GERTRUDE.

HAMLET. Now Mother, what's the matter?

GERTRUDE. Hamlet, thou hast thy father much offended.

HAMLET. Mother, you have my father much offended. (*Holds her.*)

GERTRUDE. What wilt thou do? Thou wilt not murder me? Help! Help! Ho!

POLONIUS. (*Behind the arras.*) Help!

HAMLET. How now? A rat? (*Stabs* POLONIUS.) Dead for a ducat, dead!

GERTRUDE. O me, what hast thou done?

HAMLET. Nay, I know not.

GERTRUDE. Alas, he's mad.

HAMLET. I must be cruel only to be kind. Good night, Mother. (*Exit* HAMLET *dragging* POLONIUS. *Exit* GERTRUDE, *sobbing. Arras hinges back. End scene.*)

Another room in the castle. Flourish of trumpets. Crown hinges up. Enter CLAUDIUS *and* HAMLET.

CLAUDIUS. Now, Hamlet, where's Polonius?

HAMLET. At supper. (*Hiding his sword clumsily.*)

CLAUDIUS. Hamlet, this deed must send thee hence.
Therefore prepare thyself,
Everything is bent for England.
               (*Exit* HAMLET.)
And England, if my love thou holds't at aught,
Thou may'st not coldly set our sov'reign process,
The present death of Hamlet. Do it, England! (*Exit* CLAUDIUS. *Crown hinges down. End scene.*)

At sea. Sea music. A sail appears above stage left screen. Enter HAMLET *on platform, swaying as if on ship's bridge. He wipes his eyes, and becomes seasick. End sea music. Exit* HAMLET, *holding his hand to his mouth.*

Yet another room in the castle. Flourish of trumpets. Enter CLAUDIUS *and* LAERTES.

LAERTES. Where is my father?

CLAUDIUS. Dead. (*Enter* OPHELIA *in mad trance, singing and carrying a bouquet of flowers wrapped in cellophane and with a*

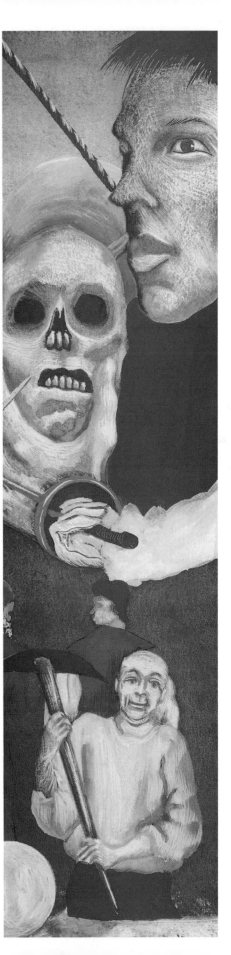

201

red ribbon. Lute music.)

OPHELIA. They bore him barefaced on the bier.
>   (*After her first line she gives a flower to* LAERTES.)
>   Hey nonny nonny, hey nonny. (*After her second, she slams the bouquet in* CLAUDIUS'S *stomach. It is, of course, the missing bouquet from the speech-day ceremony.*)

OPHELIA. And on his grave rained many a tear ...

(*Half-way through her third line she disappears behind the screen stage left and pauses.* CLAUDIUS *and* LAERTES *peer round the side she disappeared and she runs round the other behind them.*)

LAERTES. O heat dry up my brains — O kind Sister,
>   (OPHELIA *falls to ground. She catches a flower thrown*
>   *from stage right screen.*)
>   Had'st thou thy wits, and did'st persuade revenge
>   It could not move thus.

CLAUDIUS. And where the offence is, let the great axe fall. (*Exit* CLAUDIUS *and* LAERTES. OPHELIA *sits up to reach gravestone which she swings down to conceal her. Bell tolls four times. End scene.*)

A churchyard. Enter GRAVEDIGGER *and* HAMLET.

HAMLET. Ere we were two days at sea, a pirate of very warlike appointment gave us chase. In the grapple I boarded them. On the instant they got clear of our ship; so I alone became their prisoner. They have dealt with me like thieves of mercy.

GRAVEDIGGER. What is he that builds stronger than either the mason, the shipwright or the carpenter?

HAMLET. A gravemaker. The houses he makes will last till Doomsday. (GRAVEDIGGER *gives skull to* HAMLET.) Whose was it?

GRAVEDIGGER. This same skull, Sir, was Yorick's skull, the King's jester.

HAMLET. Alas, poor Yorick. (*Returns skull to* GRAVEDIGGER.) But soft — that is Laertes. (*Withdraws to side.*) (*Enter* LAERTES.)

LAERTES. What ceremony else?
>   Lay her in the earth,
>   May violets spring. I tell thee, churlish priest ...
>   (*Enter* CLAUDIUS *and* GERTRUDE.)
>   A ministering angel shall my sister be
>   When thou liest howling.

HAMLET. (*Hiding behind the brick platform.*) What, the fair Ophelia?

LAERTES. O treble woe. Hold off the earth awhile,

Till I have caught her once more in my arms.

HAMLET. (*Re-entering acting area.*)

What is he whose grief bears such an emphasis?
This is I, Hamlet the Dane!

LAERTES. The devil take thy soul. (*They grapple.*)

HAMLET. Away thy hand! (CLAUDIUS *and* GERTRUDE *pull them apart.*)

CLAUDIUS AND GERTRUDE. Hamlet! Hamlet!

HAMLET. I loved Ophelia. What wilt thou do for her?

GERTRUDE. O he is mad. Laertes! (*Exit* CLAUDIUS, GERTRUDE *and* LAERTES.)

HAMLET. The cat will mew, and dog will have his day!
(*Exeunt. End scene.*)

A hall in the castle. Flourish of trumpets, crown hinges up.
Enter HAMLET.

HAMLET. There's a divinity that shapes our ends, rough hew
them how we will. But thou would'st not think how ill all's
here about my heart. But 'tis no matter. We defy augury.
There is a special providence in the fall of a sparrow. If it be
now, 'tis not to come; if it be not to come, it will be now; if it
be not now, yet it will come. The readiness is all. (LAERTES
enters with OSRIC *bearing swords followed by* CLAUDIUS *and*
GERTRUDE *with goblets.*) Come on, Sir!

LAERTES. Come, my lord. (*Fanfare of trumpets. They draw and
duel.*)

HAMLET. One.

LAERTES. No.

HAMLET. Judgement?

OSRIC. A hit, a very palpable hit.

CLAUDIUS. Stay, give me a drink.
Hamlet, this pearl is thine, here's to thy health.
(*Drops pearl in goblet.*)
Give him the cup.

GERTRUDE. The Queen carouses to thy fortune, Hamlet.

CLAUDIUS. Gertrude, do not drink!

GERTRUDE. I will, my lord. (*Drinks.*)

LAERTES. My lord, I'll hit him now.
Have at you, now! (*They grapple and fight.*)

CLAUDIUS. Part them, they are incensed.
They bleed on both sides. (OSRIC *and* CLAUDIUS *part them.*)

LAERTES. I am justly killed by my own treachery.
(*Falls.*)

GERTRUDE. The drink, the drink! I am poisoned!

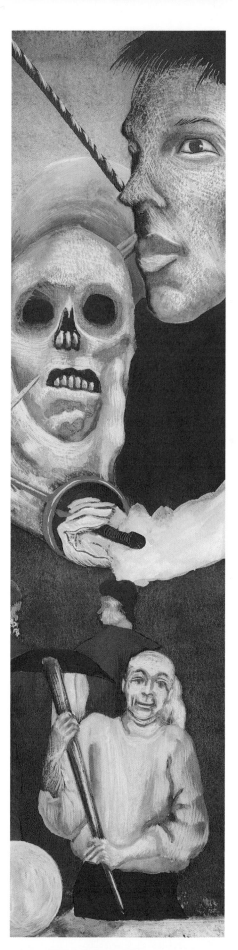

(*Dies.*)

HAMLET. Treachery! Seek it out. (*Enter* FORTINBRAS.)
　　Do it, England.

LAERTES. It is here, Hamlet. Hamlet thou art slain.
Lo, here I lie, never to rise again.
The King, the King's to blame.

HAMLET. The point envenomed too?
Then venom to thy work. (*Kills* CLAUDIUS.) (*Crown hinges down.*)

LAERTES. Exchange forgiveness with me, noble Ha . . .
m . . . (*Dies.*)

HAMLET. I follow thee.
I cannot live to hear the news from England.
the rest is silence. (*Dies*)

HORATIO. Good night sweet prince,
And flights of angels sing thee to thy rest.
(*Turns to face away from audience.*)
Go, bid the soldiers shoot.

(*Four shots heard from off-
stage. ALL stand, bow once and exit.
End.*)

❧　❧　❧

This compressed version of *Hamlet* is usually performed at a fever pitch. In order to read the play quickly, it .be necessary to prepare in advance. In groups of five (doubling of parts will be necessary) prepare a presentation of the play.

Has Stoppard captured the essence of the play in his version? Would someone not familiar with *Hamlet* be able to follow the characters and the plot of the play?

ELEGY OF Fortinbras

for C. M.
by Zbigniew Herbert

✠ ✠ ✠

Shakespeare's Fortinbras does not have much to say about Hamlet at the end of the play. If Fortinbras were given a second opportunity to deliver a eulogy, what would he say?

Now that we're alone we can talk prince man to man
though you lie on the stairs and see no more than a dead ant
nothing but black sun with broken rays
I could never think of your hands without smiling
and now that they lie on the stone like fallen nests
they are as defenceless as before The end is exactly this
The hands lie apart The sword lies apart The head apart
and the knight's feet in soft slippers

You will have a soldier's funeral without having been
    a soldier
the only ritual I am acquainted with a little
There will be no candles no singing only cannon-fuses and bursts
crepe dragged on the pavement helmets boots artillery
    horses drums drums I know nothing exquisite
those will be my manoeuvres before I start to rule
one has to take the city by the neck and shake it a bit

Anyhow you had to perish Hamlet you were not for life

Related Readings

you believed in crystal notions not in human clay
always twitching as if asleep you hunted chimeras
wolfishly you crunched the air only to vomit
you knew no human thing you did not know even how
   to breathe

Now you have peace Hamlet you accomplished what you had to
and you have peace The rest is not silence but belongs to me
you chose the easier part an elegant thrust
but what is heroic death compared with eternal watching
with a cold apple in one's hand on a narrow chair
with a view of the ant-hill and the clock's dial

Adieu prince I have tasks a sewer project
and a decree on prostitutes and beggars
I must also elaborate a better system of prisons
since as you justly said Denmark is a prison
I go to my affairs This night is born
a star named Hamlet We shall never meet
what I shall leave will not be worth a tragedy

It is not for us to greet each other or bid farewell we live on
   archipelagos
and that water these words what can they do what can they do
   prince

What significant differences does Fortinbras see between himself and Hamlet? What
does he find most praiseworthy about Hamlet?

REVIEWERS

The publishers and editors would like to thank the following educators for contributing their valuable expertise during the development of the *Global Shakespeare Series*:

Nancy Alford
Sir John A. Macdonald High School
Hubley, Nova Scotia

Dr. Philip Allingham
Golden Secondary School
Golden, British Columbia

Carol Brown
Walter Murray Collegiate Institute
Saskatoon, Saskatchewan

Rod Brown
Wellington Secondary School
Nanaimo, British Columbia

Brian Dietrich
Queen Elizabeth Senior Secondary
School
Surrey, British Columbia

Alison Douglas
McNally High School
Edmonton, Alberta

Kim Driscoll
Adam Scott Secondary School
Peterborough, Ontario

Burton Eikleberry
Grants Pass High School
Grants Pass, Oregon

Gloria Evans
Lakewood Junior Secondary School
Prince George, British Columbia

Professor Averil Gardner
Memorial University
St. John's, Newfoundland

Joyce L. Halsey
Lee's Summit North High School
Lee's Summit, Missouri

Carol Innazzo
St. Bernard's College
West Essendon, Victoria, Australia

Winston Jackson
Belmont Secondary School
Victoria, British Columbia

Marion Jenkins
Glenlyon-Norfolk School
Victoria, British Columbia

Dr. Sharon Johnston
Boone High School
Orlando, Florida

Jean Jonkers
William J. Dean Technical High School
Holyoke, Massachusetts

Beverly Joyce
Brockton High School
Brockton, Massachusetts

Judy Kayse
Huntsville High School
Huntsville, Texas

Doreen Kennedy
Vancouver Technical Secondary School
Burnaby, British Columbia

Ed Metcalfe
Fleetwood Park Secondary School
Surrey, British Columbia

Janine Modestow
William J. Dean Technical High School
Holyoke, Massachusetts

Steve Naylor
Salmon Arm Senior Secondary School
Salmon Arm, British Columbia

Kathleen Oakes
Implay City Senior High School
Romeo, Michigan

Carla O'Brien
Lakewood Junior Secondary School
Prince George, British Columbia

Bruce L. Pagni
Waukegan High School
Waukegan, Illinois

Larry Peters
Lisgar Collegiate
Ottawa, Ontario

Margaret Poetschke
Lisgar Collegiate
Ottawa, Ontario

Jeff Purse
Walter Murray Collegiate Institute
Saskatoon, Saskatchewan

Grant Shaw
Elmwood High School
Winnipeg, Manitoba

Debarah Shoultz
Columbus North High School
Columbus, Indiana

Tim Turner
Kiona-Benton High School
Benton City, Washington

James Walsh
Vernon Township High School
Vernon, New Jersey

Kimberly Weisner
Merritt Island High School
Merritt Island, Florida

Ted Wholey
Sir John A. Macdonald High School
Hubley, Nova Scotia

Beverley Winny
Adam Scott Secondary School
Peterborough, Ontario

About the Series Editors

Dom Saliani, Senior Editor of the *Global Shakespeare Series*, is the Curriculum Leader of English at Sir Winston Churchill High School in Calgary, Alberta. He has been an English teacher for over 25 years and has published a number of poetry and literature anthologies.

Chris Ferguson is currently employed as a Special Trainer by the Southwest Educational Development Laboratory in Austin, Texas. Formerly the Department Head of English at Burnet High School in Burnet, Texas, she has taught English, drama, and speech communications for over 15 years.

Dr. Tim Scott is an English teacher at Melbourne Grammar School in Victoria, Australia, where he directs a Shakespeare production every year. He wrote his Ph.D. thesis on Elizabethan drama.

ACKNOWLEDGEMENTS

Permission to reprint copyrighted material is gratefully acknowledged. Every reasonable effort has been made to contact copyright holders. Any information that enables the publisher to rectify any error or omission will be welcomed.

Hamletology by Norrie Epstein from THE FRIENDLY SHAKESPEARE by Norrie Epstein. Published by The Penguin Group. *Shakespeare Changed My Life* by Robert MacNeil from WORD-STRUCK. Published by Penguin Books. *Amleth's Revenge* by Saxo Grammaticus. Copyright © 1983 by Philip S. Jennings from MEDIEVAL LEGENDS by Philip S. Jennings. Reprinted by permission of St. Martin's Press Incorporated. *The Night Watch* by James McLean. "The Night Watch" is from THE SECRET LIFE OF RAILROADERS by James McLean, published by Coteau Books, 1982. Used by permission of the publisher. All rights reserved. *The Senioritis of a Modern Hamlet* by Christoper G. Inoue. Reprinted by permission of the author. *Well, Frankly...* by Charles, Prince of Wales from THE FRIENDLY SHAKESPEARE by Norrie Epstein. Published by The Penguin Group. *Alive or Dead? To be, or not to be* from *The British Magazine*. *At the Court of King Claudius* by Maurice Baring from DEAD LETTERS. A.P. Watt Ltd. *Gertrude Talks Back* by Margaret Atwood. Copyright © O.W. Toad Ltd., 1983, 1992, 1994. A Nan Talese Book. First Published in GOOD BONES (Coach House Press). Reprinted by permission of the author and Doubleday, A Division of Bantam Doubleday Dell Publishing Group, Inc. *They All Want to Play Hamlet* by Carl Sandburg from SMOKE AND STEEL by Carl Sandburg, copyright 1920 by Harcourt Brace & Company and renewed 1948 by Carl Sandburg, reprinted by permission of the publisher. *Ophelia's Song* by Marya Zaturenska from THE HIDDEN WATERFALL by M.Z. Gregory. Copyright 1974 by M.Z. Gregory. Vanguard Press Inc. Excerpt from *Remembering Ophelia* by Diane Fahey. Diane Fahey is a widely published Australian poet who has won numerous awards and fellowships for her poetry. Her fifth collection of poetry is THE BODY IN TIME (Spinifex, 1995). She lives by the sea in Victoria. "Remembering Ophelia" first appeared in "Westerly." *Alas, Poor Bauer* by Richard Woollatt. Reprinted by permission of the author. *Intimations* by Robert Currie from THE HALLS OF ELSI-NORE. Reprinted by permission of the author. *Meditation at Elsinore* by Elizabeth Coatsworth. Reprinted with permission of Simon & Schuster Books for Young Readers, an imprint of Simon & Schuster Children's Publishing Division from DOWN HALF THE WORLD by Elizabeth Coatsworth. Copyright © 1968 Elizabeth Coatsworth Beston. *Spring* by Charlotte Reedy from THE ENGLISH JOURNAL. *Hamlet* by Albert Wendt from THE BIRTH AND DEATH OF THE MIRACLE MAN. Reproduced with permission of Curtis Brown Ltd, on behalf of Albert Wendt. Copyright © Albert Wendt, 1986. *The Imagery of Hamlet* by Caroline Spurgeon from SHAKESPEARE'S IMAGERY. Reprinted by permission of Cambridge University Press. *Shakespeare in the Bush* by Laura Bohannan from THE ARCH OF EXPERIENCE. Harcourt Brace and Company. *15-Minute Hamlet* by Tom Stoppard from DOGG'S HAMLET. Reprinted with permission of Faber and Faber Ltd. *Elegy of Fortinbras* by Zbigniew Herbert, from POSTWAR POLISH POETRY by Czeslaw Milosz, translation copyright 1965 by Czeslaw Milosz. Used by permission of Doubleday, a division of Bantam Doubleday Dell Publishing Group, Inc.

ARTWORK

Wayne Mondok: cover, 10, 28-29, 37, 38, 46-47, 59, 60, 68-69, 80-81, 89, 90, 102-103, 116, 118, 134-135, 141, 142; **IGNITION Design and Communications**: series logo, 12, 13, 14, 19, 22, 48, 53, 54, 57, 63, 67, 72, 86, 101, 106, 121, 128; Hamlet 1604 title page reprinted by permission of the Folger Shakespeare Library: 6; **John James**: 7, from *Shakespeare's Theatre* (Simon and Schuster, 1994); **Tom Taylor**: 8; **Nicholas Vitacco**: 9; Sledded Polacks reprinted by permission of The Houghton Library, Harvard University: 13; Travelling Players from *Scarron's Comical Romance of a Company of Stage Players, 1676*: 57 **Amanda Duffy**: 145; **Tom Taylor**: 152; **Harvey Chan**: 158; **Tracey Wood**: 164; Ophelia by J. Millais from The Tate Gallery: 170; **Leon Zernitsky**: 172; **Pierre Fortin**: 174; **Thom Sevalrud**: 175; **Andrew Peycha**: 177, 181; **Alison Lang**: 189; **James Richardson**: 196.